EFFECTIVE

BUSINESS

POLICY

Effective Management
Series Editor: Alan H. Anderson

Effective Personnel Management
Alan H. Anderson

Effective Business Policy
Alan H. Anderson and Dennis Barker

Effective General Management
Alan H. Anderson

Effective Organizational Behaviour
Alan H. Anderson and Anna Kyprianou

Effective Labour Relations
Alan H. Anderson

Effective Marketing
Alan H. Anderson and Thelma Dobson

Effective International Marketing
Alan H. Anderson, Thelma Dobson and James Patterson

Effective Marketing Communications
Alan H. Anderson and David Kleiner

Effective Entrepreneurship
Alan H. Anderson and Peter Woodcock

Effective Enterprise Management
Alan H. Anderson and Dennis Barker

Effective Accounting Management
Alan H. Anderson and Eileen Nix

Effective Financial Management
Alan H. Anderson and Richard Ciechan

EFFECTIVE BUSINESS POLICY

a skills and activity-based approach

ALAN H. ANDERSON
and
DENNIS BARKER

BLACKWELL
Business

First published 1994

Blackwell Publishers
108 Cowley Road
Oxford OX4 1JF
UK

238 Main Street
Cambridge, Massachusetts 02142
USA

British Library Cataloguing in Publication Data

A CIP catalogue record for this book is available from the British Library.

Library of Congress Cataloging-in-Publication Data

Anderson, Alan H., 1950-
     Effective business policy: a skills and activity-based approach / Alan H. Anderson and Dennis Barker.
          p. cm. – (Effective management)
     Includes bibliographical references and index.
     ISBN 0-631-19125-9 (pbk.: acid-free paper)
     1. Strategic planning. 2. Industrial management. 3. Organizational effectiveness.
I. Barker, Dennis. II. Title. III. Series: Effective management (Oxford, England)
     HD30.28.A52 1994
     658.4'012–dc20   93-47324
                                                                                CIP

Designed and typeset by VAP Group Ltd., Kidlington, Oxfordshire

Printed in Great Britain by T J Press (Padstow) Ltd.

This book is printed on acid-free paper

*I would like to dedicate my contribution to our book to my wife
Maureen, daughter Kerry and son Ross.*

Alan H. Anderson

To my wife.

Dennis Barker

Contents

Figures

Boxes

Activities

Introduction to the Series

❝ He that has done nothing has known nothing.❞

Carlyle

The Concept

In this series 'effective' means getting results. By taking an action approach to management, or the stewardship of an organization, the whole series allows people to create and develop their skills of effectiveness. This interrelated series gives the underpinning knowledge base and the application of functional and generic skills of the effective manager who gets results.

Key qualities of the effective manager include:

- **functional expertise** in the various disciplines of management;
- an understanding of the **organizational context**;
- an appreciation of the **external environment**;
- **self-awareness** and the power of **self-development**.

These qualities must fuse in a climate of **enterprise**.

Management is results-oriented so action is at a premium. The basis of this activity is **skills** underpinned by our qualities. In turn these skills can be based on a discipline or a function, and be universal or generic.

The Approach of the Series

These key qualities of effective management are the core of the current twelve books of the series. The areas covered by the series at present are:

People	*Effective Personnel Management*
	Effective Labour Relations
	Effective Organizational Behaviour
Finance	*Effective Financial Management*
	Effective Accounting Management
Marketing and sales	*Effective Marketing*
	Effective International Marketing
	Effective Marketing Communications
Operations/Enterprise	*Effective Enterprise Management*
	Effective Entrepreneurship
Policy/General	*Effective Business Policy*
	Effective General Management

The key attributes of the effective manager are all dealt with in the series, and we will pinpoint where they are emphasized:

- *Functional expertise.* The four main disciplines of management – finance, marketing, operations and personnel management – make up nine books. These meet the needs of specialist disciplines and allow a wider appreciation of other functions.
- *Organizational context.* All the 'people' books – the specialist one on *Effective Organizational Behaviour*, and also *Effective Personnel Management* and *Effective Labour Relations* – cover this area. The resourcing/control issues are met in the 'finance' texts, *Effective Financial Management* and *Effective Accounting Management*. Every case activity is given some organizational context.
- *External environment.* One book, *Effective Business Policy*, is dedicated to this subject. Environmental contexts apply in every book of the series: especially in *Effective Entrepreneurship*, *Effective General Management*, and in all of the 'marketing' texts – *Effective Marketing*, *Effective International Marketing* and *Effective Marketing Communications*.
- *Self-awareness/self-development.* To a great extent management development is manager development, so we have one generic skill (see later) devoted to this topic running through each book. The subject is examined in detail in *Effective General Management*.
- *Enterprise.* The *Effective Entrepreneurship* text is allied to *Effective Enterprise Management* to give insights into this whole area through all the developing phases of the firm. The marketing and policy books also revolve around this theme.

Skills

The functional skills are inherent within the discipline-based texts. In addition, running through the series are the following generic skills:
- self-development
- teamwork
- communications
- numeracy/IT
- decisions

These generic skills are universal managerial skills which occur to some degree in every manager's job.

Format/Structure of Each Book

Each book is subdivided into six units. These are self-contained, in order to facilitate learning, but interrelated, in order to give an effective holistic view. Each book also has an introduction with an outline of the book's particular theme.

Each unit has *learning objectives* with an overview/summary of the unit.

Boxes appear in every unit of every book. They allow a different perspective from the main narrative and analysis. Research points, examples, controversy and theory are all expanded upon in these boxes. They are numbered by unit in each book, e.g. 'Box PM1.1' for the first box in Unit One of *Effective Personnel Management*.

Activities, numbered in the same way, permeate the series. These action-oriented forms of learning cover cases, questionnaires, survey results, financial data, market research information, etc. The skills which can be assessed in each one are noted in the code at the top right of the activity by having the square next to them ticked. That is, if we are assuming numeracy then the square beside Numeracy would be ticked (✓), and so on. The weighting given to these skills will depend on the activity, the tutors'/learners' needs, and the overall weighting of the skills as noted in the appendix on 'Generic Skills', with problem solving dominating in most cases.

Common cases run through the series. Functional approaches are added to these core cases to show the same organization from different perspectives. This simulates the complexity of reality.

Workbook

The activities can be written up in the *workbook* which accompanies each book in the series.

Handbook

For each book in the series, there is a *handbook*. This is not quite the 'answers' to the activities, but it does contain some indicative ideas for them (coded accordingly), which will help to stimulate discussion and thought.

Test bank

We are developing a bank of tests in question-and-answer format to accompany the series. This will be geared to the knowledge inputs of the books.

The Audience

The series is for all those who wish to be effective managers. As such, it is a series for management development on an international scale, and embraces both management education and management training. In management education, the emphasis still tends to be on cognitive or knowledge inputs; in management training, it still tends to be on skills and techniques. We need both theory and practice, with the facility to try out these functions and skills through a range of scenarios in a 'safe' learning environment. This series is unique in encompassing these perspectives and bridging the gulf between the academic and vocational sides of business management.

Academically the series is pitched at the DMS/DBA types of qualification, which often lead on to an MA/MBA after the second year. Undergraduates following business degrees or management studies will benefit from the series in their final years. Distance learners will also find the series useful, as will those studying managerial subjects for professional examinations. The competency approach and the movement towards Accredited Prior Learning and National Vocational Qualifications are underpinned by the knowledge inputs, while the activities will provide useful simulations for these approaches to management learning.

This developmental series gives an opportunity for self-improvement. Individuals may wish to enhance their managerial potential by developing themselves without institutional backing by working through the whole series. It can also be used to underpin corporate training programmes, and acts as a useful design vehicle for specialist inputs from organizations. We are happy to pursue these various options with institutions or corporations.

The approach throughout the series combines skills, knowledge and application to create and develop the effective manager. Any comments or thoughts from participants in this interactive process will be welcomed.

Alan H. Anderson
Melbourn, Cambridge

The Series: Learning, Activities, Skills and Compatibility

The emphasis on skills and activities as vehicles of learning makes this series unique. Behavioural change, or learning, is developed through a two-pronged approach.

First, there is the **knowledge-based (cognitive)** approach to learning. This is found in the main text and in the boxes. These cognitive inputs form the traditional method of learning based on the principle of receiving and understanding information. In this series, there are four main knowledge inputs covering the four main managerial functions: marketing/sales, operations/enterprise, people, and accounting/finance. In addition, these disciplines are augmented by a strategic overview covering policy making and general management. An example of this first approach may be illustrative. In the case of marketing, the learner is confronted with a model of the internal and external environments. Thereafter the learner must digest, reflect, and understand the importance of this model to the whole of the subject.

Second, there is the **activity-based** approach to learning, which emphasizes the application of knowledge and skill through techniques. This approach is vital in developing effectiveness. It is seen from two levels of learning:

1 The use and application of *specific skills*. This is the utilization of your cognitive knowledge in a practical manner. These skills emanate from the cognitive aspect of learning, so they are functional skills, specific to the discipline.

   For example, the learner needs to understand the concept of job analysis before he or she tackles an activity that requires the drawing up of a specific job evaluation programme. So knowledge is not seen for its own sake, but is applied and becomes a specific functional skill.

2 The use and application of *generic skills*. These are universal skills which every manager uses irrespective of the wider external environment, the organization, the function and the job. This is seen, for example, in the ability to make clear decisions on the merits of a case. This skill of decision making is found in most of the activities.

There is a relationship between the specific functional skills and the generic skills. The specific functional skills stand alone, but the generic skills cut across them. See figure SK.1.

In this series we use activities to cover both the specific functional and the generic skills. There are five generic skills. We shall examine each of them in turn.

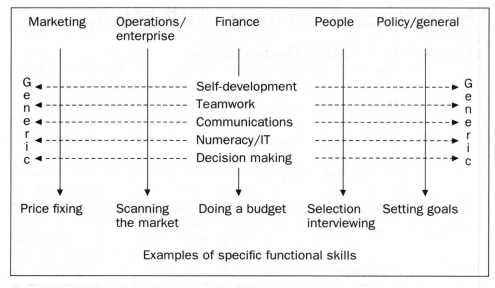

Figure SK.1 Series skills matrix: functional and generic skills.

Self-development

The learner must take responsibility for his or her learning as well as 'learning how to learn'. Time management, work scheduling and organizing the work are involved in the procedural sense. From a learning perspective, sound aspects of learning, from motivation to reward, need to be clarified and understood. The physical process of learning, including changing knowledge, skills and attitudes, may be involved. Individual goals and aspirations need to be recognized alongside the task goals. The ultimate aim of this skill is to facilitate learning transfer to new situations and environments.

Examples of this skill include:

- establishing and clarifying work goals;
- developing procedures and methods of work;
- building key learning characteristics into the process;
- using procedural learning;
- applying insightful learning;
- creating personal developmental plans;
- integrating these personal developmental plans with work goals.

Teamwork

Much of our working lives is concerned with groups. Effective teamwork is thus at a premium. This involves meeting both the task objectives and the socio-emotional processes within the group. This skill can be used for groups in a training or educational context. It can be a bridge between decision making and an awareness of self-development.

Examples of this skill include:

- clarifying the task need of the group;
- receiving, collating, ordering and rendering information;
- discussing, chairing and teamwork within the group;
- identifying the socio-emotional needs and group processes;
- linking these needs and processes to the task goals of the group.

Communications

This covers information and attitude processing within and between individuals. Oral and written communications are important because of the gamut of 'information and attitudinal' processing within the individual. At one level communication may mean writing a report, at another it could involve complex interpersonal relationships.

Examples of this skill include:

- understanding the media, aids, the message and methods;
- overcoming blockages;
- listening;
- presenting a case or commenting on the views of others;
- writing;
- designing material and systems for others to understand your communications.

Numeracy/IT

Managers need a core mastery of numbers and their application. This mastery is critical for planning, control, co-ordination, organization and, above all else, for decision making. Numeracy/IT are not seen as skills for their own sake. Here, they are regarded as the means to an end. These skills enable information and data to be utilized by the effective manager. In particular these skills are seen as an adjunct to decision making.

Examples of this skill include:

- gathering information;
- processing and testing information;

- using measures of accuracy, reliability, probability etc.;
- applying appropriate software packages;
- extrapolating information and trends for problem solving.

Decision making

Management is very much concerned with solving problems and making decisions. As group decisions are covered under teamwork, the emphasis in this decision-making skill is placed on the individual.

Decision making can involve a structured approach to problem solving with appropriate aims and methods. Apart from the 'scientific' approach, we can employ also an imaginative vision towards decision making. One is rational, the other is more like brainstorming.

Examples of this skill include:

- setting objectives and establishing criteria;
- seeking, gathering and processing information;
- deriving alternatives;
- using creative decision making;
- action planning and implementation.

This is *the* skill of management and is given primary importance in the generic skills within the activities as a reflection of everyday reality.

Before we go about learning how to develop into effective managers, it is important to understand the general principles of learning. Both the knowledge-based and the activity-based approaches are set within the environment of these principles. The series has been written to relate to Anderson's sound principles of learning which were developed in *Successful Training Practice*.

- *Motivation* – intrinsic motivation is stimulated by the range and depth of the subject matter and assisted by an action orientation.
- *Knowledge of results* – ongoing feedback is given through the handbook for each book in the series.
- *Scale learning* – each text is divided into six units, which facilitates part learning.
- *Self-pacing* – a map of the unit with objectives, content and an overview helps learners to pace their own progress.
- *Transfer* – realism is enhanced through lifelike simulations which assist learning transfer.
- *Discovery learning* – the series is geared to the learner using self-insight to stimulate learning.
- *Self-development* – self-improvement and an awareness of how we go about learning underpin the series.

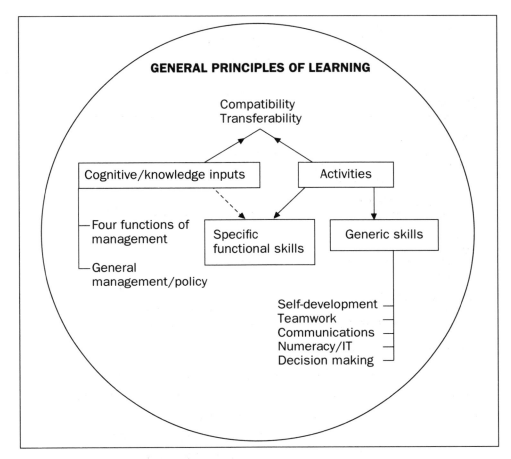

Figure SK.2 Series learning strategy.

- *Active learning* – every activity is based upon this critical component of successful learning.

From what has been said so far, the learning strategy of the series can be outlined in diagrammatic form. (See figure SK.2.)

In figure SK.2, 'compatibility and transferability' are prominent because the learning approach of the series is extremely compatible with the learning approaches of current initiatives in management development. This series is related to a range of learning classification being used in education and training. Consequently it meets the needs of other leading training systems and learning taxonomies. See figures SK.3–SK.6.

Functional knowledge and skills	An educational classification
People:	
Personnel management ———	People
Labour relations	
Organizational behaviour	
Marketing/sales:	
Marketing ———	Marketing
Marketing communications	
International marketing	
Operations/enterprise:	
Entrepreneurship ———	Operations/enterprise
Enterprise	
Finance:	
Accounting management ———	Finance
Finance	
Policy/management:	
Policy ———	Business environment/
General management	business administration
Generic skills	
Self-development ———	Managing and developing self
Teamwork ———	Working with and relating to others
Communications ‹‑‑‑	Communications
	Applying design and creativity
Decisions ‹———	Managing tasks and solving problems
Numeracy/IT ‹———	Applying technology
	Applying numeracy

———	direct relationship
‑‑‑‑‑‑‑‑‑	indirect relationship

Figure SK.3 Series knowledge and skills related to an educational classification.

Source: Adapted from Business Technician and Education Council, 'Common skills and experience of BTEC programmes'.

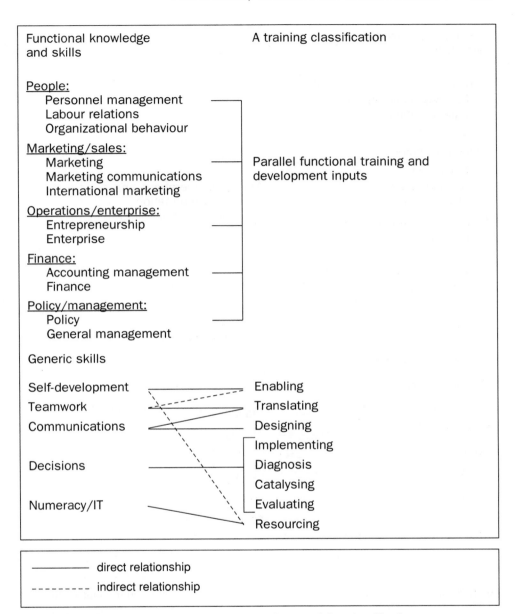

Figure SK.4 Series knowledge and skills related to a training classification.

Source: Adapted from J.A.G. Jones, 'Training intervention strategies' and experience of development programmes.

Functional knowledge and skills	MCI competency
People:	Managing people
Personnel management	
Labour relations	
Organizational behaviour	
Marketing/sales:	
Marketing	Managing operations and
Marketing communications	managing information
International marketing	(plus new texts pending)
Operations/enterprise:	
Entrepreneurship	
Enterprise	
Finance:	Managing finance
Accounting management	
Finance	
Policy/management:	Managing context
Policy	
General management	
Generic skills	
Self-development	Managing oneself
Teamwork	Managing others
Communications	Using intellect
Decisions	Planning
Numeracy/IT	

——————— direct relationship

--------- indirect relationship

Figure SK.5 Series knowledge and skills related to Management Charter Initiative (MCI) competencies.

Source: Adapted from MCI diploma guidelines.

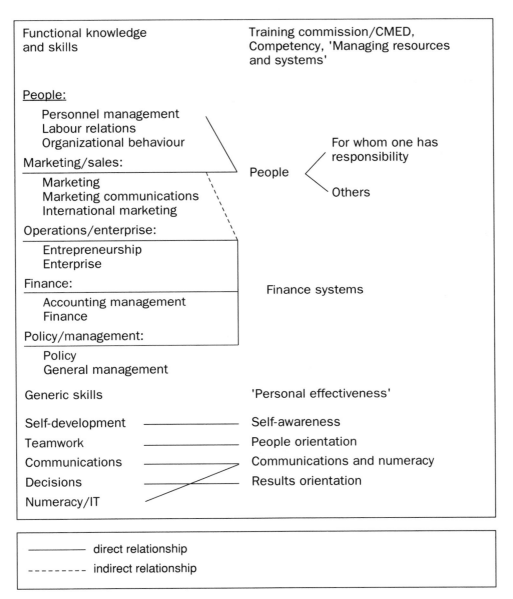

Figure SK.6 Series knowledge and skills related to Training Commission/Council for Management Education (CMED) competencies.

Source: Adapted from Training Commission/CMED, 'Classifying the components of management competencies'.

Preface

> " Many companies have been living from day to day for too long. Clear and explicit consideration of long range strategy must be restored to our business consciousness and decision-making, or we shall find that we have mortgaged the future irretrievably. "
>
> *B. Hedley*[1]

Themes and Rationale

The external environment can be very fickle and lay waste great human achievements almost at a stroke. Similarly in business, the firm's external environments can make or break it. These environmental influences can be political, economic, social/sociological, technological or competitive. However, far from leading us towards some Hardy-like philosophy of blind fate, almost wilfully destroying the plans of people, it suggests that the internal environment of the organization needs to be able to adapt and adopt ideas to counter harmful external environments which may provide more threats than opportunities. The firm needs defensive policies to counter real or foreseeable threats, offensive strategies to exploit potential opportunities and, above all, flexible policies and approaches which will allow the organizational animal to survive and be successful in its external environments.

This book is called *Effective Business Policy* and a policy implies a procedure to be followed. However, it has been found in management that policies that were highly effective in one firm would not work in another. In fact, the results differ because the situations are different. Therefore, it is the task of a manager to identify which business policy will help to achieve the organization's goals in a given situation and at a particular time. The manager needs to ask, 'What will work best both now and in the future?' This implies a wide knowledge of business policies from which selection can be made, together with an awareness of the environment in which the manager operates.

Terms such as business policy, management policy, corporate policy, strategic management and corporate strategy are often used for the same general area of management covered in this book. We have termed it 'policy' to reinforce a coherent, if flexible, approach to the external environments. It is not a recipe such that if you do X, success Y will happen. We have focused on the fundamental concepts and the interaction of the various environments, both external and internal, which the policy maker or advisor needs to understand before making a policy decision.

When we began writing this book it was very tempting to adopt the almost prescriptive approach of seeking the 'right' policies, which, with some luck or risk reduction, would lead to success. This temptation was resisted.

Fundamental truisms may not be so apparent in the business area, but the proactive policy manager and advisor, and indeed *all managers*, must understand the wider external environments. This should automatically lead on to the competitive environment and then to the environment of the business itself. In other words, the manager should gradually narrow down his or her viewpoint but still keep the external environments in view. The Japanese concept of developing peripheral vision is just as important as the skills of actually running the business.

Once the environments are understood, the manager should be capable of developing and considering options for change and, eventually, choosing, implementing and evaluating them. This line of reasoning became the framework for this book and should provide an effective business policy for all managers.

The generally accepted philosophy that strategy is defined at the top of an organization and then passed down through it is not one with which we agree. Every manager, no matter at what level, has an interest in the long-term sustainable success of the organization. Therefore, since strategy is about gaining long-term sustainable success for the organization, every manager should be involved in thinking and managing strategically. This book is designed to get managers to do that through following some of the policies recommended herein.

A list of the largest and most successful firms in 1912, 1952 and 1992 will show that few leaders survive over long periods of time. Is this the result of poor decision making and strategic management, changes in objectives, or chance? It appears that some firms do not learn to adapt to new situations as quickly as their competitors. This leads to the idea of a learning organization and the use of management learning in order to make the correct decisions. In this way, feedback from management decisions is used to modify the firm's view of the future.

We have to find ways of developing learning organizations and this implies developing learning managers. This book sets out to do just that: to develop a manager's skills so that innate creativity and competitiveness can operate freely and so lead to the most appropriate decisions. So the themes draw heavily upon the influence and impact of the external environments. The internal or business environment is seen through a specific framework which covers seven key aspects of the firm. Parallel to this approach, and on a smaller scale, we also consider a functional approach to the internal competence of the organization and to the implementation of policy. For clarity we interchange the terms 'enterprise', 'business', 'firm' and 'organization'.

The Learning Objectives

The learning objectives of this book are:
- To analyse critically the external environments at local, national and international levels.
- To focus on environmental turbulence and change and qualify and quantify accordingly.
- To analyse the competitive environment.
- To determine the organizational objectives.
- To conduct an 'internal environmental' analysis in an organization.
- To relate objectives with the themes and trends of the internal and external environments.
- To develop a range of policies for change.
- To put a range of policies into effect and to control, monitor and evaluate them.

Overview of the Content and Skills

The diagram in figure 0.1 illustrates the interaction between all the units of this book. Although the book narrows down the approach from the external environment through to implementation and evaluation there is no reason why you should start at the beginning and work through to the end. However, the final Activity does act as a link between all the units and Unit Six gives evaluative mechanisms for the whole cycle.

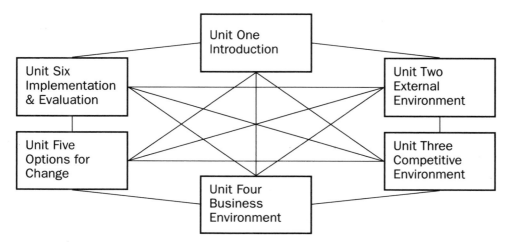

Figure 0.1 The interaction between the units in this book.

Specific policy skills reflecting this framework are linked to the generic skills outlined in the learning, activities, skills and compatibility chapter.

Note

1 Hedley, 'Strategy and the "business portfolio"'.

Acknowledgements

Dennis Barker would like to thank his wife Christine for reading the early drafts of this book and for her support during the past year. In addition, the authors would like to thank Blackwell Publishers and VAP for their work assistance, commitment and encouragement.

The authors and publisher would also like to thank Steve Culliford, Rosemary Hathaway and Evelyne Lee-Barber for their advice and assistance in the development of this book.

Unit One

Introduction

Learning Objectives

After completing this unit you should be able to:

- understand the concepts of policy and strategy and how they developed;
- describe the tasks of management;
- realize that strategies are often the result of a stream of decisions;
- understand how the units are organized and the best ways to get the most out of them;
- realize the interlinked nature of the decisions made by managers in various parts of the organization;
- realize that adapting to the environment and predicting the future are two of the keys to successful management;
- apply the generic skills.

Contents

Unit One

" In short, the organization must learn to think of itself not as
producing goods or services but as **buying customers**, as
doing the things that will make people **want** to do business
with it. And the chief executive himself has the inescapable
responsibility for creating this environment, this viewpoint, this
attitude, this aspiration. He himself must set the company's
style, its direction, and its goals. This means he has to know
precisely where he himself wants to go, and to make sure the
whole organization is enthusiastically aware of where that is.
This is the first requisite of leadership. "

                                                    T. Levitt[1]

Overview

 Managers have to make the best use of an organization's resources in a
changing environment. To do this managers have to make a stream of
decisions. These decisions determine whether a firm is successful, just
survives or fails completely and together have been termed strategic
management or business policy management.

External environmental turbulence, particularly through recession and
highly competitive international markets, makes those policy decisions
critical. Further, we believe that we need to spread the appreciation of the
subject matter to all managers, rather than limit the policy perspective to
senior managers and corporate advisors/planners. Policy appreciation is
fundamental to the whole business and should be an integral part of *every*
manager's repertoire.

In this unit we cover the topics shown in the flowchart in figure 1.1.

The Concept of Strategy

" The best strategy is always to be very strong. "

                                                    Anon

It is difficult to define the term 'strategy' since it encompasses so many
different activities. We see policy and strategy in business as broadly
synonymous. Strategy has been defined in many ways:

■ A strategy is a means to achieve ends.
■ A strategy links all the parts of an organization.

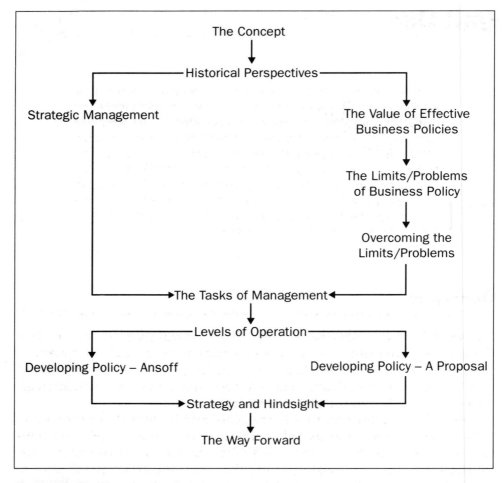

Figure 1.1 Flowchart for Unit One.

- A strategy covers all the major aspects of an organization.
- A strategy is a long-term plan.
- A strategy ensures that all parts of the plan are compatible.
- A strategy identifies basic issues such as:
  - What is our business?
  - What should it be?
  - What are our products/services, functions, markets?
  - What should we do to achieve our objectives?
- A strategy is the result of analysing the strengths and weaknesses of the organization and determining opportunities and threats.
- A strategy is an organization's planned response to its environment over time.

At this point you should read the note on strategy in Box BP1.1.

BOX BP1.1

Strategy

The word strategy is very old and comes from the Greek word *strategeia* which means the art or science of being a General. The importance of generalship in battle in ancient times was obvious. Quinn explains the classical approaches to strategy with the example of Philip and Alexander in Greece during 338BC. Effective generals choose the lines of supply, decide when and when not to fight and build relationships with people, politicians and diplomats. Generals not only plan but act as well and so these two concepts form the basis for a strategy.

Quinn identifies several necessary features such as:

Strategies have three elements:

- Goals/objectives to be achieved.
- Policies for action.
- Programmes to achieve goals within the limits set.

Strategies develop around a few key concepts and thrusts which give the strategy balance, cohesion and focus. However, some thrusts can be short-lived and some cost more than others. Therefore, sufficient resources must be allocated so that each thrust will succeed.   *imprevisto*

The essence of a strategy is to build a position so strong that the organization will achieve its goals no matter what unforeseeable forces attack it (changes in bank rates, new competitors, technologies, oil crises, wars etc.).

There should be a number of hierarchically related and mutually supportive strategies, each, as far as possible, complete in itself and congruent or synergistic with every other strategy.

Therefore, effective strategies should:

- contain clear and decisive objectives. Sub-goals may change in the heat of battle but the over-riding objective provides continuity over time.
- maintain the initiative.
- concentrate power at the right time and place.
- have built-in flexibility so that one can use minimum resources to keep opponents at a disadvantage. This involves reserves and flexibility in the organization.
- have committed and co-ordinated leadership.
- include correct timing and surprise.
- make resources secure and prevent surprises from opponents.

Source: Quinn, *Strategies for Change: Logical Incrementalism*

For an alternative view you should also read Box BP1.2 on the five Ps.

Strategic decisions are the means to achieve the ends and have implications for the organization, its products/services, markets to be served, functions to be performed and the plans and policies required for the organization to achieve its objectives. Plans and policies assign tasks and allocate resources.

BOX BP1.2

The five Ps

Mintzberg identifies five Ps for strategy:
1 Strategy as a **plan** for action.
2 Strategy as a **ploy**, a manoeuvre to outwit opponents.
3 Strategy as a **pattern** of actions – plans may go unrealized but patterns may appear.
4 Strategy as a **position** in an environment – it is the link between the organization and the environment.
5 Strategy as **perspective** – the character or culture of the organization; the ways of acting and responding and what the organization stands for. This implies sharing and uniting organization members.

It is relatively easy to change the first four **Ps** but to change the perspective of an organization is much more difficult. Many strategies have failed because of this factor.

Source: Mintzberg, 'Five Ps for Strategy'

Managers need to have a view on policy. The case of Ford is illustrative, so complete Activity BP1.1.

ACTIVITY BP1.1

FORD

Activity code
✓   Self-development
☐   Teamwork
☐   Communications
☐   Numeracy/IT
✓   Decisions

Just before the First World War, Henry Ford began to put into operation some ideas about production suggested by F.W. Taylor. The idea was to break down each of the processes of building a car into small units so that the process could be mechanized and speeded up. The small units were joined together to make a larger unit and larger units joined together to make even larger units and so on. He started first with the magneto coil assembly which was being made by one worker at the rate of 30–40 per day. He broke the process down into 29 operations performed by 29 different people on an assembly line, thus reducing the time to make a magneto from 20 to 13 minutes.

This process was repeated throughout the factory and produced a bottleneck at the final assembly where workers scrambled over the stationary chassis putting on the bits and pieces. In order to speed up the process they tried an experiment, pulling the chassis across the factory floor past piles of strategically placed parts and workers. The workers picked the parts up and fitted them as the chassis passed by. The process was developed so that Ford was able to assemble a car in a few hours instead of the 700 hours previously involved. This innovation reduced the price of the Model T from $780 in 1910 to $360 in 1914 and at the same time increased the market share from 9 per cent to 48 per cent. Subsequently Ford opened factories in Europe but resisted his managers' attempts to modernize the cars. Suggestions for improved gearboxes, transmissions, six- and eight-cylinder engines and hydraulic brakes were all refused. Owing to this short-sightedness General Motors eventually overtook Ford as market leader.

What does this tell us about management policies?

Historical Perspectives and Policy Implications

Until the 1750s most people worked on the land, at crafts in the home or in small groups. The Industrial Revolution changed all that with the development and widespread use of machinery. This technological innovation was also associated with social innovations, the move from the land into the factories and towns and the development of industrial and commercial organizations.

The period from about 1880–1930 focused on the development of mass production in order to reduce unit costs. The production of standard products at lowest cost, exemplified by Ford (see Activity BP1.1), was the route to success. There was a basic demand which was either local or national and the greatest need was to satisfy people's major comfort and security requirements. This meant that the competitive environment was quite open and an insatiable mass demand existed. The wider external environment was as turbulent as ever with new technologies, great social upheaval, political turmoil and drastic economic cycles. Yet industry and commerce were unfettered by government controls or indeed by social controls, except for trade unionism which did curb some of the raw managerial prerogatives. Within the organization, efficiency was the keyword and control systems, procedures and budgets were being installed. In spite of the trade unions, managerial authority was largely seen as an accepted part of the social order.

The period from 1930–50 saw the demand for basic products approach saturation. This caused the move from standard to differentiated products. Advertising, promotion and sales became the major concerns for managers. This move to marketing signalled the change from internally to externally focused organizations. This caused power changes in firms and the acquisition of new skills and technologies. These changes, the Depression and World War II caused problems, but essentially management was able to operate by extrapolating from the past. The development of budgets for both operations and capital expenditures occurred together with management by objectives and long-range planning. (This assumed the future was predictable through the extrapolation of historical growth and involved extending the yearly budgeting processes to three or perhaps five years so that rolling plans could be produced.) These techniques are still in use by managers today.

Changes tended to be evolutionary rather than revolutionary and there was a focus on new product development. By this time people's aspirations were rising from comfort and safety towards affluence.

The 1950s saw the arrival of this affluence, which shifted demand away from quantity to quality and began to question the growth ethic. Thus both the increasing turbulence in the environment and the increase in affluence had to be taken into account by managers.

As the years went by this turbulence was indicated by increasing inflation, government controls, consumer power and foreign competitors. Technological changes and changes in work attitudes were additional factors which had to be taken into consideration by the firm. The environment began to exert pressure on the firm so that those firms which ignored the environment, concentrated on production and marketing and relied on the past as the key to the future began to run into trouble. Therefore, there was a need to anticipate change and the development of strategic planning occurred. As turbulence increased further, management had to become increasingly flexible, develop contingency plans, identify strategic issues and deal with surprises.

By the mid-1970s the speed of change was such that events occurred and developed too rapidly to allow for the preparation of plans. Mid-year surprises which occurred faster than the planning cycle caused problems. This required the identification of strategic issues by:

1 the establishment of an environmental surveillance system covering business, political, economic, social and technological trends;

2 an estimate of the impact and urgency of the trends;

3 prioritization of issues.

At this point please read Box BP1.3 entitled 'Policy – dried up options?' This gives an historical scan of policy options and approaches.

BOX BP1.3

Policy – dried-up options?

To Kiechel[1] both the concepts and the application of strategic management, even in the early 1980s, were in tatters: 'We're going to miss corporate strategy, that sweet collection of surefire concepts – matrices, experience curves – that promised an easy win. Oh, it'll still be around here and there, showing its by now slightly grimy face in this corner or that ...'.

As in manpower (HR) planning, the early strategists seemed to promise the moon but the results were mixed. The macro (HR) plan gave way to the micro plan and perhaps to no plan at all in some organizations. A similar frantic global activity, followed by a move to micro techniques, seems to have occurred in policy management. There is a need to integrate concept and techniques which we pursue in this book.

In spite of the pessimism of Kiechel's critique his summary of the various 'phases' of business policy is very useful.

- **Extrapolation of past trends** As the market-place becomes more turbulent, clearly this approach has its limitations.
- **Strategic business units (SBUs)** Segmentation occurs in the external market-place for most companies, so a similar 'internal' segmentation occurs through the use of SBUs. These business units become strategic as they are almost free-standing mini-companies. They can identify their competitors and plan a mini-strategy accordingly.
- **The experience curve** This is based on unit costs reducing as volume increases, particularly for standardized products. The concept is an old chestnut of economists. The competitive edge, though, is derived from a vicious pricing policy as the market leader(s) undercuts others, so there is considerable fallout from the followers as they compete in this suicidal price cutting without any cost advantages.
- **Portfolio** Market share and market growth are seen as the dynamics of this approach. A growth area with a high share is sought; a mature area with a high share may provide money at least in the short term; low shares in a growth market could make you an also-ran or it could suck in your money in an attempt to gain more of the share; the low share/non-growth area is to be avoided.
- **From strategy to tactics** Increasingly, through fiercer foreign competition and a saturation policy on portfolio analysis being used by consultants, according to Kiechel, the onus has moved to the tactical implementation of the strategic master plan.
- **Tactics and issues** The 'downsizing' of strategic plans seems now to be complete with issues rather than master plans coming to the fore. The hunt for niche markets would fall into this category.
- **Core competency** The inward-looking approach now has a focus not only on separate tactics or issues but also on the exploitation of company-wide skills. The competitive edge seems to come from the distinct competence that you can offer the market-place. This assumes that the market-place wants/needs such a skill.
- **Culture vultures** This distinctive skill is not an holistic strength according to some writers for it can be a factor of the organizational personality or culture. Peters and

Waterman,[2] for example, advocate this cultural approach of combining skills, style, staff, and shared values with systems, structures and strategy. Assuming we can define it and find it, cultural change seems to be the current panacea.

Sources:
1   Some of these methods adapted from Kiechel, 'Corporate strategists under fire'
2   See Peters and Waterman, *In Search of Excellence*

Strategic Management

When someone starts a small business it is possible for that person to co-ordinate the activities easily. However, as the organization grows there comes a time when products/services, sales areas, places of operation and functions increase to such a degree that the integration of the organization requires more formal procedures. Thus policies that communicate broad guidelines for making decisions and taking actions are formulated.

This concept of 'business policy' began to prove inadequate, so that by the end of the 1950s long-range planning had developed. However, this approach was also inadequate as these plans were produced by extrapolating the past into the future and, since the environment was changing, the past was no longer the key to the future and organizations were growing larger and more complex in an unpredictable environment. For instance, up to the 1950s most of the major companies were single product/key idea firms, but by 1970 most of these had become multi-industry and multinational organizations. In order to integrate the needs of such diverse organizations in a complex environment one needs a strategy.

According to Chandler[2] a strategy was becoming necessary for 'the determination of the basic long-term goals and objectives of the enterprise, and the adoption of courses of action and the allocation of resources necessary for carrying out these goals'. This led to the development of strategy as a process rather than a policy and so 'corporate strategy' was born.

The Value of Effective Business Policies

A strategy enables organizations to prepare for and deal with a rapidly changing environment. The disadvantage is that organizations sometimes create a bureaucracy of strategic planners who lose contact with the organization's products and services. Another disadvantage is that the vetting system may restrict management decisions to the most sensible and risk-free options. In such situations innovations must be able to survive the detailed analysis of the planning process which eliminates many opportunities that are risky or difficult to explain. Therefore, the extent to which risk should be part of the strategic process must also be considered by managers. If managers do not take risks it is unlikely that they will be able to gain competitive advantage.

 In a review of organizations which used strategic planning, Armstrong[3] concluded that it paid off. The winners identified their areas of competence and took advantage of them, but the losers simply reacted to the environment.

Strategic planning implies that a firm's ability to move into new business areas depends on its ability to perform well in those areas. This, in its turn, implies that the key criteria for a strategy would be the historical strengths of the firm. However, many firms have found that there are no business areas in which their historical strengths are applicable. Their historical strengths may even be weaknesses. Ford's concentration on black standard cars was a factor leading to their loss of leadership in the car industry. Their strength in producing a standard product became a weakness in a new multi-model market.

 Strategic management brings benefits in the form of:

- providing a guide for the organization;
- alerting other managers and employees to change;
- providing a rationale for resource allocation;
- providing congruence/synergy across the organization;
- encouraging a proactive approach to management.

This is important since successful organizations do not simply react and defend but innovate and lead.

Policies are essential to organizations in order to ensure that daily decisions and actions are consistent with the organization's objectives, strategies and values. Organization policies help organizations to:

- achieve efficiency;
- co-ordinate activities;
- communicate the desired image both internally and externally;
- develop human resources – managers take responsibility, exercise discretion and develop themselves and others.

Procedures and rules, however, describe precisely the action to be taken in particular situations. They permit little or no discretion and are often in the form of employee handbooks or standard operating procedures. Managers also see the value of preparing budgets and so create planning and control systems. However, the need for individual managerial discretion is paramount and the procedures/control mechanisms should not become laws unto themselves. The debate on planning, policies, procedures and bureaucracy is taken up in Activity BP1.2 on the Domsec company. Complete this Activity before you go any further.

ACTIVITY BP1.2

DOMSEC: PLANNING

Activity code
- ✓ Self-development
- ✓ Teamwork
- ✓ Communications
- ✓ Numeracy/IT
- ☐ Decisions

Ted 'Plodder' Harvey was not really a businessman, or so he liked to think. He was a policeman by training and by inclination. Sitting in the Managing Director's office, he mused to himself that only ten years ago he had left the force as his wife Penny had worried about the high-risk business of London policing.

He had got a security advisor's job very quickly – and not through the Masonic link, as that young radical student son of his liked to say. The security job had been at Black's brewery, a major Essex company based near Romford. Theft and fiddling from timesheets to expenses had almost been on an organized basis when he first started but good detective work and his 'presence' had marginalized the 'shrinkage' and wholesale fiddles. He had liked working in Black's and it had given him an insight into the workings of organizations from the inside looking out as opposed to his police role of looking 'in' to organizations and to domestic 'situations'. He had met 'Boots' Smith, the safety advisor there, and mutual interests in angling and the Masonic society into which 'Plodder' had increasingly moved cemented the friendship. 'Boots' was a stickler for discipline, hence the ambiguous nickname based on 'wear your safety boots' or, more likely, on Smith's rather heavy-footed managerial style. The 'Plodder' title came from his own background. PC Plod was a children's favourite on TV or something. The relationship between the men both at work and at leisure blossomed. They became the best of friends.

The whole business thing started almost as a joke. Security and safety were linked to the basic health of the individual and the enterprise. After months of saloon-bar planning and banter, they had come up with a plan to have a company specializing in their strengths: security and safety. Sanctioned by the bank manager, agreed by their accountants and helped by a local estate agent, suitable premises had been found and Black's, the brewery firm, provided their first main ongoing contract. Domsec, domestic security, had been established. There is an adage that nothing succeeds like success and it applied to Domsec. The firm went from strength to strength. The firm rested on meeting the growing needs of the market-place and the expertise of 'Plodder' and 'Boots'. The name itself was a bit of a misnomer as the work involved safety and security in both domestic and industrial settings; it was both consultancy advice and the fitting of a range of security and safety devices.

In a sense, there were really two operating units, the security firm with its emphasis on the domestic market and the safety firm with its orientation on the business-to-business or industrial market. The domestic security market to date could be termed 'low tech'. There were no closed circuit TVs or access controls, no video entry systems or security grilles or doors. They would put in window bars if the customer demanded it but 'Boots' was against the concept on safety grounds. So it was not a state-of-the-art electronic detection. Nor did it involve highly trained 'officers' or dog handlers to protect property or people. It was on a basic level: door spy-holes, intercoms, bolts, snibs and digital locking systems whereby the homeowners could punch in their number. But even this digital system had been quite a recent innovation. The industrial security market had demanded greater technical specialization and manpower, so the company to date had majored on the new building, refurbishment and security-conscious owner market segments.

The health and safety part of the business was co-ordinated by 'Boots'. The firm provided 'any safety piece of equipment', or so it boasted. It manufactured nothing as a deliberate policy but it provided safety shoes, goggles, gloves, breathing apparatus, protective uniforms and suits, and so on. In addition, the firm provided guidance on safety to the industrial users and consultancy-cum-training skills for representatives. It also crossed over to the other 'division' in giving advice on such things as fire alarms to domestic users but this advice had largely become routine apart from at the initial sales pitch for large construction contracts.

The business was very successful. Security was the watchword of the troubled times while industrial and commercial safety were statutory requirements which had to be met.

The business continued to grow without conscious planning as it seemed to satisfy the needs of customers. The growth meant the employment of a marketeer, Amid Hamin. Amid was a great believer in planning and soon after joining the firm, the issue of a planned approach to policy began to arise.

Ted and 'Boots' were entrepreneurs and subject specialists, while Amid knew his stuff but was more of a manager. The founders believed in what their instinct told them; Amid believed in his mind. The following exchange took place at the monthly conference for the senior executives.

Amid: 'Planning will mean that the firm can control the environment. Not only that, but you guys keep a plan of sorts in your head and by writing it down the rest of the team can keep up to date with your ideas. The alternative to a planned approach is to live by the seat of our pants.'

Boots: 'With respect, Amid, we've been doing this for a long time now. We have an intuitive "feel" for what we are about – we don't need plans of action or more bureaucracy.'

Amid: 'The issue is not bureaucracy but growth in good times or survival in bad times. Markets can go, competition can move in, our products can be substituted, health and safety laws can be relaxed ... need I go on?'

Ted: 'We want results as well, but we have a "plan", as you call it. We know what we're about, we know the business – or the two businesses, in our case, or at least, the two sides of the business. Granted we could monitor things a bit better with budgets and things but we're OK – the market dictates and we are in the right market.'

The meeting dragged on and the debating points were becoming repetitive.

Assume that you are Amid.

1 How would you go about blunting their argument?
2 Advancing your own?
3 It may be worthwhile noting the limits of your own planning arguments as well.

The Limits and Problems of Business Policy

The danger for strategic management is the growth of a large group of planners who lose contact with the firm's products and customers. They may make decisions based on theoretical concepts rather than the real needs of the business. There can be a large investment in time, money and people which can take years to pay off and the running-in period may result in lost opportunities. The major problem, however, is that strategic planning often tends to restrict firms to the most rational risk-free option. Managers only develop those strategies that they know will survive the firm's planning process. Managers have to devise ways to overcome such defects. Nevertheless, research has shown that firms with clear well-defined strategies outperform those with informal unclear ones as mentioned earlier.[4]

Overcoming the Limits and Problems

In order to take account of the deficiencies of strategic planning, Ansoff[5] believed there was a need for capability planning. This is because the success of any strategy depends on the internal functional and managerial capabilities of the firm. The concept of capability planning is understood in the functional areas in terms of marketing, finance, human resources and so on, but not in the management area.

Ansoff believes management capability is dependent on five factors:

1 The quality and mentality of the manager.
2 The culture of the firm.
3 The power structure.
4 The management systems and organization structure.
5 The work capacity of the manager.

This is because when a firm faces a new situation the implementation of plans to overcome it meets resistance. Thus the *management of resistance to change* is implicit in strategic management.

The Tasks of Management

Following a study of the literature, Hofer and Schendel[6] proposed six tasks for strategic management:

1 Identify the organization goals.
2 Forecast the future environmental conditions.
3 Formulate strategy.
4 Evaluate past strategy in order to estimate the success of future strategy.
5 Implement the strategy.
6 Control and monitor the strategy.

Of course these have to be adapted for low-level managers but in broad terms they are acceptable.

It is always necessary for managers to become more **effective** (by doing the right things) and **efficient** (by doing things right) in what they are doing, but the environment also changes and they have to adapt to change. It is the manager's job to interpret the winds of change. **Strategic management**, therefore, is a stream of decisions and actions that lead to the implementation of a successful strategy.

Strategic management is an ongoing process and is carried out not in isolation but alongside all the other jobs involved in managing an organization – planning, organizing, leading and controlling. On the other hand, strategic management does not make continuous demands on a manager's time since change is not orderly or predictable. Once the strategy has been decided the management's job is really a strategy-supporting one – managers have to get the best performance out of the organization in order to achieve the objectives of the strategy. This means that every manager is a strategy maker, implementer and evaluator since every part of an organization has a strategic role to play. When managers themselves are involved in making strategy it is difficult for them to avoid responsibility for the results from it. Managers should know when to initiate strategic change and the kind of change to initiate.

The anticipation of possible changes, particularly in the external environment, can be critical to the success of the business. Managers must:

■ examine and anticipate trends;
■ estimate the impact or urgency of the trends;
■ prioritize the issues.

The urgent issues are dealt with immediately and the process is monitored for effectiveness.

Both strong and weak issues should be identified and both should be prioritized. If a firm waits for a weak issue to become strong before it begins to plan for it, the correct response will be late or may not be made at all.

This leads on to the problem of dealing with surprises and the ability to set up an emergency surprise system. The example in Box BP1.4 on Union Carbide is instructive and should be read next.

BOX BP1.4

Union Carbide: the need for a 'surprise system'

Some companies such as airlines and shipping firms have contingency plans for emergencies. However, most organizations do not foresee any possibility of emergencies occurring in their business. Therefore, they find themselves unable to respond to catastrophes either immediately or in the long term.

This happened to Union Carbide on the morning of 3 December 1984. Its pesticide plant in Bhopal, India, leaked lethal methylisocyanate gas into a crowded city of 700,000 people. The death toll started at 200 and eventually climbed to 2,000 with over 100,000 injured. There was a delay in the accident being reported to the Union Carbide headquarters in Connecticut, USA, since there were only a few telephone lines into Bhopal. Consequently, Union Carbide had to obtain further information from its Bombay subsidiary. As soon as the magnitude of the disaster became apparent the management of the plant had been placed under arrest, so detailed information was limited.

Having failed to get any answers to his questions, Warren Anderson, the Chief Executive Officer of Union Carbide, flew to India to assess the situation and organize help. However, he was immediately placed under arrest and was consequently unable to sort out the situation. Indian officials also closed the plant in order to prevent staff tampering with the evidence.

Anderson was eventually freed on bail and Union Carbide were expected to pay damages far in excess of their insurance. Worldwide production of the chemical was stopped and Union Carbide lost over $800 million in value on the stock market within a week. The firm's safety policies and procedures came under detailed scrutiny and its public relations had to be repaired.

Levels of Operation

Strategy is useful at several levels in an organization – corporate, business, functional and operating. There is also an institutional strategy which pervades all levels of the organization.

Before we enlarge upon this, take stock of your views on operations and policy. Traditionally we have divided managerial tasks into two categories – operations and policy. It is important that we know our starting point before we can develop a policy perspective. Please complete Activity BP1.3 on roles.

ACTIVITY BP1.3

ROLES

Activity code
✓ Self-development
✓ Teamwork
☐ Communications
☐ Numeracy/IT
✓ Decisions

A range of statements from managers is shown below. Some are Policy (P) roles whilst others are Operational (O) roles. Some may have elements of both (P/O). Allocate P, O or P/O accordingly.

Statement   *Role*

 1 Our objectives are pre-established here.
 2 My identification is with my profession.
 3 The function is the key to business.
 4 Innovation makes for goal setting.
 5 The perspective must be company-wide.
 6 The external environment is the dynamo around here.
 7 Our subject matter is often unfamiliar.
 8 Incentives are critical for goal achievement.
 9 Each culture has 'rules of the game'.
10 Past experience is my teacher.
11 My duties tend to be familiar and concrete.
12 A long time-scale is needed to evaluate results.
13 Risk is always present.
14 Objectives are fluid.
15 Prompt feedback on goals is essential.
16 New areas must always be considered.

A business strategy answers questions such as:

■ What products or services are/should be provided?
■ Which markets do/should we serve?
■ What functions are needed?
■ What facilities are needed and where?
■ What technology is required?
■ What core competencies do we have/need?

The aim here is:

- to compete successfully and gain competitive advantage;
- to respond to environmental changes;
- to unify the strategies of the functional areas;
- to manage the business successfully and develop the capability of the organization.

The **functional strategies** guide the activity in the functional areas of finance, human resources, manufacturing, marketing, research and development and so on. Strategy at this level uses the internal expertise of the organization to achieve organization objectives at the business unit level and answers questions such as:

- How do we get where we want to go?
- What cross-functional programmes are needed?
- How do stakeholders affect the organization and its plans?
- What is our plan for action?
- How do we allocate resources?
- What is our operating budget?
- What is our strategic budget?
- What is our stakeholder budget?

The aim here is to support the business strategy, meet functional area objectives and manage the organization successfully.

Operating strategies are for the basic operating units, distribution centres, plants, sales areas and so on and the departments within the functional areas such as advertising, purchasing, stock control and distribution. They add the detail and support the functional and business strategies by achieving the operating unit objectives. The importance of this level is obvious since any weakness here can affect the image of the organization with regard to its customers and so influence the overall strategy.

The **institutional strategy** gives the organization a distinctive character and answers the question: What do we stand for?

Small organizations may operate with fewer levels by including corporate level strategy, for instance, with the business level.

There must be some way of **monitoring** any strategy, so a control system must be instituted to answer questions such as:

- How do we know if the organization is on track?
- What assumptions have we made about stakeholders?

The overall strategy is often determined at the top and pushed downwards, where the details are filled in and then pushed back upwards. Much discussion is usually involved in order to rationalize the various levels and strategies. This process is important since the time taken to respond to environmental changes and competitors is often critical.

Therefore, it is also important to be able to harness new ideas which may be lying dormant at low levels in the organization. In what ways can these be identified and utilized? The decisions made at quite low levels in an organization often affect the long-term development of the organization, for example, the decision to use the Nicest People campaign by the Honda management in the US (see Box BP1.9 on the Honda Motor Company later in this unit).

A sound strategy:

- is congruent with the organization's internal and external environments;
- is congruent with its capability and culture;
- leads to long-term sustainable competitive advantage;
- leads to profitability and is easily communicated to the employees.

So we need to ask ourselves 'Is strategy really a form of planning?' Please read Box BP1.5 on strategy versus planning.

BOX BP1.5

Strategy versus planning

Hayes and Wheelwright identify five characteristics that differentiate strategy from planning:

1 Time horizon – a strategy implies an extended time period for both implementation and impact.
2 Impact – although the consequences of a strategy may not be obvious for a long time, the impact will be significant.
3 There is a concentration of effort on a narrow range of activities.
4 There is also a pattern of decisions which support one another over time.
5 The strategy pervades the organization, affecting all aspects of it from resource allocation to day-to-day operations.

Source: Hayes and Wheelwright, *Restoring our Competitive Edge*

Corporate strategy is for the organization as a whole, sets the direction and guides the allocation of resources. It is decided by senior management and answers such questions as:

- Where are we going?
- What business(es) are we in?
- What business should we be in?
- Who are the stakeholders?

Decisions made at this level involve establishing priorities and the use of resources for buying new businesses, developing new ideas, liquefying assets, making joint ventures or mergers and so on. It may well be that in the small business the owner makes these decisions. Congruency and synergy are important in making the whole greater than the sum of its parts. It is also important to monitor the strategy over time.

The **business strategy** applies to the **strategic business unit** (SBU) which operates independently of others. This could be a small business, a division of a large corporation or a part of a public service organization which can operate independently.

Developing Policy – Ansoff

Ansoff[7] developed a strategic success hypothesis which stated that a firm's performance is optimized when its aggressiveness and responsiveness match its environment. This has been validated by a number of research studies and should therefore form a good basis on which to proceed.

Ansoff defines **environmental turbulence** as a measure of the changeability and predictability of a firm's environment. Changeability depends on the complexity of the environment and the familiarity of the challenges to the firm, whereas predictability is a combination of the rapidity of change and the ability to foresee the future. Ansoff identified five levels of turbulence:

Level 1   Environments are repetitive in the sense that the market is stable; the challenges repeat themselves; change is slower than the organization's ability to respond; the future is expected to be the same as the past.

Level 2   Complexity increases but managers can still extrapolate from the past and forecast the future with confidence.

Level 3   Complexity increases further but the organization's response is too slow. The future is still predictable with some degree of confidence.

Level 4   Turbulence increases with the addition of global and socio-political changes. The future is only partly predictable.

Level 5   Turbulence increases further with unexpected events or situations developing more quickly than the organization can respond.

Over the years management systems have been developed to deal with these levels of turbulence and these are shown in figure 1.2.

Aggressiveness is described by the degree of discontinuity with the past of the firm's new products/services, competitive environments and market strategies, and the timeliness of the introduction of new products and services. **Level 1** is usually only found in not-for-profit organizations which do not change unless forced by a threat to their survival. **Level 2** is characterized by Henry Ford, who standardized production. **Level 3** organizations are those which shape and influence a customer's needs, perhaps by using artificial obsolescence. **Level 4** organizations scan their environment for future opportunities. The aim is to be where the action is by entering and exiting industries. **Level 5** organizations aim to remain at the cutting edge of design and technology.

Environment	Level 1 Repetitive	Level 2 Expanding	Level 3 Changing	Level 4 Discontinuous	Level 5 Surprising
Future	Predictable	Forecastable by extrapolation	Predictable threats and opportunities	Partially predictable opportunities	Unpredictable surprises
Management	By control	By extrapolation	By anticipating change	By flexible and rapid response	Management of surprises
Systems	Policy and procedure manuals	Financial control and capital budgeting	Long range planning	Strategic planning Strategic management	Strategic management Strategic issues Crisis management

Figure 1.2 Turbulence levels and management systems.

Source: Adapted from Ansoff, 1989.

The **responsiveness** of the firm must also match the environment and it is described by the climate, or management's propensity to respond in a particular way, for example to welcome, control or reject change; the competence, or management's ability to respond; and the capacity or volume of work the management can handle. **Level 1** organizations are change-rejecting, precedence-driven, highly structured, hierarchical and centralized. Management is custodial or control-driven. **Level 2** organizations are efficiency-driven and adapt to change. Power is in the production function. Management is production-driven. **Level 3** organizations are market-driven, extrovert and future-oriented but based on historical strengths. Management is market-driven. **Level 4** organizations are environment-driven. The seat of power is dependent on the challenge. Management is strategy-driven. **Level 5** organizations are environment-creating, may be driven by the market or research and development and are committed to creativity. Management is by flexible response.

According to Ansoff, strategic activities (doing the right things) and the operational activities (doing things right) compete for resources and management attention in firms at Levels 4 and 5.

Ansoff provides worksheets for diagnosing the level of turbulence, managers' profiles, management climate profiles and management competence profiles. These are used to diagnose an organization's current and future capability.

Level	Environment	Aggressiveness	Responsiveness
5	Surprising	Creative	Flexible
4	Discontinuous	Entrepreneurial	Strategic
3	Changing	Anticipatory	Marketing
2	Expanding	Reactive	Production
1	Repetitive	Stable	Custodial

Figure 1.3 Chart for optimizing a firm's performance.

Source: Adapted from Ansoff, 1989.

For our purposes, the chart shown in figure 1.3 can be used to optimize an organization's performance by comparing its present profile with its required future profile. Steps can then be taken to bring them into line if necessary.

For example, a group of managers could be asked to identify the current positions of their organization under each of the headings – Environment, Aggressiveness and Responsiveness – in the chart. If they then predict that the turbulence of the environment for their organization will soon be at a higher level, the difference between the present and future levels will indicate the amount of change the organization will have to experience in order to prepare itself for the future. Read Box BP1.6 for an example of the application of the Ansoff approach.

BOX BP1.6

An example of the Ansoff approach

A few years ago, one of our postgraduate students was examining the operational strategies required for a new project his company was planning. He was shocked when his Board of Directors cancelled it. This was the result of a series of environmental bombshells that exploded on the company.

On taking stock of the situation the manager decided to evaluate the original strategy and its relevance in the light of the environmental changes that occurred. Why was the company not able to adapt to change?

To answer this question, the manager turned to Ansoff in order to position the company's organization culture. Ansoff identified five types of organization culture – custodial, production, marketing, strategic and flexible. These are based on the managers' capability profiles, management climate profiles and management competence profiles. The manager used these profiles as questionnaires to position the company's organization culture.

He discovered that the culture of the company was to reject change, reject risk, focus on repetitive operations, not to 'rock the boat' and to respond only to a crisis. In Ansoff's terms, these were characteristics of a custodial organization culture.

Again, in Ansoff's terms, the internal characteristics of management competencies were also custodial. The main focus was in production, the management systems were by policy and procedure manuals and the management information system was largely informal. There was no structured environmental surveillance and problems were solved by trial and error as they arose. These are all characteristics of a custodial/production-oriented culture. However, the environment had become turbulent over the previous five years and the company had been unable to alter its strategy, until hit by a crisis.

For optimum profitability, the responsiveness of the organization must match the turbulence of the firm's environment. In this case there was a strong mismatch.

The manager and two colleagues were given the opportunity to present their findings to the Board of Directors, and it was not difficult to get their acceptance of the evaluation. The group of three was empowered to develop the company's strategic management capabilities and was strengthened by the addition of two of the Board members. The group has since produced a number of strategic choices with both internal and external actions.

This action project has had an enormous effect both on the company and on the manager. From being a manager who simply implemented decisions, he has moved to a position where he can have some effect on the strategy of the company.

Developing Policy – A Proposal

While Ansoff has identified the framework within which managers operate, there are also the day-to-day decisions that managers make in order to achieve their goals. Therefore, in order to be able to develop managers who are capable of dealing with issues at this level of complexity we need to:

- develop skills in analysing the environment and identifying opportunities and threats;
- understand the concepts of products/markets/industry and how they operate, together with the opportunities and threats they provide;
- analyse a firm and identify its strengths and weaknesses including its capability and propensity for risk;
- determine the impact/urgency of the opportunities and threats;

- identify the key issues for future sustainable success;
- develop options for change;
- implement the best options;
 - evaluate the results.

The concept is illustrated in figure 1.4 on page 30. This indicates that the skills of management can be learned independently in any order. Taken together they form a process for effective business policy management.

We are now going to develop this approach by means of a series of worked examples, presented in Boxes BP1.7–BP1.9. You should read the boxes in turn and write down your answers to the questions as well as your thoughts on the manner in which policies were developed in the Honda Motor Company. These are not the usual generic activities since they give a longitudinal perspective on the developing policy of Honda. One activity leads to the next and a suggested 'answer' is given after each box. Read each box and write down your thoughts before reading the answers. Now turn to Box BP1.7 on the Honda Motor Company. These activities are based on the work of Pascale[8] and Quinn.[9]

BOX BP1.7

Honda Motor Company (1)

By the age of 25 Soichiro Honda was one of the youngest entrepreneurs in Japan. He also loved cars and engines which he built and raced. However, the war destroyed his business and he sold off his assets. After the war, Japan was devastated and all forms of transport difficult. He didn't want to ride on overcrowded buses and trains so he built himself a motorized bicycle using war-surplus engines which once provided power for radios. There was an obvious market and these mopeds began to sell well. However, Honda was more interested in engineering than profits so he almost became bankrupt. He was introduced to Takeo Fujisawa whose ponderous style contrasted sharply with Honda's impatient directness. Nevertheless, they were to become lifelong friends and Fujisawa's financial and marketing skills set the foundation for the entire future development.

Just as before the war, Honda was not commercially motivated but used the company to express his innovative engineering ability. It was Fujisawa who saw the need for a four-stroke engine to keep up with competitors. In a short time Honda doubled the horsepower of four-stroke engines. Demand was high but the organization was chaotic and so forced investment in a simplified mass production process, integrating key components but buying in non-critical parts. In this way, owing firstly to design advantages and secondly to production methods, Honda achieved 15 per cent of the Japanese market by 1954. Fujisawa was able to turn this demand to his advantage by allocating production to distributors who would pay in advance. This provided cash flow and solved his financial problems.

1 What are the key factors that led to success in this section?
2 Read the section again and see if you can pick them out.
3 Is there any sign of a strategy?

Key success factors are:

1 Honda is an engineer who thrives on competition and technical excellence.

2 Honda did not try to develop his love for cars after the war but identified a need and set out to satisfy it.

3 There was a strong demand for his mopeds in Japan after the war.

4 He needed a partner to provide the skills he was lacking and was lucky in finding Fujisawa.

5 His innovation, doubling the power of the four-stroke engine, provided a technological edge over the competition.

6 Integration of the production of key components and the buying in of non-critical parts provided production advantages.

7 Fujisawa saw the opportunity to solve his cash-flow problems. Was this a risk?

8 So far there is no sign of a strategy to dominate the world, just a series of events, good decision making and luck.

BOX BP1.8

Honda Motor Company (2)

Honda refused to participate with both the central political committees and other business leaders directing Japan's economic recovery. Indeed, from time to time these committees and other leaders effectively blocked the development of Honda.

Honda built on his competitive advantage by racing his motorcycles and by 1956 his experience began to pay off in even more efficient engines and sales.

By this time Fujisawa had realized that there was a wider market and asked Honda to design a new moped. He sensed an untapped market niche for local delivery vehicles which needed a step-through frame, automatic transmission and one-hand controls. The Honda Supercub was the result.

The company was swamped with orders and sought finance to build a new factory with a capacity of 30,000 units a month, although at the time the Japanese market for two-wheelers was only 20,000. They did not think this was a speculative venture as they had the technology and the market. The demand was there, so that by 1959 Honda was in first place among Japanese motorcycle manufacturers.

This success enabled Fujisawa to restructure Honda's distribution channels. Since Honda was a late entry to the business, his motorcycles were carried as secondary lines by the distributors. Also, all sales were on a consignment basis. Fujisawa characterized the Supercub as more like a bicycle than a motorcycle and the traditional distributors agreed. In this way he was able to sell direct to retailers, mainly bicycle shops which were small and numerous. This produced over 12,000 outlets and enabled a cash-on-delivery system to be installed.

From this base Honda began to look overseas.

1 What do you see as the key success factors in this section?
2 Read the section again and pick them out.
3 Is there any sign of a strategy yet?

Key success factors are:

1 Honda wanted to stay independent.
2 Honda continued to build on his technological advantage by racing motorcycles.
3 Fujisawa identified a new market. Is this the same market in which Honda started out? Is he 'sticking to his knitting'?
4 They invested in a large new factory. Was this a risk?
5 Fujisawa changed the distribution channels and solved his cash-flow problems in one move. Was this a risk?
6 Honda now had the capacity and the technological advantage. In order to keep his capacity fully occupied he had to find ways of expanding his market. This could only be done overseas.

Until this time Honda had achieved success simply by luck and making good business decisions rather than following a strategy. Fujisawa realized the importance of cash flow and seized every opportunity to increase it. Now they were beginning to think about the future.

BOX BP1.9

Honda Motor Company (3)

For several years Honda tried to break into the market in South-East Asia without success. Honda also began to race his motorcycles overseas and was more successful. He collected the Manufacturers' Team Prize in 1959 and the first five places in the 1961 Isle of Man TT races.

Fujisawa believed American preferences could set trends for the rest of the world so he eventually targeted the United States. At first they tried an agent but soon set up their own company. The Ministry of Finance allowed them to invest only $250,000 in the United States and only $110,000 of that in cash: the rest had to be in motorcycles and spare parts.

The US market was 450,000 motorcycles per year, of which 60,000 were imported from Europe. It did not seem unreasonable to aim for 10 per cent of that market. Their only strategy was to see if they could sell something in the United States and take it from there. They simply took the same number of each of their four products. In money terms their stock was heavily loaded towards the larger bikes.

In late 1959, the end of the selling season, they set up in Los Angeles where there was a Japanese community, a climate which encouraged motorcycling and a growing population. The two executives were short of cash and lived in one room, rented an old shed and did all their own labouring. The first year was not a success – they had difficulty in signing up dealers. Then disaster struck – the Honda reputation was almost destroyed because the bikes were driven longer distances at faster speeds than in Japan. They leaked oil and the clutches failed. The new company had to use precious cash to return the motorcycles to Japan for testing in order to solve the problem.

While the Supercub was a success in Japan, Honda was trying to compete with the big European bikes in the United States. However, the Honda team used the Supercubs to ride around Los Angeles and attracted a lot of attention. Indeed, a Sears buyer showed interest and when the disaster of the larger bikes occurred, Honda had to concentrate on selling the Supercub. In fact, the retailers who wanted to sell the bikes were sports goods stores, not motorcycle dealers.

Honda reinvested their sales in stock and advertising. However, the advertising still pushed the four products equally. The retailers repeatedly told them that the buyers were ordinary people, but Honda hesitated against targeting this segment since they feared alienating the high-margin end of the business.

In 1963, a student of advertising at the University College of Los Angeles submitted an advertising campaign for Honda as his project, taking the theme 'You meet the nicest people on a Honda'. He contacted Grey Advertising who wanted the Honda account.

The Honda team had since grown to five members, who failed to reach a unanimous decision about the campaign. The sales director believed that the 'Nicest People' campaign was the right one and it was eventually accepted. The campaign fanned the flames of Honda sales and by 1964 50 per cent of all motorcycles sold in the United States were Hondas.

Owing to the customer profile, there was a move away from dealer credit to consumer credit companies and banks. This gave Honda the base on which to cease shipping on a consignment basis and ask for cash on delivery. Honda transferred power from the dealer to the manufacturer and this became the pattern for the industry in later years.

1 What do you see as the key success factors in this section?
2 Read the section again and pick them out.
3 Is there any sign of a strategy yet?

Key success factors are:
1 The company accepted the challenge of taking on the West Europeans in the United States. There was a higher margin on large motorcycles.
2 The company set out to see if they could sell something and made a start in a small way.
3 The company's technology nearly failed them as the bikes were operating under different conditions from those in Japan.
4 The company was forced to sell the Supercub to survive but did not refocus their marketing until 1963–4.
5 The sales director saw the potential in the advertising campaign which focused on a large untapped segment of the market.
6 The company moved to cash on delivery and solved the cash-flow problem.

Again, there is no sign of a strategy other than the move to solve the cash-flow problem which has appeared before. However, a number of trends do seem to run through this case, not really forming a strategy but indicating good management practice.

1 Emphasis was placed on technological competitiveness and quality, both on the race tracks and in the products.
2 The importance of the small-engined mass market with small margins provided a base for the larger-margin big-engine bikes. This was forced on Honda in the United States but should have been obvious from the domestic experience.
3 There were moves to large numbers of retailers and cash on delivery. This provided access to the market and cash flow.
4 Honda and Fujisawa operated as a team.
5 The Honda executives did not continue to push the original objective of attacking the big-bike market.
6 The junior sales director was able to persuade more senior colleagues to choose the 'Nicest People' campaign.
7 Honda management appeared to be able to adapt to the environment but could at times be as slow to react as anyone else.
8 European manufacturers did not become aware of the threat from Japan until it was too late.

In fact by 1973 Honda had captured the US market and reduced the UK share of that market from 49 per cent to 9 per cent, effectively destroying the British industry.

Strategy and Hindsight

According to Pascale,[10] the Boston Consulting Group wrote a report for the British Government in 1975 which business schools soon analysed. They identified the following as Honda's strategy:

- High productivity.
- Technical superiority.
- High investment per employee – double the European norm.
- Development of a market region by region.
- Establishment of a subsidiary rather than dependence on distributors.
- Starting the push in the USA with their smallest motorcycle.
- Separating their motorcycles from the 'Hell's Angels' brigade.
- Aggressive pricing and advertising.

It was only later that the true story emerged as described in the case above. Thus there is a tendency for consultants and academics to oversimplify and overlook the way in which organizations adapt, experiment and thereby learn, sometimes making mistakes and sometimes being lucky. Perhaps it is the way firms deal with mistakes and chance events outside their field of vision that is important in business. Indeed, the Japanese tend to be distrustful of a single 'strategy' since that focuses attention at the expense of peripheral vision. Perhaps peripheral vision is a key to the survival of Japanese firms over the long term. The Japanese try to detect changes in the customers and their needs, the technology and the competition. A strategy, therefore, may be a weakness which can be detected in competitors and exploited.

Thus we come back to the idea of a learning organization and how it can be developed. Perhaps we should use a contingency approach rather than a strategy. In other words, the decision depends on the situation rather than the overall strategy.

Honda did not aim to be the top motorcycle producer in Japan but they did try to do everything well and followed good business practice. Their design, production and quality were the best. They based their products on racing and research and they focused on cash flow and investment. They made good profits so could let their US subsidiary take risks and learn from its mistakes. Honda was not happy to sit on its laurels, but set out to improve its products and look for new niches in the market to exploit. Aren't these policies that any manufacturing firm should follow?

The Way Forward

So many textbooks in the past have provided a method which has proved to be successful in a particular situation but has failed under different conditions. It is therefore important for managers to continually update their thinking. Although useful at the present moment, their skills may be leading them into trouble as conditions change, unless they adapt to the change taking place.

A change does not necessarily start at the top of an organization but can be initiated at much lower levels, as mentioned above in connection with Honda. Therefore, it is management attitudes to change and decision making which are important for success in the long term.

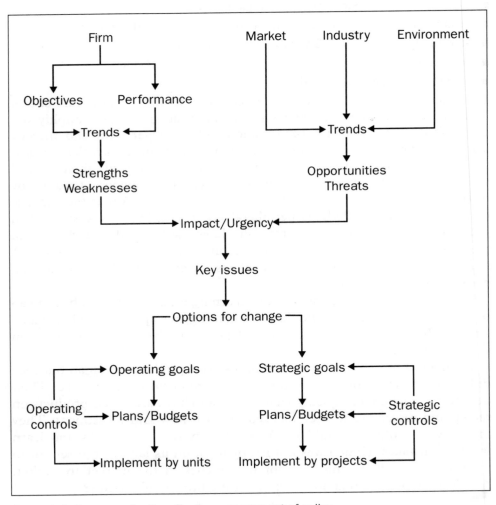

Figure 1.4 A process for the effective management of policy.

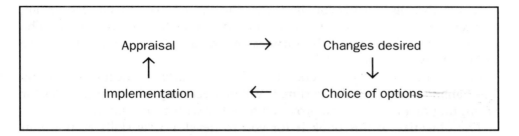

Figure 1.5 The policy process for management.

For instance, one could start at any point in figure 1.4 and work downwards. Ultimately the results of the implementation will feed back into the firm at the top of the figure and interact with the industry, market and environment. Therefore it is a matter of thinking and learning at all levels of the organization. Only by understanding the process in this way can we improve management effectiveness (that is, doing things right).

The process of managing an organization can be summarized in a diagram (see figure 1.5). The figure is designed to show a process that is occurring all the time in an organization. The process, repeated by managers many times a year, is outlined in more detail in the rest of this book. A manager is continually appraising the organization and its environments and deciding the changes to be made.

Appraisals consist of observing all the relevant factors in the external, competitive and business environments of the organization. The results of this process tell the manager something about the business and trigger decisions about changes which must be made in response to the observations.

The methods for making the changes and the methods for implementation are then decided upon. Usually these will occur at the same time, since there is no point in deciding on a change that cannot be implemented properly. Finally, the results are appraised and the process repeated.

This book will look at the broader aspects of business through the environment and gradually focus down to the firm. The skills necessary for analysing each of these aspects and making decisions will be explained. The objective is not to provide a catalogue of techniques but to provide a few key skills which will aid your thinking about change. It is the thinking that is important, not the technique.

Through using these skills, the strengths, weaknesses, opportunities and threats will be determined and the key issues identified. The various options available will be described and explained so that managers will be able to use them as and when necessary.

It is in the implementation stage that the chosen options succeed or fail, so techniques of implementation will be discussed and practised. The importance of all facets of the business working together during this stage cannot be over-emphasized.

Finally, the evaluation of change is discussed and the necessary criteria for change to be successful outlined. Where necessary, charts and tables for prompting managers will be provided together with cases and questions.

The objective of this book is for you to develop new skills so that you will become a better manager, rather than to develop a subject called policy management. Opportunities for practice will be provided in order to increase your efficiency and effectiveness so that your organization will survive and ultimately be successful.

Notes

1 Levitt, 'Marketing Myopia'.
2 Chandler, *Strategy and Structure*.
3 Armstrong, 'The value of formal planning for strategic decisions'.
4 Ibid.
5 Ansoff and McDonnell, *Implanting Strategic Management*.
6 Hofer and Schendel, *Strategy Formulation*.
7 Ansoff and McDonnell, *Implanting Strategic Management*.
8 Pascale, 'Perspectives on strategy: the real story behind Honda's success'.
9 Quinn, 'Honda Motor Company'.
10 Pascale, 'Perspectives on strategy'.

Unit Two

The External Environment

Learning Objectives

After completing this unit you should be able to:

- make a PEST analysis of your organization and identify the key opportunities and threats;

- identify the critical internal and external stakeholders;

- identify the key assumptions, beliefs and values behind your decisions;

- identify 'What do we stand for?';

- apply the generic skills.

Contents

Overview

The Climate

► Political

► Economic

► Sociological

► Technological

Stakeholders

► Internal stakeholders

► External stakeholders

► Generic strategies for dealing with stakeholders

Intangible Variables

► Assumptions

► Beliefs

► Values

What Do We Stand For?

► Stakeholder analysis

► Values analysis

► Social issue analysis

Unit Two

ρ

" Long range planning became a frustrating activity ... There
was little attention paid to the wider environmental (economic,
demographic, social, legal, technological) changes and operating market characteristics"

P. McKiernan, on an historical overview on long-range planning[1]

Overview

An organization's ability to cope with its external environment is probably
the major factor for its success or failure in a free enterprise society.
Changes in customer needs, political conditions and technology not only
affect an organization but can make or break an entire industry. The
successful organization, therefore, has learned to interact profitably with its
environment.

We believe that managers have a tendency to focus on the working of
the organization, that is, its internal environment, and underestimate the
effect of the external environment on the business. This tendency is
perhaps more acceptable as long as the external environment is stable and
predictable. When the external environment becomes turbulent managers
need to pay much more attention to it. Current developments around the
Pacific, the breakup of former eastern bloc communist countries, changes
in the EC and inflation have all affected business and industry in the last
two decades. Within individual countries there have been other changes –
political, legal, fiscal, demographic, ecological and so on – which have also
affected organizations.

Over the same period standards by which managers are judged have also
changed. In earlier years managers set out to maximize profits in order to
benefit the shareholders. Currently, managers must also take into account
quality of life and make themselves responsible to a wide variety of
stakeholders.

Figure 2.1 illustrates the overall environment in which an organization
operates. The forces and factors identified in the figure determine the
organization's future position. In this unit the way in which the external
environment or climatic factors, stakeholders and intangible variables may
determine the future position of an organization is explained. Other factors
will be discussed in Unit Three. It is important to take each of these
variables into consideration during management decision making and the

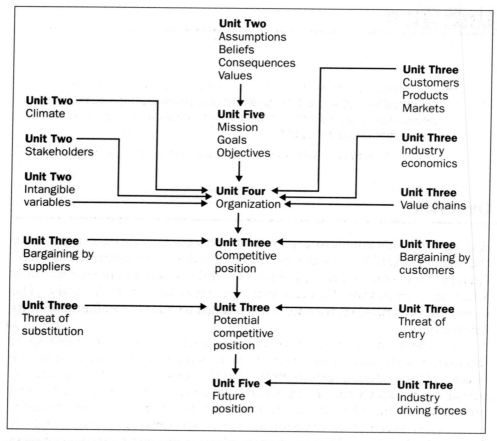

Figure 2.1 How the various forces and factors operating in an environment affect an organization.

prioritizing of these factors will need considerable conceptual ability in the context of your specific situation.

The Climate

The external environment or climate in which an organization operates has implications for a firm's strategy and its implementation. The major sub-climates to consider are the **P**olitical, **E**conomic, **S**ociological and **T**echnological (**PEST**). Managers should examine the ways in which each of these influences the organization. The detail to which this is taken will depend on the resources available and the ability to make sense of the data collected. However, simply keeping an eye on a few key factors will enable the manager to identify opportunities and threats to the organization. Please read Box BP2.1 on the wider external environment.

BOX BP2.1

The wider external environment

The interaction of political, economic, sociological and technological factors provides a context to the 'macro' environment of the organization and its market-place(s). These variables influence the market, providing both opportunities and constraints. Examples include:

- **Political** Legislation can inhibit a market-place, for example by the control of pornography and television advertising. The political stability of a country, region or area can certainly influence the market. The wealthy area of Iraq suffering under Saddam Hussein's regime is a good example. If and when the regime goes, the market will probably open up.

- **Economic** The amount and quality of skilled labour in one area compared to others can provide a wealthier market. The movement of labour in the EC can be cited here. Savings can be wiped out by price inflation as in some Latin American states or in Eastern Europe in the early 1990s.

- **Sociological** A greater ecological awareness can mean that products such as car exhausts must be altered to take account of the environment. The ethnic mix of a population can lead to cultural trends in eating, for example, that can be exploited.

- **Technological** Energy changes, information technology (IT), improved communication systems and so on make information and knowledge more readily available to everyone from competitor to customer. Change can have a drastic effect on the products; for example, the market for riding whips declined sharply with the advent of the motor car industry.

Political

The **political climate** consists of the factors related to the use and/or allocation of power. It is produced at several levels – local, national and international – and is tempered by special interest groups and other political entities. This climate is supported by the legal and judicial framework of the societies in which the organization operates.

It is impossible to determine a list of environmental factors that are important for all organizations but some key factors to watch are:

- employment and environmental protection legislation;
- foreign trade regulations;
- government stability and power bases;
- health and safety regulations;
- monopoly legislation;
- taxation.

An example from Holland can be seen in Box BP2.2

BOX BP2.2

The political environment

The green issue seems to be on the political agenda of the 1990s. It even affects corporate giants like Shell.

Tough procedures by the Dutch on the granting of licences have meant that Shell had to propose an eco-plan costing some £1.5 billion for its refinery near Rotterdam.

This plan is necessary before the plant's operational permit is agreed by the State.

Source: Adapted from Spinks, 'Dutch eco laws prompt Shell to clean up Rotterdam refinery'

Economic

The **economic climate** consists of all the factors related to the flow of energy, information, money, products and services. It is obviously critical to the success of the organization. There are two types of economic change that are important to managers, structural and cyclical. **Structural** changes challenge our basic assumptions about how the economy works. Sudden changes in energy costs or a shift from an industrial to a service economy are examples. Such changes may be permanent or temporary. **Cyclical** changes are periodic swings in economic activity such as interest rates and inflation.

Structural changes often need fundamental rethinking of strategies for organizations whereas cyclical changes are a function of the normal economic climate.

Some key factors to watch are:

- business cycles
- disposable income
- energy availability and cost
- gross national product (GNP)
- inflation
- interest rates
- investment
- money supply
- prices
- productivity
- unemployment
- wage rates

BOX BP2.3

The economic environment

We make an artificial distinction between the four components of the PEST environment, but this is for the sake of analysis only as clearly they do inter-act.

This interaction can be seen in the example below of a two-way process combining sociological trends and economics.

Martin and Mason, for example, examine four different 'end-of-century scen-arios' in the leisure sector with variables of high/low economic performance interacting with changes/static positions in sociological values, working pat-terns, and so on.

For example, we can have low economic growth and changing sociological values and attitudes to give us what the researchers term 'self-restraint'. If this economic growth is fused with no change or environmental type of val-ues, 'frustration' will then ensue. If these values remain fixed and economic growth is high, 'conventional success' will occur. The other option involves economic growth and changed values which will result in 'transformed growth'.

Source: Adapted from Martin and Mason, 'Leisure and Work'

Regional variations and trends are important.

An example of the economic environment can be seen in Box BP2.3.

Sociological

The **sociological climate** consists of the factors that affect the way people live and is produced by three variables: demography, lifestyle and social values. Both the demographic and lifestyle variables will influence the composition, expectations and location of the organization's labour supply and customers, whereas social values determine the choices people make in life and how managers and organizations operate. Our values change and adjust over time so that policies acceptable a few years ago may not be acceptable today. Values in one country may be incompatible with those in another. Variations in values may also explain differences between one sector of a population and another.

Some key factors to watch are:

- attitudes to work and leisure
- consumerism
- income distribution
- levels of education

BOX BP2.4

The sociological environment

The investment in people to give a country a competitive edge over others has been addressed in a study by the National Economic Development Office (NEDO) and the former Manpower Services Commission (MSC).

A comparative analysis was made between Germany, the United States, Japan and the United Kingdom. Some of the main findings included:

- **Qualifications** The average competitor nation has a higher take-up rate for off-the-job training and education than in the UK. For example, in the USA, 1 in 5 of the workforce is qualified to first degree level.
- **Youth policy** At the time of the writing of the report, some two-thirds of the 16–18-year-olds in the UK entered the labour market while some 94 per cent of Japanese youth stayed on to continue their education up to the age of 18.
- **Engineering** The output of graduate engineers in Japan totalled some 70,000 per annum compared to 15,000 in the UK, while apprenticeship training in the UK was difficult to find.
- **Education and training** In the competitor states, funding of education and training is a necessary capital investment, not just a cost. Employers in Germany, for example, foot most of the bill for apprentice training.
- **Information on opportunities** There is a need for an information type of agency in the UK not dissimilar to the American experience.

Perhaps some movement has occurred since the writing of the report in 1984, but the UK still looks to be at a considerable disadvantage compared to its economic rivals in the core strengths of its work-based knowledge and skills.

Source: Adapted from NEDO and MSC, *Competence and Competition, Training and Education in the Federal Republic of Germany, the United States and Japan*

- lifestyle changes
- population demographics
- social mobility and values

Now refer to Box BP2.4.

Technological

The **technological climate** is related to the development of knowledge about machines, materials, processes and tools. It is based on advances in science, new materials, products and processes. The level of technology in an organization, industry or society determines the kinds of products and services that can be produced, the equipment used and the methods of management required.

Technology can be a driving force in shaping the future of an organization and therefore a way of gaining competitive advantage. On the other hand, failure to recognize new technology can result in an organization failing to survive.

Some key factors to watch are:

- government and industry focus
- government spending on research
- new discoveries or developments
- rates of obsolescence
- speed of technology transfer

An example of new technology illustrates these changes in Box BP2.5.

BOX BP2.5

The technological environment

Perhaps one of the quickest-changing environments in business is that of computing.

The advent of Windows has meant multi-tasking, multi-threading and built-in networking attributes which have boosted the speed and performance of products using this mechanism.

An example is provided by Pilot Software and its new process, described as 'the world's first open systems multi-dimensional database server'. For instance, this can be applied as an ongoing basis for sales and marketing data collation and application to give a rapid response to trends in the external economic environment.

Source: Adapted from *Management Consultant News*, 'Multi-dimensional Data Sensor'

Of course the key environmental issues for one organization will not be the same as for another, even in the same industry. However, the key factors mentioned above enable managers to identify the major forces at work in their environment.

Successful strategies tend to be perpetuated. There is a strong incentive to repeat that which worked in the past, to do it better, more efficiently and to get more people to do the same. This is because organizations reinforce successful behaviour by creating information and learning systems, incentives and organization structures around successful strategies. However, this approach can have disadvantages since it can continue to push the organization in the same direction long after the need for it has gone (for example Henry Ford and the Model T).

Consequently, we need alternative types of forecasting techniques and we need to examine some of the alternative approaches to environmental scans. In this connection, read Box BP2.6 before you go any further.

BOX BP2.6

Environmental scans: policy and forecasting techniques

LeBell and Krasner show the potential relationship between the phase of organizational development and given techniques of forecasting the environment. Rather than pursue this approach, we can usefully examine their range of scanning techniques open to the policy maker.

- **Expert opinion** The so-called 'Delphi technique' can be used, or highly structured interviews with experts in the sector can be useful. Alternatively, expert opinion can be used as a standing committee or panel such as exists in the UK with 'wise men' advising the current administration on economic policy.
- **Non-expert opinion** Surveys, discussions and scenario generation can be interesting to get the lay person's view of things. Trends and themes which the experts may have missed may appear.
- **Extrapolation** The lifecycle curve or mere linear extrapolation can be used, but these have clear limits in more dynamic periods – it is historians, not history, who repeat themselves.
- **Estimates** Worst-case analysis or extending the high/low limits of risk, for example, may give the worst and best cases.
- **Mapping** A form of morphology analysis where the environment is tracked, recorded and plotted can be employed.
- **Modelling** There are many types, from simpler stochastic models to more complex methods with many variables and factors. Regression analysis and probability tables can be used as well in these more complex variations.

Source: Adapted from LeBell and Krasner, 'Selecting environmental forecasting techniques for business planning requirements'

You should now be able to tackle Activity BP2.1 on the Randy brothers.

Stakeholders

Stakeholders are those groups or individuals affected directly or indirectly by a firm's pursuit of its goals. Managers have to deal with stakeholders and so balance the conflicting claims on the organization. The competing claims of customers, shareholders, workers and the local community, for instance, have to be assessed in order for the organization to survive. Whether you are a chief executive officer (CEO) or a first line manager, you can still make use of the framework which follows. As a first line

ACTIVITY BP2.1

THE RANDY BROTHERS

Activity code
- ✓ Self-development
- ✓ Teamwork
- ☐ Communications
- ☐ Numeracy/IT
- ✓ Decisions

The Randy brothers were Greek Cypriots. The invasion of Northern Cyprus by the Turks had obliged the young brothers to move south with their successful restaurant business.

Interests spread through the years into Spain, Italy and the Balearic Islands. The formula was similar: good quality food at reasonable prices.

An opportunity arose to acquire an English country house hotel near Bath. One of their compatriots, a business studies student at a London college, agreed to conduct an environmental analysis for the brothers. The specific competitive analysis would follow and he hoped to get a vacation job so that his 'intelligence' system could relate back to Cyprus concerning the internal environment of the firm.

'Geographically, the house is based in southern England, which provides a stable political environment. Terrorists are active in some parts of the country but there has been no crusade against the rich, other than the occasional flurry against business leaders in Northern Ireland and by Welsh nationalist extremists setting fire to property owned by absentee landlords. Our potential clientèle is rich but should not be affected by these forces.

'It is a Grade II listed Georgian building with 30 rooms, swimming pool, leisure centre and 29 acres of parkland. Planning permission to amend the Grade II building may be difficult.

'The government does not really interfere with the hotel and restaurant sector, believing in a climate of free enterprise, so labour is particularly cheap. Furthermore, the rural area means that wages are already depressed. Legislation does exist in health and safety and there are very strict hygiene requirements.

'Within a 35-mile radius there are 11 other hotels and, with the inclusion of this country house, some 300 rooms are provided by these hotels. Prices are in line with the competition at about £130 per night and an average dinner costs approximately £30 per head. There are no real high-quality restaurants in this 35-mile area. A good report in the wine and food guides is critical for business.

'Some conferences and seminars for senior managers are occasionally held here. The locals in the area do not frequent the hotel, although some 'A/B' socio-economic categories do frequent the restaurant. It certainly has 'snob' value.

'The technological aspect of the external environment does not really apply. The house is served by a good transport and distribution network, it has old-world charm, there is some modern technology in the leisure areas, but this industry, and indeed the hotel, is not at the forefront of the technology, and no 'threat' is expected from this quarter. Some would argue that a kitchen revolution has occurred in terms of food preparation and the speed of cooking, but this has not affected the house.'

Assume that you are one of the Randy brothers. Conduct a PEST analysis of this hotel and its environment based on the information above. Make conclusions on both opportunities and threats.

manager, you may not be able to identify the same stakeholders as a CEO, but you must know who they are.

The external environment of an organization is continually changing and the forces involved create groups or individuals who become stakeholders. Stakeholders are of two types: **internal** stakeholders and **external** stakeholders (see figure 2.2). Critical stakeholders can be identified using figure 2.3.

Internal stakeholders	**External stakeholders**
Employees	Competitors
Owners/shareholders	Customers
Board of directors	Financial institutions
	Governments
	Local community
	Multiple stakeholders
	Suppliers
	Unions

Figure 2.2 Typical stakeholders.

Internal stakeholders

Internal stakeholders are part of the environment for which a manager is responsible. The firm's **employees** are important stakeholders, especially during periods when the workforce is changing. Changes in the birth rate, the influence of ethnic minorities, skill shortages and employee involvement are increasing the stake of the employee in the organization.

Stakeholders	Major assumptions which give rise to:	Knowledge about assumptions *Scale: 0–100%*	Impact on strategy *Scale: 0–100%*
Competitors e.g. Company X	Opportunities: X has weaker product line	80%	90%
	Threats: X has greater financial and marketing strength	90%	90%
	X has better distribution	90%	80%
Customers	Opportunities: Threats:		
Employees	Opportunities: Threats:		
Owners/ shareholders	Opportunities: Threats:		
Regulators	Opportunities: Threats:		
Special interest groups	Opportunities: Threats:		
Suppliers	Opportunities: Threats:		

Figure 2.3 The critical stakeholders for an organization.

Source: Adapted from Rowe et al., 1989.

Employees can also be sources of new ideas and must be regarded as company assets and nurtured in order for the organization to prosper.

Shareholders have a stake in the organization in that they expect a return on their investment and also expect it to grow in value. There are different types of shareholder both private and institutional, each of which makes demands on the organization which have to be reconciled by the manager.

The **Boards of directors** have a duty to ensure the continuity of management; protect the shareholders' investment; ensure management is prudent; approve major financial and operational decisions of management; represent the organization in society; and enforce, maintain and revise the corporate charter and bye-laws. The Board is a legal entity and a representative of the owners. However, outside representation on the Board is becoming more common and can be an effective way of involving major stakeholders with the organization. Boards are also tending to become smaller in order to get more done in the time available, since the environment is becoming more turbulent.

External stakeholders

There are many different external stakeholders, the most important of whom are the **customers**. Who are they? Where are they? What do they want? How can the product or service be provided at the right price? In what ways can the number of customers be increased? These are just some of the questions which need to be answered.

High quality standards, customer service and the influence of new technology in the form of communications and transportation have made possible the concept of a 'global' rather than 'national' product and international customers may need to be catered for.

Within the organization itself, everyone is a customer of everyone else and this has wide-ranging effects with regard to customer service.

In order to sell its products or services, an organization must gain more customers and so must compete against others. Therefore **competitors** are important stakeholders.[2] Competitors have a stake in your business because their success depends on what you do. Therefore, they will do everything in their power to influence your decisions and to gain your customers. A manager must provide superior customer satisfaction in order to beat the competition. It is important to think who your competitors are now as well as who your competitors could be in the future. Many firms have disappeared because a competitor appeared unexpectedly and they were unable to respond quickly enough. Foreign competition, laws and cultures may require additional resources to assess competition properly.

Discussion of competition leads to the role of **governments** as stakeholders. They act as watchdogs, regulating business and industry in the public interest and to ensure that market principles are followed.

Governments shape an organization's strategy by the way they control financial, fiscal and legal policies. Managers have to deal with local, national and international controls for employment, health, laws, resources, safety and taxes, amongst others.

Consideration of the resources for your business will identify **suppliers** as stakeholders. Suppliers provide energy, equipment, finance, labour, raw materials and services to the organization which then uses them to produce products and services. Organizations are therefore dependent on their suppliers in order to survive. Sources of supply need to be kept under constant observation in order to detect potential threats or opportunities.

Managers must look for a competitive edge, and this could be in better and/or cheaper supply lines. Quality and standards are important, as are shortages, poor delivery times and fluctuating prices. The place of stock in the organization must also be critically examined and a policy developed to optimize its effect on the organization. This may involve capital investment. The effect of new technology in terms of computer control and robots has produced significant changes in this area over the last decade.

The need for supplies of labour brings into focus **unions** as major stakeholders. Major changes in labour relations have taken place in recent years owing to changes in the environment and other stakeholders. Unions are becoming more interested in the quality of life and work, and confrontation is being increasingly avoided so as to enable firms to survive in the turbulent environment.

The turbulent environment demands the help of **financial institutions**, who are therefore major stakeholders in many organizations. Changes have occurred in the financial markets over the last decade and many new products and services have been developed to meet the needs of international trade. The presence of new technology has also allowed 24-hour trading of stocks, shares and money as well as instant access to the money situation both inside and outside the organization.

New mass-communication technologies have enabled the media to open organizations to **public scrutiny**. The visual impact of television and investigative reporting have made managers more aware of the impact of their decisions on society. New skills are having to be cultivated in order to deal with public relations and minimize the damage of unforeseen occurrences, for example, the scare concerning the presence of benzine in Perrier mineral water in the early 1990s.

These unforeseen occurrences and the needs of society which develop out of the climate of the environment have led to the growth of **special interest groups**. Consumer and environmental groups and those with special health, safety and ethical interests all have a stake in one organization or another.

Dissatisfied customers either complain or take their custom elsewhere. **Customer loyalty** will tend to decide whether a firm is successful or not, hence the importance of brand names and brand loyalty. Complaints should lead to the improvement of the product or service, whereas the loss of a customer can contribute to an organization's decline.

Each organization has to satisfy its own unique set of stakeholders, so it is important for managers to identify and prioritize their stakeholders regularly. At the same time, there is a complex network of relationships and coalitions between stakeholders which also varies from time to time. For instance, employees, unions and ecology groups could unite against a proposed innovation that could cause some form of pollution. These **multiple stakeholders** may also develop and change over time.

In order to identify significant relationships, a matrix of the external stakeholders should be produced (see figure 2.4). You should describe each of the stakeholder groups in detail for your particular organization and then compare them with one another. Then describe the ways in which they interact in the squares provided in the matrix.

Actions taken by one stakeholder or coalition may affect other stakeholders. Over time, stakeholder relationships become more complex

	1	2	3	4	5	6	7	8
1 Employees								
2 Owners/shareholder								
3 Board of directors								
4 Competitors								
5 Customers								
6 Regulators								
7 Special interest groups								
8 Suppliers								

Figure 2.4 A matrix of the major stakeholders, used to show their interactions with one another.

and produce a need for new, faster, more reliable responses and better ways of predicting the effects of the responses. All stakeholders are affected by the opportunities and threats generated by these responses. The complexity causes the relationships to become more impersonal.

Rowe et al.[3] believe that the success of any strategy depends on the validity of the assumptions made about an organization's stakeholders,

Stakeholders	Major assumptions which give rise to:	Knowledge about assumptions Scale: 0–100%	Impact on strategy Scale: 0–100%
Competitors	Opportunities: Threats:		
Customers	Opportunities: Threats:		
Employees	Opportunities: Threats:		
Owners/ shareholders	Opportunities: Threats:		
Regulators	Opportunities: Threats:		
Special interest groups	Opportunities: Threats:		
Suppliers	Opportunities: Threats:		

Figure 2.5 The critical stakeholders for an organization.

Source: Adapted from Rowe et al., 1989.

particularly about how they will respond as the strategy unfolds. In order to identify and validate the assumptions made about each stakeholder, we have to identify the assumptions and rank them with respect to their importance and certainty. This can be done using the chart in figure 2.5.

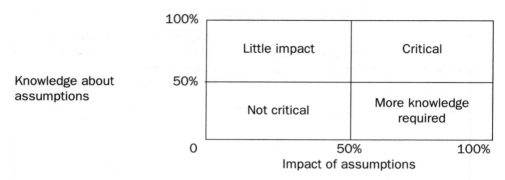

Figure 2.6 How knowledge about assumptions and their impact on strategy can be used to make better management decisions.

Source: Adapted from Rowe et al., 1989.

A successful strategy is one which takes advantage of opportunities and minimizes the impact of threats. A simple chart to show knowledge about assumptions against impact of assumptions on strategy (from figure 2.5) will identify assumptions requiring further investigation (see figure 2.6).

Another approach is to total the assumptions reporting opportunities and the assumptions reporting threats. If the total number of threats outweighs the total number of opportunities then the strategy has little chance of success. On the other hand, some of the threats may be turned into opportunities by creative thinking. If the total number of opportunities is greater than the number of threats then the strategy has more chance of success.

The climate or environmental factors (PEST) should also be assessed as to their importance and impact. A chart similar to figure 2.6 can be produced for each environmental factor – political, environmental, sociological and technological – in order to assist management decision making (see figure 2.7).

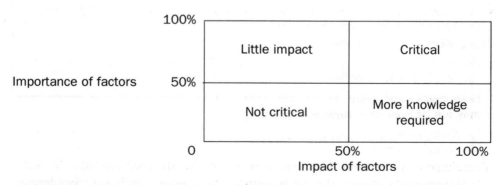

Figure 2.7 How the importance of environmental factors and their impact can be used to make better management decisions.

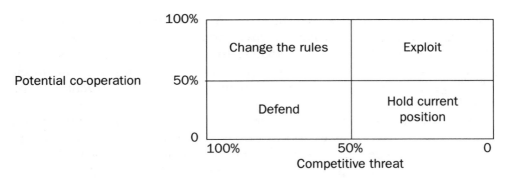

Figure 2.8 Generic stakeholder strategies.

Source: Adapted from Freeman, 1984.

Generic strategies for dealing with stakeholders

Freeman[4] developed a set of generic strategies for dealing with stakeholders which are valid regardless of which industry is involved. The potential co-operation (to what extent can the stakeholder help us to achieve our objectives?) and the competitive threat (to what extent can stakeholders prevent us from achieving our goals?) for each stakeholder are determined and plotted on a graph (see figure 2.8).

Once the stakeholders are plotted on the graph it will be possible to decide how to deal with them. For example stakeholders with:

- high co-operative potential and low competitive threat indicate the need for the adoption of an offensive strategy to get these stakeholders to co-operate.
- high competitive threat and low co-operative potential indicate the need for the adoption of a defensive strategy to prevent the threat they pose for us.
- both high co-operative potential and competitive threat indicate the need to adopt a strategy to change or influence the rules which govern the stakeholder interactions.
- both low co-operative potential and low competitive threat indicate the need for the firm to continue with the current strategy.

There are a number of drawbacks to the stakeholder concept:

1 Openness may lead to problems owing to difficult issues being brought to the surface. It also highlights the knowledge or ignorance of the managers.

2 Both management and employees must be involved and the knowledge base may not be present in these groups.

3 Paralysis by analysis may occur. This involves time, effort and costs. One must take action – hopefully, action which has, of course, been thought through.

We believe this is a useful approach for dealing with stakeholders.

It is important to sense changes in both the stakeholders and the climate in order to flag the need for changes in strategy. This can be done by identifying opportunities and threats. There is evidence to show that organizations good at sensing the environment are the better performers. However, simply being able to analyse the environment is not sufficient. Organizations have to be able to respond to change. This will depend on the flexibility, quality and culture of management and the structure of the organization.

Since managers tend to over-emphasize the strengths and opportunities and neglect the weaknesses and threats of their businesses, a vulnerability analysis was suggested by Hurd.[5] This is explained in Box BP2.7 and provides a risk averse approach which you might wish to consider.

Now that you understand the stakeholder concept you should be able to complete Activity BP2.2 on page 54.

BOX BP2.7

Vulnerability analysis

A **vulnerability analysis** was suggested by Hurd in order to answer the question: 'Which supporting elements (underpinnings), if taken away, might seriously damage or even destroy the organization?'

This vulnerability analysis helps managers to identify:

- the underpinnings on which the organization depends;
- the threats to the underpinnings;
- the impact of the threats to the organization and the organization's ability to compete effectively.

According to Hurd there are several key steps:

1 Identify underpinnings under headings such as:
   Customer needs and wants
   Resources and assets
   Cost position relative to competition
   Customer base
   Technology
   Special skills, systems etc.
   Corporate identity
   Barriers to competition
   Social values
   Sanctions, supports and incentives
   Goodwill
   Complementary products
2 In what ways would removal of an underpinning threaten the organization?
3 Rank the impact of the worst consequences of each threat.
4 Rank the ability of the organization to deal with each threat – the reaction.
5 Plot impact against reaction: refer to the following chart.

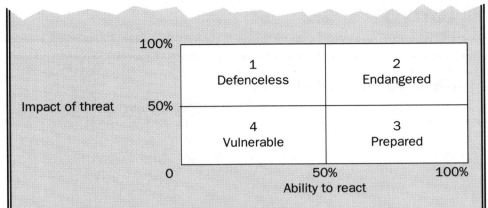

Chart to show how the impact of threats and the ability of an organization to react to threats can be used for management decision making (adapted from Rowe et al.).

- Any threats that occur in area 1 demand immediate attention and indicate that the organization is defenceless. Management should upgrade the organization's ability to react and so move the threat at least to area 2.
- Any threats in area 2 imply that threats are dangerous but the organization can react or retaliate.
- Threats in area 3 imply that the organization is prepared.
- Threats in area 4 are light to moderate and little needs to be done other than monitor and be prepared for them.

Source: Adapted from Hurd, 'Vulnerability analysis in business planning'

Intangible Variables

A strategy is a means to an end. Clearly this implies that an organization needs to develop a clear idea of where it is going and why. This starts with a vision of where the organization intends to be at some time in the future. The vision might require the present policies to continue, or there might be a need for new ones. Choosing the vision and finding the route to get there are relatively simple in themselves. However, the task becomes more difficult when considered in the context of the organization and its environment. Many variables, such as the assumptions, beliefs and values held by members of the organization, are difficult to measure objectively and we shall now briefly consider how to deal with them.

ACTIVITY BP2.2

COLLEGE OF EDUCATION

Activity code
- ✓ Self-development
- ✓ Teamwork
- ✓ Communications
-   Numeracy/IT
- ✓ Decisions

Assume that you are a senior manager at the College of Education.

1 Using the stakeholder approach, critically appraise the views of the staff in this case.

2 Report on methods to tackle the issues raised by the staff.

This state-funded College of Education is based at four sites within a 15-mile radius in the south of England. It has approximately the following number of students: 1,900 full-time students, predominantly school leavers undertaking technician-type courses; 600 day-release students from local industry and commerce, undertaking professional and technician-type courses; 2,800 students who attend one afternoon and two evenings per week from their place of work; and 6,000 students who attend in the evenings only. It has some 220 full-time academic staff, 195 part-time-cum-associate help, and 150 administrative staff, technicians, porters and so on.

In many ways it is a community college rather than an academic centre of excellence. It is involved in adult education in the broadest sense, although it is becoming increasingly vocation-oriented, with a strong presence in business studies, finance and languages for business. The specialisms are reflected in the organizational structure, although older specialisms are still predominant, perhaps at the expense of the newer growth areas of business and languages. There are five faculties:

1 TAD – technology, art and design
2 communications and media
3 social studies (English, literature, sociology and psychology)
4 business and finance
5 languages

The support areas include learning resources, which is supposed to keep academics abreast of 'best practice'; student counselling and welfare; and a new innovation for the College, the marketing liaison group. This marketing group reflects the educational changes at national level, whereby funding from government is being slowly and deliberately reduced per student, while the number (and, arguably, the quality) of students is increased. The marketing team's role is to find additional funding from short courses and language seminars, and from encouraging the enrolment of overseas students, with or without English as their first language, as they pay the full tuition fees without government funding or support. The marketing team would like all students to pay the full tuition fees and envisage this happening as the government increasingly withdraws financial support from the education sector. An administrative section co-ordinates all non-academic staff.

There is a senior management team of administrators with personnel and labour relations support from the human resources team. The senior management (six in all) are joined by the five faculty heads to form the directorate. Each head of faculty is supported by the set leader, who assists with resources, timetabling, staff management and academic development. In addition, there are a range of standing committees and subcommittees of the directorate covering areas from academic standards to sexual and racial equality. The organizational structure is shown in the chart.

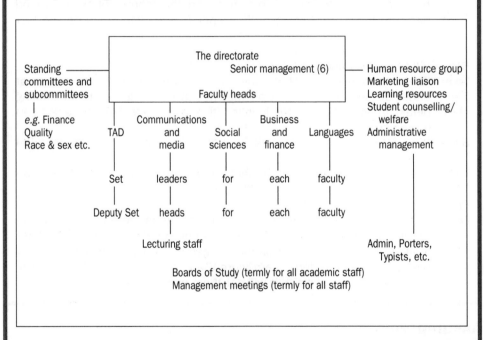

An independent government assessors' report had emphasized the competence, if not the excellence, of the language department and of the business section. These points confirmed what the staff already knew. Tom, the unit leader for languages, and Bill, who ran the business courses, discussed matters as follows.

Tom: 'Frankly, Bill, your business courses have come out top and so have my language team. With a joint academic staff of ten people, we should start a Business English College.'

Bill:	'A buy-out.'
Tom:	'No, don't be daft, Bill, we can't buy them out. But, at the end of the day, this place pays a salary which is none too impressive, and the number of students increases daily, with more and more tutorials, marking and demands being placed on us. Add to that the 1950s scientific management view of the directorate who wish to treat us like proletarians while they award themselves bonuses for additional student numbers, and where does it leave us?'
Bill:	'Nowhere, and things are going downhill fast. What can we do, though? Most of the lecturers in the business area may get work outside the college, but the language people are trapped – unless some nice translation job comes up in the EC. I'm tired of the whole thing: we used to be a college, now we're a factory for degrees and technical business qualifications at the lower end of the educational spectrum. The lecturers are demotivated, they are sick of all these new bureaucratic controls, the management style stinks and the labour relations around here are not worth a candle! This appraisal system could be the last straw. Even the finances are a shambles.'
Tom:	'What appraisal is this?'
Bill:	'I'll tell you all about it later, Tom.'
Tom:	'Well, I suppose there's no point in just moaning about it – we must either do something or get on with it, but things are certainly looking bleak. In fact, we're both in our fifties and we're already looking to retirement.'
Bill:	'Yes, retirement out of here looks a great idea, but I'm too young and I need some stimulus.'
Tom:	'I did see the union–management circular on early retirement with an enhanced pension.'
Bill:	'So did I.'
Tom:	'What it all comes down to is that this college is mere bricks and mortar with a degree-granting facility for young people to enter the labour market or to get on in the promotion game. To that extent most of my post-experience students earn more than I do – the irony is, I'm teaching them the very skills that will get them even more money.'

Assumptions

Managers propose strategies on the basis of assumptions in which they have varying degrees of belief. Though strategies are based on data, the interpretation of that data involves assumptions and beliefs. Managers make assumptions because they cannot predict the future, since prediction involves risk and possible consequences. Some managers are risk takers while others, faced with the same facts and data, are risk averse. Only the consequences will tell which manager is right. Nevertheless, most managers do not identify the consequences of their strategies and so invite disaster. Therefore, managers should always assess the Assumptions,

Beliefs and Consequences (the **ABC**s) behind their proposed strategies. This involves:

■ identifying the **assumptions** behind each strategy;

■ estimating the strength of each assumption;

■ identifying all the **consequences**, both good and bad, for each assumption.

A chart can be constructed in order to assess the assumptions behind strategies (see figure 2.9).

Assumptions behind strategies	Strength of assumptions	Consequences

Figure 2.9 Chart to enable managers to assess the assumptions behind their strategies.

Beliefs

Real change or even the possibility of adapting to change, quite apart from anticipating environmental change, may well begin with changes in belief. Perhaps before we even begin to scan the external environment discussed earlier in the unit we should examine our beliefs. To us, the belief and value systems of management are critical components of business policy.

Behind our assumptions are **beliefs**. Peters and Waterman[6] identified seven beliefs held by successful managers. These are:

1 Belief in being the best.

2 Belief in the importance of doing a job well.

3 Belief in treating people as individuals.

4 Belief in superior quality.

5 Belief that people should be innovators and that, as a result, organizations should be willing to support failure.

6 Belief that informality helps communication.

7 Belief in the importance of growth and profits.

Peters and Waterman found that in successful companies managers focused on these beliefs and were able to get other people, down to the lowest levels, to share them. Strategy is based partly on shared beliefs about an organization's environment. The strength of these beliefs and their validity influence the success of the organization. Managers who are averse to risk tend to reject new ideas, no matter how much data support the idea. We shall develop these ideas later in the book.

The rejection of new ideas implies that real change begins with changes in belief. Therefore there is a need to identify the organization's beliefs and compare them to current and future reality. Any differences must be reconciled and new beliefs developed to meet new circumstances. The belief audit suggested by Zakon[7] is useful to this end. He believes the process should be a continuous one in order to detect early warning signals and patterns. The beliefs should be obtained from the organization's competitors, customers and suppliers and from the way the organization operates.

Answers to questions such as the following need to be obtained:

1 What makes our business successful?
2 Will today's advantages still be relevant five years from now?
3 How can we change our competitive advantage?
4 How can we exploit advantages in the future?

Early warning signals may come from the market-place, distribution channels, competitors and the organization itself.

Managers need to be able to log the assumptions behind their decisions and think through the consequences of the assumptions. Figure 2.10 provides a chart for you to make a belief audit.

What makes us successful?	What will the future be like?	Change needed?
Beliefs: *e.g.* branch network necessary	Beliefs: *e.g.* fewer branches	*e.g.* reduce number of branches
Strategy:	Strategy:	?
Actions:	Actions:	?

Figure 2.10 Chart for making a belief audit.

Before we turn to the values of managers, it would be a good idea for you to complete Activity BP2.3 'Value systems – a self-analysis'.

ACTIVITY BP2.3

VALUE SYSTEMS – A SELF-ANALYSIS

Activity code
- ✓ Self-development
- ☐ Teamwork
- ☐ Communications
- ☐ Numeracy/IT
- ☐ Decisions

Below is a range of statements organized in five groups. In each group, select one statement only which most closely fits your own values in the context of business. There are no right or wrong answers. Refer to the Handbook and Workbook for scoring.

1 I am quite pragmatic in my approach. ☐

2 I am very pragmatic in my approach. ☐

3 Business should be conducted with a high degree of morality. ☐

4 Achievement is important. ☐

5 Growth is important. ☐

6 People are important. ☐

7 We need to be competent. ☐

8 Size is important. ☐

9 A humanistic vision is important. ☐

10 Profit maximization, efficiency and productivity must be emphasized. ☐

11 We need to achieve. ☐

12 Growth and profit maximization are not high on my values. ☐

13 The workgroup is an important reference group for value systems. ☐

14 Change is endemic and best handled through a shared value system. ☐

15 Different values exist as people are all different. ☐

Source: The core research on these values comes from England, 'Managers and their value systems'. The quiz is adapted from this research

Values

Values are general, abstract ideas that guide our thinking and actions. They can be broadly classified as aesthetic, moral, religious and social. They are a set of attitudes about what is good or bad, desirable or undesirable. Values underlie the beliefs managers have about people and their organization. Managers' values are demonstrated by the actions they take, what they think, and how they allocate time, energy and skills. Since about 1900, managers' ethical and performance values have passed through several stages to reach those currently held – from profit maximization, through trusteeship, to an emphasis on the quality of life and a more ethical approach. Waterman[8] identified the following values and attitudes which he believed successful organizations require:

- Informed opportunism – keeping up to date to maintain strategic advantage.
- Direction and empowerment – identifying what needs to be done and allowing subordinates to find ways of doing it.
- Friendly acts and congenial controls – using financial controls but giving managers freedom to be creative.
- A different mirror – ideas can come from a variety of sources, such as competitors, customers and employees.
- Teamwork, trust, politics and power – accepting that fighting will occur but stressing teamwork and trust to get the work done.
- Stability in motion – allowing rules to be broken when necessary.
- Attitudes and attention – attention is more effective than exhortation and symbolic behaviour makes words come true.
- Causes and commitment – being aware of the 'grand cause' so that it permeates the actions.

In successful organizations effective leaders make values become infectious. Values affect a person's thinking habits, ways of relating to one another, the technology they use and the job descriptions, policies, procedures and rules by which they operate.

Spranger[9] identified six types of person based on the values they held:

Theoretical Truth was dominant. The aim was to systematize knowledge. Theoretical types included intellectuals, philosophers and scientists.

Aesthetic Beauty and harmony in terms of fitness, grace and symmetry were important.

Social Love, co-operation and humanism were reflected in kindness, sympathy and unselfishness.

Political Power was dominant; this type is a characteristic of many leaders.

Religious   Unity was important together with belief, faith and the mystical.

Economic   Efficiency and the pursuit of wealth are dominant.

A manager does not necessarily behave as one type but has a profile of values which is characteristic for the manager. That is, certain value types are stronger than others for each manager. The strategies produced by managers tend to reflect their personal value profile.

At this point, read Box BP2.8 on the value systems of management.

BOX BP2.8

The value systems of management

It is a cliché to say that we live in changing times. It is probably inaccurate, too, for times have always been changing, but perhaps the difference is one of degree as the pace of change seems to have quickened over the years. Traditional value systems, however these are defined, may also change under these pressures.

Stuart Hampson took over the role of chairman of the John Lewis Partnership in February 1993. The firm, a major quality retailer in the UK, has more than just a polished image; it has distinct value systems based on a traditional vision of virtues. Laurence quotes Hampson's virtue system, value and assortment, service and honesty. On an anecdotal level, of all the UK retailers in this segment, the firm's obsession with service and value for money is difficult to match.

The firm's vision of partnership between its staff seems to become a partnership between the firm and its customer. In the 1990s, difficult trading times exist for many retailers and it will be interesting to speculate whether traditional value systems enable this firm to grow from strength to strength.

Source: Laurence, 'Old-fashioned way ahead at John Lewis'

In contrast to the values which can be used to describe a person, Peters and Waterman[10] identified eight operating values held and acted on by successful managers:

1 They value action – 'do it, try it, fix it' – with a view to gaining competitive advantage.

2 They value customers, quality and service. Customer needs and wants are important.

3 They value autonomy and innovation and being allowed a reasonable number of mistakes.

4 They value people.

5 They value actions which convey values to co-workers, customers and suppliers.

6 They value underlying themes and a sense of direction.

7 They value reducing bureaucracy and red tape.

8 They value flexibility, decentralization and an entrepreneurial spirit with sensible controls.

Peters and Waterman's operating values identify means rather than ends and can be used to satisfy Spranger's personal values.

Social values are an important part of an organization's external environment. For instance, the values associated with agrarian, industrial and post-industrial societies are different. Therefore, managers should be aware of the values, both current and developing, in their society. Sometimes organizations deliberately incorporate the current social values into their strategies. For example, the Swedish car manufacturer Volvo replaced their assembly lines by teams that built cars from start to finish in order to combat boredom.

All strategies are based on values and should be appropriate for the conditions, place and time in which the organization operates. That is to say the values are neither good nor bad, but *appropriate*. Inappropriate values create products and services that customers will not pay for. However, more than one set of appropriate values can create a successful organization. Whether a strategy is successful or not depends on the values that underlie it and are part of an organization's culture. McDonald's core values are **Quality**, **Service**, **Cleanliness** and **Value** (**QSCV**) and these values are rewarded as part of its systems and procedures.

Now complete the tasks in Activity BP2.4, 'Value systems: bucking the trend – for a while'.

ACTIVITY BP2.4

VALUE SYSTEMS: BUCKING THE TREND – FOR A WHILE

Activity code
- ✓ Self-development
- ✓ Teamwork
- ☐ Communications
- ☐ Numeracy/IT
- ✓ Decisions

The Body Shop

The Body Shop, that well-known High Street retail outlet specializing in skin and hair care products, is an innovative retailer. Environmental issues dominate its innovative formulations to create a caring image throughout the stores. Honesty and integrity provide its value system and describe its mission. Its owner, Anita Roddick, has summarized the business policy of the firm as 'going in diametrically the opposite direction to the rest of the cosmetic industry'.

The company's growth is legendary: from a single shop in Brighton, UK, selling a mere 15 products, to a global operation from Sweden to Singapore with a range of nearly 300 products and a total of 400 shops worldwide.

The products buck the trend. They are not tested on animals and are not over-elaborately packaged. There are five different sizes for each item of the mainstream products, reflecting perhaps the company's narrow product range at the outset. Prices are relatively lower than those of the competition. Choice is given by the five sizes, and the environmental 'green' vision includes biodegradable carrier bags and refillable containers. Clearly the firm has kept pace with, or actually given a lead to, an increasing green lobby in consumerism.

A relatively small factory in west Sussex and an empire based on franchises has meant that expansion has been not only rapid but also not too costly.

Natural ingredients dominate the product range and worldwide research into skin and hair care from different cultures is conducted by Anita Roddick. This core approach has been maintained since the start of the business.

Competition is never far away. Other retail multiples copied and adopted a similar environmental approach. Recession hit the High Street leader and its products may have been more of a 'luxury' item than a necessity for some people. The Body Shop suffered. It had (legitimately) broken the rules of the game, but the other players can also break the rules – legitimately or otherwise.

1 Outline the key determinants of The Body Shop's initial success. Weight these factors in importance.
2 To what extent are these factors transferable to other competitive situations?

What Do We Stand For?

Value judgements are important for the success of the organization's strategy and are involved both in its formulation and implementation. This means that the values of those affected by the strategy must be taken into account. Therefore, if the same values are shared throughout the organization, the implementation of a strategy is relatively easy and successful.

For thousands of years military and religious organizations have practised the principle of depending on the shared values of their members. However, managers of commercial and industrial organizations have traditionally focused on the hard facts from the functional areas.

Over-reliance on the analytical aspects of strategic management has produced long and involved processes involving complicated flowcharts and lots of data.

These business factors are impersonal, logical and rational but the business world does not operate like that. Additionally, moral and ethical values in terms of social responsibility have recently begun to be recognized and these add more complexity to the situation. Therefore, we believe it is important for every organization to determine 'What do we stand for?'

Determining an organization's strategy is not a simple process, as it involves every level of the organization through any changes in policy, reallocation of resources and changes in the stakeholders and their relationships. These changes involve taking into account the assumptions, beliefs and values of the people concerned. Therefore, before a manager can consider formulating a corporate strategy, a set of questions must be asked which are focused on the **stakeholders**, **values** and **social issues**. It is only when these questions have been answered that the business opportunities available can be explored. We will build on these issues in the next section.

Stakeholder analysis

Freeman[11] suggested that in order to determine 'What do we stand for?' we need to answer some key questions about stakeholders, values and social issues (see figure 2.11).

This process can be extended by considering the various effects each stakeholder has on the organization and the effects the organization has on

Stakeholder analysis	Value analysis	Social issues
Who are our stakeholders?	What are the dominant organization values?	What are the major issues facing society over the next 10 years?
What effects do we have on each in political, economic and social terms?	What are the values of the top management?	How do these issues affect the organization and the stakeholders?
How do these stakeholders perceive these effects?	What are the values of the key stakeholders?	

Figure 2.11 Chart to determine 'What do we stand for?'

Source: Adapted from Freeman, 1984.

Stakeholder's Name:	
Effects of the organization's actions on the stakeholder	**Effects of the stakeholder's actions on the organization**
Political:	Political:
Economic:	Economic:
Social:	Social:
Technical:	Technical:
Managerial:	Managerial:

Figure 2.12 Chart to explore the cause and effect relationships between the organization and stakeholders.

Source: Adapted from Freeman, 1984.

each stakeholder. Stakeholders and organizations affect one another politically, economically, socially and technologically.

Management also has a part to play since stakeholders may cause changes in management processes, systems, styles and values. Management must be able to understand all stakeholders and deal with them successfully. By completing the chart in figure 2.12, managers should be able to understand the cause-and-effect relationships between the organization and stakeholders.

The chart is designed to help managers think through the effects of their actions. They must determine whether these actions are or will be acceptable to the stakeholders of the organization.

As we have discussed earlier, there are of course pitfalls in using the stakeholder concept in that, by exposing the stakeholders to examination, a number of difficult issues may surface and difficult decisions may have to be made. Therefore, it is important to involve as many interested parties as possible. Furthermore, since it is important to take action, time, effort and costs are involved. At the same time it is necessary to prioritize as well as identify the stakeholders in order to focus attention on the key issues.

Values analysis

People experience conflicts as a result of the roles they take in society – as a spouse, parent, citizen, manager or expert, for instance. How is it possible to get some kind of consistency between our roles in society? Are there some underlying values that each person carries from one role to another?

There is also the question of the values of the organization. These are shaped by tradition, culture and leadership and many values outlive the organization's members. However, the personal values of members may not be identical with the values of the organization but there should be a high degree of congruence. If there is a large difference in values between the organization, its stakeholders and its managers, then it is unlikely that the organization can be successful. Therefore, it is important to identify the values of these three entities and their similarities, inconsistencies and conflicts (see figures 2.13 and 2.14).

Values of managers	Similarities? Inconsistencies? Conflicts?	Values of organization
1	?	1
2	?	2
3	?	3
etc.	etc.	etc.

Figure 2.13 Chart to compare the values of managers with those of the organization.

Values of organization	Similarities? Inconsistencies? Conflicts?	Values of stakeholders
1	?	1
2	?	2
3	?	3
etc.	etc.	etc.

Figure 2.14 Chart to compare the values of the organization with those of the stakeholders.

This approach should enable you to identify value issues in your organization that need to be addressed before corporate strategy can be explored.

It is important for managers to understand the importance of values in planning business strategy. The values on which strategy is based should be appropriate for the conditions, place and time in which the organization operates. These values should be embedded in the organization's culture, its atmosphere, attitudes and behaviour. Culture will be dealt with later when the internal environment of the organization is examined.

Social issue analysis

Stakeholders, managers and organizations operate in society so it is necessary to identify as far as possible the critical issues of that society, both now and in the future. It is useful to look at the major issues facing society today, compare them to those issues expected to be faced in five or ten years' time and to identify the reasons for the changes. This is also probably best done by means of a chart (see figure 2.15).

Major social issues today	Reasons for change if any	Major social issues expected in 5–10 years
Political:	?	Political:
Economic:	?	Economic:
Social:	?	Social:
Technological:	?	Technological:
Managerial:	?	Managerial:

Figure 2.15 Chart to identify the key social issues both now and in the future.

Source: Adapted from Freeman, 1984.

In a sense we have completed a full circle and come back to the traditional PEST analysis, but the perspective is now wider and includes managerial issues.

Finally, we can combine the results of our analysis of the stakeholders, values and social issues in a statement of what the organization stands for. In order for the organization to survive there must be a 'fit' between the values of the organization, its managers and stakeholders, and the social issues. Therefore, regardless of the quality of its strategy, managers, productivity, standards and so on, the organization cannot be successful unless the values are congruent.

The next unit will focus on the decisions managers have to make with regard to competition in products or services, markets and industries.

Notes

1 McKiernan, 'Strategy formulation and the growth share matrix'.
2 At first glance this argument may look a little perverse. We often assume that competition means a fight to the death, but there can be a knock-on effect if a major competitor goes under, since the whole of the 'shared' product may be harmed and this could have a negative impact on the industry. The rush by UK building societies to protect each other when a colleague or competitor is in trouble is illustrative of this point.
3 Rowe et al., *Strategic Management: a methodological approach*.
4 Freeman, *Strategic Management: a stakeholder approach*.
5 Hurd, *Vulnerability Analysis in Business Planning*.
6 Peters and Waterman, *In Search of Excellence*.
7 Zakon, *The Beliefs Audit*.
8 Waterman, *The Renewal Factor*.
9 Spranger, *Types of Men*.
10 Peters and Waterman, *In Search of Excellence*.
11 Freeman, *Strategic Management: a stakeholder approach*.

Unit Three

The Competitive Environment

Learning Objectives

After completing this unit you should be able to:

- identify who and where your customers are and what they want;
- understand the concepts of product, product mix and product, market and industry life cycles;
- use the life-cycle concept to manage a business;
- understand and use the concepts of market and marketing mix in order to make market and product assessments;
- make a report on your industry prospects and overall attractiveness;
- use the PIMS approach to compare business and industry norms;
- use value chain analysis to gain sustainable competitive advantage;
- use a functional approach to gain a sustainable competitive advantage;
- apply the generic skills.

Contents

Overview

Competition

The Competitive Environment

► The customer

   Monitoring customers

   Types of customer

   Demand factors

► The product

   The product mix

   The product life cycle

► The market

   The marketing mix

   Market and product assessment

Industry and the Competitive Environment

► Dominant economic characteristics

► Industry driving forces

► The strength of the competitive forces

   Rivalry among existing firms

   Threat of entry

   Substitute products

   Power of suppliers

   Power of buyers

► The competitive positions of the competitors

► Predicting competitors' moves

► Key success factors

► Industry prospects and overall attractiveness

Gaining Competitive Advantage

► Value chains

    Value chain analysis

► Resources and the value chain

► A functional approach to competitive advantage

Unit Three

" Competition comes first in the government's policies, but it must be fair competition. "

Nicholas Ridley, former UK Transport Secretary[1]

Overview

In Unit Two we looked at the environment external to an organization. In this unit we look at the same environment, but *from the viewpoint of the competition within it*. Evidence of this competition can be found in the organization's distribution methods, the products or services it provides, its prices and the promotion methods used. We shall also look at ways of gaining a sustainable competitive advantage over the competition through the value chain.

The success of an organization depends on the management understanding its competitive environment. If managers know the competitive environment and its products and resources well, they will be able to choose how and where to compete.

The competitive environment is very complex but can be as narrow as that for an X-ray machine or as wide as that for a commodity such as copper. Competitors can be few or many, the environment local or global and products differentiated or standardized. Variables such as these make it very difficult to compete successfully.

It is obvious that industries differ in their competitive environment, economic characteristics and long-term viability. The speed of technical change can vary widely between industries. Capital requirements may be large or small, the market local or worldwide, the products standard or differentiated, competitive forces strong or weak and focused on price, quality or service and so on, and demand can be rising or falling. In spite of this complexity managers must be able to make decisions about whether an industry is attractive or not for placing company funds. This unit therefore sets out to help you to understand your competitive environment.

Figure 3.1 shows how Unit Three fits in with Unit Two and the subsequent units.

Now read Box BP3.1 which gives two different perspectives on how to analyse the competitive environment. These are useful as background before we begin to develop this unit in depth.

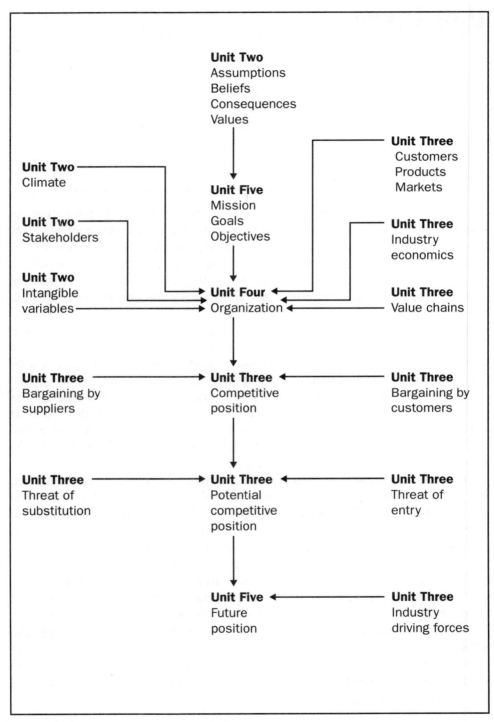

Figure 3.1 How the various forces and factors operating in an environment affect an organization.

BOX BP3.1

The competitive environment

We will examine two approaches to this specific environmental analysis. The first is by Bates and Eldredge[1] and the second by Porter.[2]

For Bates and Eldredge, the analysis is fourfold: demand, inputs, competition and the synthesis of all three to give the critical factors for success in the sector, the industry opportunities and the longer-term prospects.

Demand is gauged and classified by necessity or luxury, durability or non-durability and whether it is self-standing or derived. The market potential is examined and the stage of the product life cycle is touched upon. Opportunities and potential volume of sales can now be derived.

The supply side is also calculated as 'inputs' to ensure that costs do not exceed potential profits. The productive capacity, labour and raw materials are all considered.

Next we turn to the competition to try to predict their behaviour and to enable us to counter their tactics. The structure of the industry and the willingness and ability to change are noted while competition is analysed using the 4Ps – price, product, place and promotion. Thereafter, a synthesis of these three stages occurs.

Porter takes a different view. The immediate competitive environment is seen as the opposition producing close substitutes for each other. This 'substitutability' is the key. It can cover products, process or geographical markets.

There is not just opposition from substitutes, though, as Porter believes in 'extended rivalry'. Existing competition, the threat of new entrants to the game, the bargaining power of both suppliers and buyers and this threat of substitution make up the 'structural determinants of the intensity of competition'. These points are developed in the text, so we will look briefly at Porter's proposition on competitive opposition, which is that rivalry will *increase* in the following situations:

- as the number of competitors increases, they become more similar in size and in relative power;
- as the industry slows;
- where fixed costs are high or where efficient means to meet capacity are large or where excess capacity exists;
- as products become more standardized in the industry.

Rivalry becomes even more volatile as diverse companies with different backgrounds enter and compete in the industry.

Sources:

1　Adapted from Bates and Eldredge, *Strategy and Policy, Analysis, Formulation and Implementation*
2　Adapted from Porter, *Competitive Strategy: techniques for analyzing industries and competitors*

Competition

Organizations may face different types of competition, for example, from:

- producers of directly similar products or services, such as a car manufacturer faced with competition from other car manufacturers;
- producers of substitute products, such as a tape cassette producer faced with competition from producers of laser discs and other types of home entertainment;
- a customer's limited buying power, for example a producer of garden mowers may be faced with competition if a customer has to decide between a garden mower, a new outfit or having the television repaired.

It is essential that managers know which of these types of competition are important to them. They must also realize what kind of market structure they are operating in. There are four basic types of market structure in the UK economy: pure competition, monopolistic competition, oligopoly and monopoly. These are summarized in figure 3.2.

	Pure competition	Monopolistic competition	Oligopoly	Monopoly
Number of competitors	Lots	Many	Few	One
Size of competitors	Small	Variable	Large	None
Nature of product	Homogeneous	Differentiated	Homogeneous or differentiated	Unique
Seller's control of price	None	Some	Some	Complete
Entry into industry	Very easy	Easy	Difficult	Very difficult

Figure 3.2 Typical market structures.

Pure competition is rarely found but exists when there are many small buyers and sellers, each with complete market information. No single buyer or seller controls market demand, supply or price. The product is homogeneous since each seller markets the same product and it is easy to enter or leave this type of market. The marketing of fruit and vegetables is close to pure competition.

In **monopolistic competition** there are many buyers and sellers but they lack complete market information. Each seller attempts to gain a differential advantage over competitors by means of product, brand, packaging, distribution system, promotion or customer service. The idea is to attract buyers through perceived differences. Even though the sellers are marketing essentially similar products they have more control over their prices and products. Most products and services are marketed under monopolistic competition.

An **oligopoly** is a market structure with a few large sellers marketing similar products and accounting for all or almost all of an industry's sales. For example, aluminium, beer, cars and cigarettes are oligopolistic industries. The strong competition and/or the large capital investment make it difficult for new firms to enter the market.

The reactions of competitors are the keys to marketing strategies since all firms charge similar prices. If a firm raises its prices, sales will drop and if it lowers prices, the competition will follow and the price will settle at the lower level. Thus the last thing that an oligopoly wants is a price war. Competition tends to be based on quality, service or advertising.

A **monopoly** occurs when one firm markets a particular product or service and there is no close substitute, for example public utilities such as gas, electricity and water. This situation soon leads to heavy regulation by governments. Patents may provide some firms with a monopoly position, for example in the pharmaceutical industry.

The Competitive Environment

There are several concepts which must be understood in order to make a useful assessment of the competitive environment. These are the customer, product, market and industry and they will be outlined below.

The customer

To achieve an organization's goals it is important for managers to consider their customers together with their needs. Figure 3.3 illustrates the process which will be considered in this section.

One of the beliefs of Peters and Waterman[2] quoted in Unit Two concerned getting close to your customers – supplying their needs for high quality products and services at a price they can afford.

Monitoring customers
Information is necessary in order to manage an organization successfully and the most important information is to know what the customer wants.

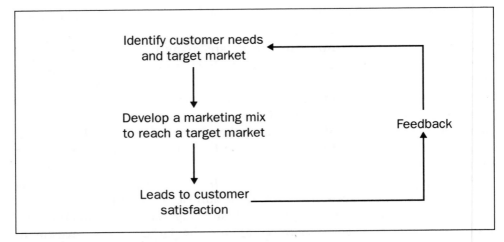

Figure 3.3 The importance of the customer to any organization.

Therefore, in the same way that an environment monitoring system was suggested in Unit Two, we need a customer monitoring system. A system must be set up to find out who the customers are or will be and what they want. It must be oriented towards the future and the concept of the customer broadly defined.

Taken to the extreme in an organization, each person can be a customer of every other person inside the organization. From this viewpoint, customers are not only buyers of products but also recipients of services provided by each person in the organization free of charge. Each recipient has a need for high quality service, so the problem for managers is how to develop a quality culture in the organization. Total Quality Management (TQM) and 'getting it right first time' are just two popular managerial themes of the 1990s. However, in this book we must concentrate on the actual or potential buyers of the organization's products and services.

Types of customer
There are three major groups of customers:
1 **Consumers** – who are influenced by availability, convenience, credit, price, quality, reputation, variety, guarantees, and so on.
2 **Retailers and wholesalers** – who are influenced by availability, competitive products, consumer recognition, product line breadth, product turnover, profit potential, promotional and merchandising support, supply dependability, and so on.
3 **Industrial and institutional buyers** – who are influenced by availability, financing, legal conformity, price, product information, product lines, product performance, profitability, technical assistance, and so on.

Demand factors

There are also two primary demand factors, **demographic** and **geographic**, which affect the market for goods and services for different industries. Demographic factors include changes in population, age changes in the population and income distribution in the population. Such changes can provide threats or opportunities to an organization and have to be taken into consideration. Geographic factors must also be considered since new locations for expansion or relocation are often required. The need for such changes may be owing to customer demand or operating costs.

The product

In order to satisfy customer needs we need **products**. Products are concepts, objects, places, personalities, organizations and services that can be offered for sale. Organizations may have many different products.

The **product concept** is based on:

- providing a core benefit or service;
- a formal product in terms of styling, features, brand name, packaging and quality;
- augmentation, which includes installation, service, guarantees and delivery.

The product mix

The **product mix** is the full list of products offered by an organization and can vary from a single product to multi-lines with multi-products. The product mix has breadth in terms of the number of product lines and depth by the assortment of colours, models and sizes offered on each product line. For example, Ford sell lines of cars, vans and trucks and within each line are several models, sizes, colours and so on which are needed or desired by the customers. Managers must understand the contribution of each line and product to the organization's costs and profits. This is important for management control and also for monitoring the product life cycle from development through growth and maturity to decline.

The product life cycle

Products, like people, go through a life cycle, since products grow in sales, then decline and are eventually replaced. The period from birth to death is the life cycle. The **product life cycle** reflects product demand as the product moves from introduction through saturation to obsolescence (see figure 3.4).

The life cycle can be considered to involve four stages: introduction, growth, maturity and decline. Figures in textbooks suggest that these

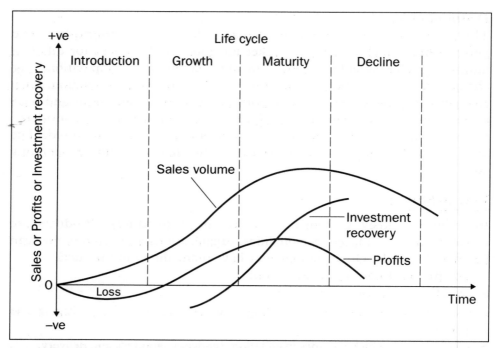

Figure 3.4   Sales, profit and investment recovery life cycles.

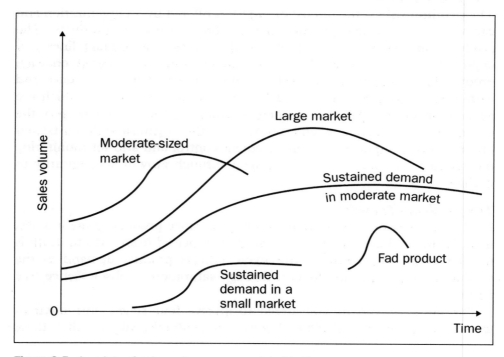

Figure 3.5   A variety of sales volume curves related to time.

stages are of equal length, though in fact they last for different periods of time. This is illustrated in the curves in figure 3.5.

These variations in stages also vary from product to product and all products do not go through all the stages. The slopes of the curves indicate the speed or rate of demand. A steep upward slope indicates high demand and the introductory or maturity periods are short. In the same way demand can decline slowly or quickly.

In general, the introduction stage consists of creating awareness and acceptance for the product. Investment continues into the growth stage which shows increasing profits which in turn attract competitors. During maturity competition reaches its peak. A decline in sales and profits follows until the product is withdrawn. However, it may not be until the decline stage that there is maximum recovery of investment.

Each of these stages has implications for managers since the competitors, distribution, pricing, products and profit margins change as one moves from one stage to another. The product life cycle, therefore, is of fundamental importance to the manager and is a key part of the strategic thinking process. See Box BP3.2 for the Japanese view of a life cycle.

BOX BP3.2

The Japanese life cycle

Particelli suggests that a reason for the industrial success of the Japanese is their different perception of the product life cycle. In the West a large amount of resources is allocated to innovation, which involves a lot of false starts for every successful product. As the market matures, more emphasis is placed on marketing and sales. Only in the mature stage is the focus turned to cost cutting.

The Japanese wait until the technology important to success has been invented and the market tested and stimulated. This is probably about the time the West begins to reduce its input to innovation. Then the Japanese enter the market. They spend heavily on innovation (in order to differentiate their products), marketing and producing at low cost. For the Japanese, the loss-making period of the introduction and its associated uncertainties (since few of the products researched are actually produced) are reduced.

Source: Particelli, 'The Japanese are coming: Global strategic planning in action'

McNamee[3] suggested that, ideally, products should be introduced in sequence so that the firm derives maximum benefit from the sales of its products (see figure 3.6).

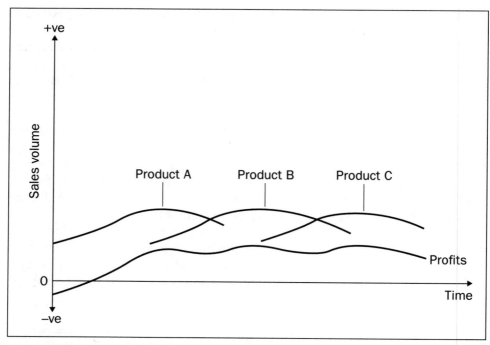

Figure 3.6   How the products of a business must be replaced over time in order to keep profits fairly constant.

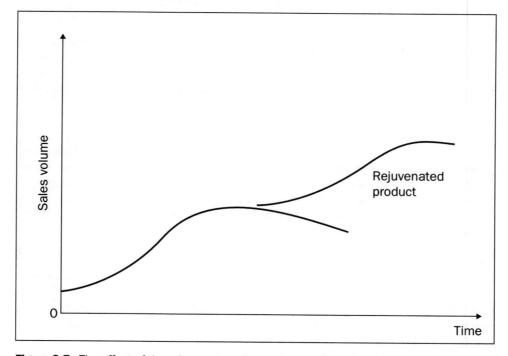

Figure 3.7   The effect of the rejuvenation of a product on the sales volume.

Alternatively, by spending on innovation and/or marketing, a manager can rejuvenate a product and achieve a similar result (see figure 3.7).

Each stage in the product life cycle has a number of characteristics, and these are summarized in figure 3.8.

The products of every organization will eventually become obsolete and as the product ages its profit declines. If ageing products are not changed or replaced then the organization's sales volume and profits will decline (see figures 3.6 and 3.7). The decline in sales occurs because:

■ the need for the product disappears;

■ a better or cheaper product appears;

■ customers become tired of the product.

Therefore, new products are essential for an organization to survive, let alone grow and make profits.

Note that in the development stage profit is often negative and that profit starts to decline while sales are still rising (see figure 3.4). This occurs because advertising and selling efforts must be increased or prices must be cut (or both) in order to continue to expand sales in the face of intensifying competition. Once a product is reaching maturity a manager must either do something to rejuvenate it or have a replacement ready to make up the drop in profits and maintain growth.

The concept poses a few problems for the manager. For example, to what extent is it possible to predict a product's life cycle? In order to do this one requires insight into technological developments or possible customer taste changes. A product's position in the life cycle may be determined, but when is it going to change to the next stage and how fast will the change be?

Answering such questions requires the monitoring of the environment described in Unit Two. Meantime, we can identify life cycles of different length and shape and also issues that cut across the various functions and stages of the product life cycle. Essentially we need to plot a product's sales volume against time and examine the shape of the curve. We can also plot sales and profits over time to see where they cross and attempt to predict future behaviour (see figure 3.9).

The shapes of the product sales and product profit curves are not predetermined since the shape can be controlled to a greater or lesser extent by management. Managers can:

1 predict the shape of a product's life cycle;

2 anticipate the marketing requirements for the next stage.

Products and customers produce demand, so the shapes of the curves produced depend on demand and the product life span which may be: short (< 2 years); moderate (2–10 years); or long (>10 years).

These ranges are quite arbitrary and depend on the product, market and industry being studied (see figure 3.5).

Features	Introduction stage	Growth stage	Mature stage	Decline stage
Products, services, processes, markets	Key factors: Product design, development and quality Control the number of designs and design changes Develop standards	Add product variants by technical and performance variations Reliability very important Make product improvements competitively Control quality	Superior quality needed Standardization Product change less rapid	Little product differentiation Product quality can fall Product lines need pruning
Production and distribution	Tendency for over-capacity and short product runs Need for highly skilled labour and management Training and development important Specialized distribution channels Economies of scale few and not important Experience curve effects can show early gains	Move to mass production causes under-capacity and increase in capital intensity Scramble for distribution channels Centralizing of production Experience curve effects very high Large production volume can create need for more employees in production, overtime or buying in Start to develop successor products	Near optimum capacity Long production runs Mass distribution channels Emphasis on efficiency and low cost May need to reduce work force	Over-capacity Mass production Speciality distribution channels

Buyers	Few customers often with high income	Demand exceeds supply Wider buyer group will accept uneven quality	Mass market Saturation Brand loyalty Repeat purchase	Buyers become sophisticated
Marketing	Need to create awareness and gain acceptance High marketing costs High advertising/sales ratio Price skimming Service often important	High advertising/sales ratio Advertising and distribution important for non-technical products Concentrate on brand development Find a niche Reduce prices	Segmentation/niches important Service important Efforts to extend life cycle Packaging important Need to promote aggressively Advertising and mass selling important. Use of defensive pricing Saturation developing	Decreased demand Low advertising to sales ratio Little marketing Phase out products High substitution
Competition	Few competitors	Many competitors Mergers and exits occur	Price competition Industry consolidates and firms exit, other firms merge or take over market share of those who leave	Exits Few competitors remain

continued...

Figure 3.8 The characteristics of each stage in the product life cycle.

Features	Introduction stage	Growth stage	Mature stage	Decline stage
Money	High risk	Risks decrease since growth covers mistakes	Falling prices owing to increases in efficiency or price cutting, lower margins and profits	Low prices and margins
	High prices and margins	Moderately high prices		Liquidate assets not needed
	Demand can be price-inelastic	Need to finance rapid expansion	Stable market structure and prices can develop	Prices very elastic
	High investment may be necessary	Still have cash outflows but profits increasing	Increasing cash inflow but profits may start to decline owing to increased marketing	Bargaining power of buyers high
	Prepare for cash outflow and low profits or losses	Demand increasingly elastic	Prices inelastic in segments	
Barriers to entry	Can be high if products protected	Decreasing	Increasing as capital intensity increases	High capital intensity gives low returns
		Technical transfer increasing		
Barriers to exit	Can be low if little investment	Low but increasing	High for large firms	Decreasing
Vertical integration	Generally low	Increasing	High	High

Figure 3.8 The characteristics of each stage in the product life cycle (continued).

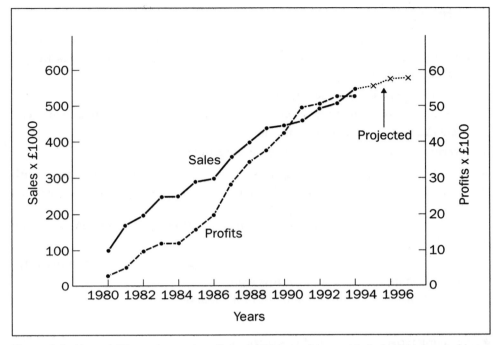

Figure 3.9 How plotting sales and profits over time can be used to help decision making.

The position within a life cycle is based on eight features of the industry in question:

■ breadth of product lines
■ entry and exit barriers
■ growth potential
■ loyalty
■ market growth rate
■ market share of competitors
■ number of competitors
■ technology

It is necessary to separate the concepts of product, market and industry life cycles. A firm might be developing a product in a market which is thinning out in a declining industry. For instance, a Scottish shipbuilder might be developing a new battleship in a shipbuilding industry which is dying in the UK and in a world which is becoming less warlike.

When a market is growing, a firm can grow simply by keeping up with the demand from the market. The situation is very different when markets are mature and demand has flattened. In this case growth can only be achieved by taking market share from competitors.

The market

Kotler[4] defines a market as 'the set of individuals or organizations who are actual or potential buyers of a product or service'. He suggests making use of four categories of market:

1 consumer markets – people buying for personal use;
2 producer markets – manufacturers buying materials or parts for their own use;
3 resale markets – people buying for the purpose of reselling;
4 government markets – those buying for government purposes.

Kotler also suggests segmenting those markets into sets of customers with distinct needs. Segments could be based on attitudes, buying practices, locations, needs, resources, size, and so on.

Once the segments have been identified, different strategies could be followed, for example:

1 an undifferentiated approach – a single marketing mix for the broadest market;
2 a marketing mix focused on a narrow segment;
3 different mixes for different segments of the market.

The choice would depend on:

- the characteristics of the products/services;
- the competition;
- the organization's resources; and
- the needs of the customers.

The marketing mix

This term is used to describe the **Product**, its **Price**, the distribution system (**Place**) and **Promotion** (the four **P**s). The marketing mix is influenced and supported by the organization's internal resources but limited by the environment.

The four Ps are interrelated in that decisions in one area usually affect other areas. Since each of the four Ps contains many variables, it is up to management to select the combination that adapts to the environment, satisfies the market and meets the organization's goals.

Under the term **product** managers need to plan and develop the right products or services; change existing products; add new products; delete old products; decide on branding, packaging, and so on.

Pricing decisions are based on various approaches: increasing profits; increasing market share; improving competitive position, and enhancing consumer impressions of the product or service or organization. Pricing based on costs depends on the relative importance of fixed and variable costs for the organization and its competitors. Economies of scale and investment in technology may be important. Organizations with high fixed costs such as airlines, hospitals and steelworks are sensitive to changes in sales volumes. Pricing policies can be based on contribution, skimming, penetration and competition.

Place or distribution implies ensuring that the organization's products or services reach the customers at the right time. Products can be sent directly from the manufacturer to the customer or go through several channels involving agents, brokers, wholesalers and retailers. The costs of transportation, storage and access to markets must also be considered.

Promotion is about communication. How do you persuade or induce customers to buy your products or services? The objectives of promotion can be to inform, educate, assist comparison, stimulate needs or directly affect the decision to buy. A manager has to decide whether to promote the organization, the product line or the product itself. Perhaps a strategy should be developed for each of these.

Promotion is often divided into four activities: advertising, personal selling, publicity and sales promotion. Managers must decide on the mix of these four activities and the budgets involved.

The promotion strategy will also depend on the position of the product in its life cycle. Different strategies need to be used at different stages in the life cycle. For instance, managers have to decide when:

1 personal selling is important;
2 advertising is important;
3 promotional efforts by retailers are important;
4 manufacturer or retailer advertising should be used;
5 manufacturers should operate a 'push' or 'pull' strategy;
6 promotion activity should be continued or changed during heavy demand or when demand exceeds capacity.

The marketing mix is important to managers because of its integrating nature between the four Ps. The mix for any product is a combination of factors which together induce a customer to buy. At the same time both the product and the buying behaviour of the consumer influence the choice of marketing mix.

Market and product assessment

Once we have understood the basic concepts of marketing we can focus on methods that will help managers assess their products and markets. An analysis of the market(s), product line(s), product(s), life cycles and the marketing mix should identify the gaps to be filled and improvements to be made. Gaps in the product line or distribution chain, for instance, could lead to management decisions to fill them.

Other factors which need to be examined are the relationships between marketing and the other functional areas in the organization such as research and development, production and finance. Can these be developed to produce a competitive edge?

	Existing market	A	Variants Imitations	Extend product line
Market options	Expanded market	Promote aggressively	Segment market, differentiate products	Diversify vertically
	New market	Develop market	Extend market	Diversify Conglomerate
		Present products	Improved products	New products

Product alternatives

Figure 3.10 Chart to determine the position of each of an organization's products and the possible product/market options.

Source: Adapted from Rowe et al., 1989.

Managers can make a product/market assessment by identifying where each of the organization's products stands in its market. Rowe et al.[5] explain growth vector analysis which examines the product, market and the alternative directions for growth. A new product in an existing market requires a different approach from an existing product in a new market.

As can be seen in figure 3.10, a chart can be used to identify the current position. Present products should be listed with their market share, sales, profits, growth, position in the life cycle, pricing policies and so on, on a separate chart, and some assessment made. The products can then be listed in block A on the chart. Possible alternatives can then be developed. This type of chart is a tool that can be developed in any way you find useful.

Industry and the Competitive Environment

So far in this unit we have considered the needs of the customer and the market-place in which the organization operates. The organization does not operate in isolation, however, but in a dynamic competitive environment. A manager has to develop a competitive edge for his or her organization and defend it over time. Therefore, this part of the unit will be devoted to understanding the industry and the competitive environment in which the organization operates.

The difference between an industry and a market is easily understood by taking the car industry as an example. The car industry is made up of several manufacturers which service several markets – luxury, small car, off-road, small vans and trucks. Some organizations compete on an industry basis while others compete only within the market. For example, Ford competes in the motor vehicle industry while Land Rover competes in the off-road market. Essentially, an industry is a group of organizations whose products compete for the same buyers.

The analysis of an industry and its competitive environment is a way of ensuring that important features of the organization's environment are not overlooked. Clues to the future are to be found in this work, which should be done periodically in order to detect gradual changes in the industry.

Industries vary in their economic characteristics and competitive environment to such an extent that a well-managed organization can find it difficult to survive in one industry while a poorly managed organization in another industry can make large profits.

In order to try to make some sense of this dichotomy we shall outline an approach to industry and competitive analysis which will help you to build up an understanding of your industry and its competitive environment. This will enable you to make decisions about both the short-term and long-term attractiveness of the industry.

Thompson and Strickland[6] suggest seven steps for analysing an industry and its competitive environment:

1 Identify the dominant economic characteristics of the industry.
2 Identify and assess the driving forces.
3 Evaluate the strength of the competitive forces.
4 Assess the competitive positions of the competitors in the industry.
5 Predict which competitor will be likely to make which competitive moves next.
6 Identify the key success factors for the industry.
7 Draw conclusions about the attractiveness of the industry both short-term and long-term.

Each of these steps will be discussed in turn in order to build up an understanding of an industry and its competitive environment.

Dominant economic characteristics

The first task is to identify the dominant economic characteristics of the industry. A checklist is provided in figure 3.11 to enable you to build up a comprehensive picture of your industry.

Economic characteristics	Priority	Details
Market size Scope of competitive rivalry Market growth rate Stage in life cycle Number of firms in industry Customers Degree of vertical integration Ease of entry/exit Technology/innovation Product characteristics Scale economics Experience curve effects Capacity utilization Industry profitability		

Figure 3.11   A checklist of the economic characteristics of your industry.

Source: Adapted from Thompson and Strickland, 1992.

Industry driving forces

The economic characteristics identified earlier are a snapshot of the present but they do not tell managers about the forces which have formed the industry in the past and which will shape its future. Managers must try to identify the key driving forces and the impact they will have on the industry in the future. Porter[7] identified the most common driving forces as follows:

- changes in the long-term industry growth rate;
- changes in who buys the product and how they use it;
- product innovation;
- technological change;
- marketing innovation;
- entry or exit of major firms;
- diffusion of technical know-how;
- increasing global trade;
- changes in costs and efficiency;
- emerging buyer preferences for a differentiated instead of a standardized product (or for a standardized product instead of a differentiated product);

- regulatory influences and government policy changes;
- changing concerns, attitudes and lifestyles;
- reductions in uncertainty and business risk.

While a large number of forces may be affecting an industry, only three or four are likely to be the driving forces for that industry. They are the ones that will determine how the industry evolves and operates. The manager has to:

- decide which forces have the greatest effect on the organization at present;
- decide which forces will have the greatest effect on the organization in the future;
- assess the implications and consequences of each of the key driving forces;
- design a strategy to take account of these key driving forces (see Unit Five).

The strength of the competitive forces

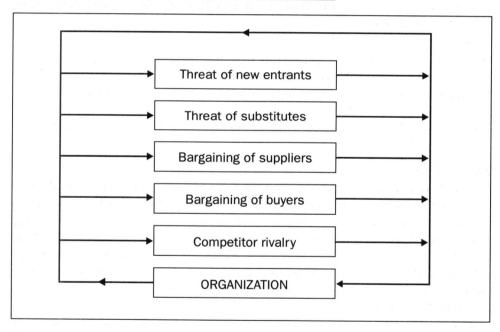

Figure 3.12 Porter's five competitive forces.

Porter's five forces model[8] is a very useful concept for identifying the key competitive forces in an industry (see figure 3.12). By understanding the five competitive forces a manager should be able to:

- build a sustainable competitive advantage;
- out-manoeuvre rivals;
- defend against competitive forces;
- strengthen the organization's market position.

Rivalry among existing firms

Porter likens this to jockeying for position, using tactics such as advertising, better distribution, guarantees, quality or services, new products or features, prices, promotions and so on. The weapons change over time as organizations attack and defend themselves.

Intense rivalry occurs when:

■ There are many competitors or they are roughly equal in size and power.

■ Slow growth in the industry induces fights for market share.

■ Products and services lack differentiation or switching costs.

■ High fixed costs or perishable goods induce price cutting.

■ Capacity has to be added in large increments, so producing periods of over-capacity and price cutting.

■ Exit barriers are high and inefficient and unprofitable organizations continue. The profitability of the healthy ones is also affected by the intense competition.

■ Competitors have different ideas about how to compete or a commitment to being number one.

Essentially competition is:

Weak when most organizations in the industry earn above-average returns on investment.

Moderate when most organizations in the industry earn average returns on investment.

Intense when competition drives down the profits of the industry in general.

Threat of entry

This can occur when organizations can see the possibility of growth and profit in the industry. Industries with low growth rates (under 6 per cent per year for normal conditions) do not encourage new entrants. Existing firms can maintain profitability if they can protect their position. The stronger the threat of entry, the more incentive there is for existing firms to strengthen their position against new entrants in order to make entry more difficult. This can be done by price reductions, aggressive advertising, promotions, brand loyalty and so on.

The decision to enter depends on the barriers to entry and the expected reaction of the existing firms to the new entrant. There are several barriers to entry:

■ access to distribution channels

■ brand preferences, customer loyalty, product differentiation

■ capital requirements

■ cost advantages independent of size

■ economies of scale

- inability to gain access to technology, specialized knowledge, raw materials, locations etc.
- learning and experience curve effects
- regulatory policies
- switching costs
- tariffs and international trade restrictions

Substitute products

These are often available from firms in another industry. The availability of competitively priced substitute products places a ceiling on the prices firms can charge. If they price too high they will give an incentive to customers to change to the substitute. This price ceiling also controls the profits that the industry can earn unless it can cut costs. If substitutes are cheaper then firms must either reduce prices and thus profits or reduce costs.

Substitutes cause customers to compare quality and performance as well as price. Therefore, existing firms have to differentiate their products or services from substitutes in some way in order to be able to compete, for example by price, quality, service and so on.

Substitutes can be weak or strong depending on the switching costs such as retraining, additional equipment or stock. Measures of the strength of substitutes are:

- the rate at which the sales are growing
- the market share
- plans for expansion of capacity
- size of profits

The environment must be monitored continuously in order to guard against substitutes surprising the industry.

Power of suppliers

Suppliers have the power to affect an industry by raising prices or reducing quality. If a firm is unable to recover the increased cost by raising prices or absorbing the loss in quality in some way then its profits will be squeezed. The power of a supplier depends on the characteristics of the market and the relative importance of its sales to the firm compared to its total sales.

A supplier is powerful when:

- Products or services are unique or differentiated or there are switching costs.
- Its products are not easily substituted.
- Forward integration into the industry is possible.
- Sales to the industry are not important to the suppliers.

Power of buyers

Buyers have the power to force down supplier prices and demand higher quality or more service at the expense of the supplier's profits.

A buyer is powerful when:
- It makes large purchases.
- Products or services are standard or can be substituted.
- The purchases form only a small part of the total cost of the final product.
- It makes small profits.
- The quality of the buyer's product does not depend on the supplier.
- The supplier's product does not save the buyer money.
- It could integrate backwards into the supplier's product.
- It can influence the consumers' decision, e.g. large retailers.

Consumers (as a buying group) have power because they are sensitive to prices when:
- They buy standard products.
- Products or services are expensive relative to their incomes.
- Quality is not important.

If all the forces are strong, rivalry is strong, entry barriers are low, competition from substitutes is strong and both buyers and suppliers have strong bargaining power, then the profitability of the industry will be low. If the industry has good long-term profit prospects then the opposite occurs. The conclusions from your study can be summarized in figure 3.13.

	Weak	Medium	Strong
Competition			
Threat of entry			
Threat of substitutes			
Power of suppliers			
Power of buyers			

Figure 3.13 Chart to summarize the conclusions from the work done on the competitive environment.

The competitive positions of the competitors

According to Thompson and Strickland[9] the competitive characteristics that differentiate firms in an industry are:
- price/quality range – high, medium, low
- geographical coverage – local, regional, national, global

	Own firm or Competitor			
	Rating R	Priority	Weight W	R × W
Price/quality range				
Geographical coverage				
Degree of vertical integration				
Product line breadth				
Distribution channels				
Degree of service				
		Total	1.00	

Figure 3.14 Chart for comparing the competitive characteristics of firms in an industry.

- degree of vertical integration – none, partial, full
- product line breadth – wide, medium, narrow
- use of distribution channels – one, some, all
- degree of service – no frills, limited, full

These can be plotted on a chart to compare firms (see figure 3.14).

Each of the characteristics is rated out of ten and then prioritized. The priorities are then used to give the characteristic a weighting. All the weights should add up to 1.00. The rating and the weighting are then multiplied and placed in the last column. Your own firm and competitors can be compared easily if the chart is extended. The priority and weighting are constant for all the firms in each industry.

An alternative functional type of approach can be seen in Box BP3.3.

BOX BP3.3

Competitor analysis – what's the opposition doing?

We need to watch our opposition while maintaining our own vision of the enterprise. Some thoughts are shown below:

- **Policy** What overall view are they taking? Is it broad-brushed or focused? What do you (and they) see as their competitive advantage? Are they vulnerable in any areas? Do they have visible weaknesses?

- **Marketing and R&D** Examine their products, innovation and new launches as well as pricing structure(s). Product ranges or portfolios, from 'cash cows' to 'dogs', may be worth looking at. Their promotion and advertising in particular segments and targets needs monitoring alongside any selling initiatives, discounting, etc. Distribution outlets and channels and 'consistency' also need an effective intelligence gathering system.

- **Finance** Are they profitable? How is the cash flow? Do they have funds for growth, policies, etc.? Is it possible to break down the profitability by product line? Do we know (approximately) their marketing expenditure patterns from research to advertising? Where are they putting their R&D monies? How profitable are they?

- **Personnel and Operations** Monitoring changes in plant, technology or sites and in staff relationships can also pay dividends concerning changes in product and staff morale.

- **Organization** How are the competitors organized? Does their organizational structure help or hinder their goal attainment?

- **Management** How well are they managed? Do they have direction and co-ordination? What is the core competence of their managers, and are they effective?

Predicting competitors' moves

Once you have recorded all your competitors you will be able to find out who are your closest rivals. It will be necessary to keep an eye on these and try to predict how they will compete in the future. It is also necessary to predict who your major competitors will be in the future, since some current competitors will lose ground while small firms may be poised to make a major attack on the market, with a new product, for instance. Ask yourself the following questions: Which firms are in favourable positions and why? Which firms are in unfavourable positions and why?

You should now complete Activity BP3.1.

Key success factors

These determine financial and competitive success in the industry. Firms can win competitive advantage in an industry by concentrating on one or two key success factors. There are many types of success factors:

- Technology-related – research, innovatory, process
- Manufacturing-related – low cost, efficiency, high utilization
- Distribution-related – low cost, fast delivery, network
- Marketing-related – sales force, packaging, service
- Skills-related – design, engineering, information technology
- Organization capability – information systems, response times, management

Other key success factors include reputation, locations, patents and so on.

ACTIVITY BP3.1

CHEAP IMPORTS AND THE COBBLER'S CHILDREN

Activity code
✓ Self-development
✓ Teamwork
✓ Communications
☐ Numeracy/IT
✓ Decisions

The UK shoe industry is hitting hard times and is 'down at heel'. The case of Clarks shoes is enlightening.

Clarks is a well-known quality shoemaker and is respected in the market-place. For generations, parents have trusted the company's shoes both for themselves and for the growing feet of their children. The shoes are not cheap, but they are not expensive either – a quality product at a reasonable price.

The total UK shoe market hovers around 300 million pairs per annum. Sears is well out in front but Clarks provide a strong second place with an overall sales turnover of some £600 million. The shoe market, like the clothing and car industries, has suffered from a flood of cheap(er) imports. Imported shoes make up almost two-thirds of the market while the British manufacturers' share has been declining steadily for some years. While appreciating quality, the market-place is price-sensitive and non-UK shoes can beat UK products 'feet down' on cost.

Clarks' main competitor, Sears, is experiencing difficulties and over 300 shops have been closed, while Clarks have closed their original factory. Profits have been falling sharply as well and have initially been halved since 1986–7 to the mid-£20 millions for 1990–1.

The problems have been noted by management and external consultants have been brought in to review strategy. Reports in the financial press indicate some division of opinion between the Clark family and some of the new senior management of the firm. For example, strains have been evident over a production versus marketing orientation and there is division on whether to allow foreign investment in the company.

1 Isolate the issues in this case.
2 What can Clarks' management do about these problems?
3 Assuming that government curbs on cheap imports are not forthcoming, what sort of recommendations do you think a strategic consultant would make in this scenario?

Source: Facts adapted from Cowe, 'As Clark loses its footing, the family falls out over chairman'

The key success factors for the industry should be identified and prioritized. How do your firm and competitors stand on each of them? Which of them are you going to adopt?

You may now wish to read the examples in Box BP3.4 and Box BP3.5.

BOX BP3.4

Don't play with the big boys – but small is not necessarily beautiful

Kyocera, Brother Industries and Citizen are all Japanese companies, quite successful in their own right, which all moved away from their core activities through diversification policies.

Kyocera's speciality is in high-technology ceramics. Its move into cameras faced the established onslaught of the 'big boys', Konica, Minolta and Canon. Brother, a force in electronic typewriters, has been hard-pushed against competition from Toshiba, Matsushita and NEC. Citizen's sortie into the computer printing business faced high-volume/low-value competition from companies such as Epsom.

Rodger notes that Citizen's experience with its diversification strategy has been reasonably successful. Its policy has been to stay away from the major players and not to enter a market-place where it would be a late entrant. For example, other companies have tapped into Citizen's skill in dealing with small components. This move towards miniaturization in tiny rods and floppy disk drives has benefited Citizen.

Market entry is not the only problem when facing the big companies. Exit from the market may have to be contemplated once the big battalions start encroaching on your territory, unless your niche-cum-advantage is very well secured, but even then you may be forced to retreat.

Source: Adapted from Rodger, 'Clocking on to diversity'

BOX BP3.5

Live in peace

Confrontation is not necessarily the best policy in a market dominated by giants. The case of Terry's chocolate illustrates this point.

The leading confectionery manufacturers are Cadbury, Mars and Nestlé. The Terry's operation is small and the mass market dominated by the giants was not really touched; for example, its 'Moments' chocolate bar has some £30 million sales of a market worth ten times that amount.

The market-place is always tough and the recession has hit the luxury area of some chocolates. Yet the firm seems quite profitable: around £18–£19 million for 1991–2 is quite creditable.

The company's takeover in 1993 by Philip Morris, a colossal company with a cash-glut 'problem', may stiffen the resolve of Terry's to confront the big boys, who somehow do not look quite so big.

Industry prospects and overall attractiveness

It is now time to review all the information you have collected about the industry. What conclusions can you make about the long- and short-term attractiveness of the industry? An attractive industry encourages the development of an aggressive, expansionist approach, while an unattractive industry encourages a protective approach. Weak firms may have to consider leaving the industry or merging with a rival. Factors to be considered include:

- growth rate potential;
- potential entry and exit of firms;
- stability or dependability of demand;
- potential of competitive forces to become weaker or stronger;
- severity of industry problems;
- degree of risk and uncertainty in the industry;
- profit prospects.

Such an analysis will enable a report to be written, which should include:

- factors which make the industry attractive, with reasons;
- factors which make the industry unattractive, with reasons;
- special issues and problems;
- profit outlook.

Study Box BP3.6 which gives an alternative approach, then complete Activity BP3.2.

BOX BP3.6

The Profit Impact of Market Strategy (PIMS)

PIMS is an acronym for Profit Impact of Market Strategy which started life in the 1960s as a research project for the General Electric Company (GE) in the United States. The research project (at the time called PROM – Profitability

Optimization Model) was set up to investigate the following:

- the relationship between market share and operating economics;
- methods for strategically managing GE's businesses;
- the factors controlling return on investment.

Historical data from GE's many businesses were used to investigate the laws of the market-place. GE was hoping to predict the future performance of its many businesses.

By 1972 the project had been taken over by the Marketing Science Institute of the Harvard Business School. The project was extended to other businesses in order to extend the size and mix of the sample. In 1975 PIMS became a commercial enterprise under the Strategic Planning Institute (SPI) in Cambridge, Massachusetts. SPI is a non-profit-making organization controlled by its member companies. Currently, hundreds of companies operating thousands of businesses subscribe to and contribute information to SPI. Most of the companies are in the USA but increasing numbers are joining from Europe and elsewhere.

The research set out to develop a database from which it could discover the laws of the market-place and make the findings available to the participating companies. It set out to answer questions such as:

- What is the normal cash flow, profit level, return on investment (ROI) for particular businesses and industries?
- Which factors determine the levels of cash flow, profit and ROI in the businesses?
- Which strategies should businesses follow to meet their objectives?

Schoeffler identified nine fundamental conclusions:

1 Business situations generally behave in a regular and predictable manner (provided the environment is fairly stable).
2 All business situations are basically alike and obey the same laws in the market-place.
3 The laws of the market-place determine about 80 per cent of the observed variance in the operating results across different businesses. (This implies that only 20 per cent of performance can be attributed to managers.) It follows, therefore, that there are some businesses that are naturally profitable and some businesses that are naturally unprofitable. Is it more important for a manager to be in the right business than to manage well?
4 There are also nine major strategic business influences on profitability and cash flow:
   (a) Investment intensity – investment/sales percentage and investment/added value percentage
   (b) Productivity – added value/employee percentage and added value/sales percentage
   (c) Market share and relative market share (firm's market share/sum of three largest competitors)
   (d) Growth of the market served – percentage per year
   (e) Relative quality of the products or services offered

(f) Innovation or differentiation – new products/sales percentage and/or marketing/sales percentage and/or R&D/sales percentage

(g) Vertical integration

(h) Are cost increases absorbed or passed on to customers?

(i) Current strategic efforts may have contrary effects to the factors above

5 The operation of these nine strategic influences is complex – do not consider one at a time.

6 Product characteristics do not matter but the strategic business influences do. Similar influences give similar operating results despite the products or services.

7 The expected impacts of strategic business influences tend to assert themselves over time.

8 Business strategies are successful if their fundamentals are good and unsuccessful if poor.

9 Most clear strategy signals are robust.

The major limitation of the PIMS approach is to consider that the past is the key to the future. Thus the strategic models suggested are limited in scope. However, the identification of key strategic influences is a useful tool for identifying trends and comparisons between businesses and between businesses and industry norms.

Sources:

1 Schoeffler, 'Nine basic findings on business strategy'
2 Schoeffler, Buzzell and Heany, 'Impact of strategic planning on profit performance'

ACTIVITY BP3.2

COMPETITIVE POSITIONS OF FIRMS AND THEIR COMPETITORS

Activity code

✓ Self-development
✓ Teamwork
✓ Communications
✓ Numeracy/IT
✓ Decisions

Your firm can be rated out of 10 for each of the factors in the chart (R). The factors can then be prioritized and the top five or so weighted (W). The weights should add up to 1.00. The rating R can then be multiplied by the weighting W. The same factors can then be rated for all your competitors and an assessment made of the competition.

	Rating (R)	Priority	Weight (W)	R x W
Market share				
Relative market share (firm's share/sum of three largest competitors)				
Quality of products or services				
Market growth (%) per year				
New products/sales (%)				
Vertical integration				
Value added/employee (%)				
Utilization of capacity				
Investment/sales (%)				
Stock/sales (%)				
R&D/sales (%)				
Marketing/sales (%)				
Others				
		Total	1.00	

1 Apply this chart to three firms of your choice. You may wish to consult company reports for details.
2 Write a report of your assessment of the three competitors.

Before proceeding to the next section on gaining competitive advantage, compare the PIMS approach with the one outlined earlier. Which do you think will be most useful to you and why?

Gaining Competitive Advantage

Value chains

This section is intended to enable you to gain a competitive advantage over your competitors. The activities of designing, producing, marketing, delivering and supporting products and services are not confined within the business but also include the suppliers, distributors and customers outside it. The extent to which products and services are valued by customers is determined by the way the various activities are performed. Thus these activities form a value chain. Successful businesses have a theme running through the value chain such as low-cost leadership, quality or service.

The concept of value started to be developed in the section on the external environment. Now we are looking at value in a slightly different way – the value chain concept of Porter.[10]

Every business receives resources, transforms them and sends them as outputs to the customer. This is the value chain and each of the activities in the chain **adds value to the output**.

Input, transformation and output consume resources in terms of administration, buildings, equipment, labour, land, management, materials and money. The consumption of resources results in costs to the business.

The value of the output is measured by the total value generated, or revenue = sales × number sold. The difference between the total costs and the revenue produces the margin, value added or operating profit, depending on the term you wish to use.

The efficiency of a business is measured by the ratio given by operating profit/total investment, or return on capital employed (ROCE) (see Unit Six).

Since what happens in the value chain affects costs and profits, the decisions about each activity in the value chain determine the nature and quality of the output.

A business that seeks to gain advantage by cost leadership tries to reduce resources and the prices it pays for them. A business that seeks to gain advantage by differentiation performs its value chain activities better than or differently from its competitors. Therefore, identification and improvement of the value chain activities are probably the best means of gaining a sustainable competitive advantage.

The process of converting inputs to outputs can involve hundreds to thousands of different activities. Porter[11] classified these as either primary or supporting activities.

The five **primary activities** that form the value chain are:

1 **Inbound logistics** – the relationships with suppliers, including the activities involved in receiving, storing and internally distributing the inputs such as equipment, finance, ideas, materials and people. The activities include stock control, materials handling, vehicle scheduling and warehousing.

2 **Production** – the activities involved in converting inputs to outputs such as products and services. Assembling, design, fabrication, machining, maintaining, packaging, process development and testing are typical activities.

3 **Outbound logistics** – the activities necessary for collecting, storing and distributing the output to the customers. Sometimes this may involve getting the customer to the product or service. Delivery, materials handling, order processing, scheduling, shipping and warehousing are typical activities.

4 **Marketing and sales** make customers aware of the product or service, induce them to buy and facilitate the purchasing process. Advertising, distributing, pricing, promoting, proposing and quoting are typical activities.

5 **Service** includes the activities necessary to keep the product or service working effectively for the customer after the sale and delivery. Activities such as consulting, distribution, fine-tuning, guarantees, installing, repairing, spare parts and training are involved.

To a greater or lesser extent all businesses perform activities such as these and must be reasonably proficient in them. Superiority in one or two activities can be a competitive advantage. For example, McDonalds is very good at production, marketing and sales.

The four **support activities** service the primary activities of the value chain and the business itself.

1 **Procurement** is the process of acquiring resources for the primary activities. This is carried out by any employee who acquires resources for the business, except for human resources.

2 **Human Resources Management** involves all of the activities involved in recruiting, selecting, hiring, training, developing, rewarding and eventually dismissing or laying off personnel. This process affects the overall cost of labour through the salary and wage levels. Overall performance of the business is affected by the level of skill and motivation in the business produced by the hiring and training programmes.

3 **Technology development**. All activities have a technology or 'know how' associated with the products, processes and resources involved, which includes all the design, hardware, software, procedures, and technical know how required to convert the inputs to outputs.

4 **Management systems** consist of the functional areas of a business, such as accounting, administration, finance, planning, public relations, quality control and general management. These functions hold the business together and can form a competitive edge if they are working well.

Support activities can be found in several unexpected parts of a business. For example, senior management may not be recruited by the personnel department and the ordering of new plant may not be done by the purchasing department. Therefore, be prepared to look for support activities in all parts of the business.

The support activities described above can provide a business with a competitive edge. For example, certain businesses concentrate on hiring the best managers and others the best technology.

Value chain analysis

The process of value chain analysis starts with the identification of the key primary and support activities. There are several steps in the process.

First, identify the key **primary activities**:

- The activities associated with the inbound logistics can be found by identifying the sources of all the incoming resources. Then ask yourself, 'What activities are necessary to obtain and handle the resources?'
- For production, you need to identify the activities necessary to convert the inputs to outputs.
- The activities in the outbound logistics can be found by identifying where all the outputs are going and what activities are necessary to move the outputs to the customer.
- Marketing and sales activities include all those needed to inform and persuade customers to buy and accept the outputs. Order-taking processes are also important.
- Service activities include all the activities needed to maintain customer satisfaction.

Next, identify **support activities**. Review the primary activities and determine in what ways each of them is helped by each of the support activities in turn – procurement, human resource management, technological development, and management systems.

Once the primary and support activities have been identified, ask yourself the following questions: 'Does this activity give the business a cost advantage?' 'Does this activity help the business to differentiate its products or services from competitors?' If the answers are yes, ask yourself whether this advantage is sustainable over time.

Now you must re-examine the activities in the value chain for anything that decreases competitive advantage. Ask yourself the following questions: 'In what ways does an error or deficiency in this activity affect later activities?' 'Is the business able to adjust or correct errors or deficiencies?'

The objective of this process is to identify or build a core competency or series of core competencies that the business does well compared to its competitors. These provide a competitive edge and represent specialized expertise that competitors do not have and hopefully cannot easily obtain.

Make sure you understand how to make a value chain analysis and then complete Activity BP3.3.

ACTIVITY BP3.3

THE DESIGNER COMPANY/KD DESIGNS

Activity code
- ✓ Self-development
- ✓ Teamwork
- ✓ Communications
- ☐ Numeracy/IT
- ✓ Decisions

KD stands for Kerry Designs. The firm started in Malaysia in 1985. It is a fashion company dealing mainly in smartly designed casual wear, T-shirts and jumpers with some fashion accessories such as scarves and jewellery. The clothes were designed and sold by Kerry and manufactured to her specifications by a local textile company, ABC textiles. The designs created the uniqueness while the cotton fabric T-shirts and the heavier sweaters were manufactured to a high standard.

After many successful trading years, KD Designs had the opportunity to become involved in a joint venture with The Designer Company. If successful, this could lead to a full merger. Delia Conningsby, the owner of The Designer Company, was keen to combine on business ventures and she sent Kerry Designs the following specification of her firm.

Delia and her best friend from art school, Marcia, successfully completed their design courses in an outstanding fashion. In the late 1960s, fresh from college with little or no business exposure or, indeed, capital, they began to design and sell headscarves and ties from their London flat.

With the assistance of a friend, they managed to obtain a continuous textile printing machine and a curing oven to fix dyes. They now had the production capacity and the design skills to supply fabrics to retailers. Selling to these firms was difficult but the product quality was good and the designs refreshingly nostalgic to many of the store buyers. This wholesale business continued to grow through the early 1970s.

Vertical integration followed. They now moved into design, fabric printing, clothing manufacturing and new retail outlets of their own within the UK, with several outlets in the USA. By 1979 sales were touching £12.5 million per annum. At the time of writing, this sales turnover has reached £18 million per annum.

The secret of the success lay and continues to lie in the company's design concept. It taps an idyllic rural English paradise of simplicity and tradition (one that probably never existed). Consumers are not historians, in the main, and the designs strike a chord with a nostalgic vision of the past – not unlike many best-selling historical romances. Natural fabrics are used and Britain's museums provide a stimulus to new designs and adaptations. A design team works under Marcia's direction while Delia has focused more on the business side.

The clothing collections focus on female attire with accessories. There is one main collection per year in the spring but the firm is considering a winter collection as well. A 'younger woman's' collection for teenage girls is also part of the main collection. There are plans for either a casual collection or entry into the bridal market. The collections can take up to one year, if not longer, to put together so the designers are very busy.

Solid marketing, customer audits and feedback sessions with retail staff play a critical role in getting the range and colours right. The production team also have an input into the process, but this is very much focused on the market-place. The whole process is extremely cost-effective.

The latest venture has been a move into interior design. With the help of a Cambridge firm, they provide a full package for the 'discerning customer'. Curtains, cushions, fabric for settees, chairs, bedcovers, lampshades and so on are all part of this package. This is very expensive and the firm subcontracts specialists in the field, including carpet-makers if necessary. A more economical version of this quality range is now appearing in the main retail outlets.

A cost-effective production system based on quality epitomizes the work. Careful pricing to a middle-range market-place (apart from the customized interior design package which is for a richer market) blends with this quality. The company always aims to respond to demand and short production runs with little changes in the overall process facilitate this response in different designs and colours. Subcontracting does occur but the firms must meet tight quality and price specifications. This allows fluctuations in demand to be met and it means that the core employees are retained on a permanent basis without the fear of redundancy and layoff.

A point-of-sale system ensures that the 'best sellers' are known almost instantaneously. Forecasts are annual, with quarterly plans which are reviewed weekly.

A new production facility has been built in the Scottish Borders. This ensures plenty of skilled labour within the textile trade and an abundant supply of wool. Patterns are produced by computer-aided design by a CAD specialist, Ray Wing of Meldreth, Cambridgeshire. This allows more layers of fabric to be cut at any one time.

Stock levels and stock control as well as overall quality assurance are handled by the production team at the small factory in north London and the new customized site in the Borders.

The firm has a divisional and functional structure. The services are provided by headquarters, which are based in the West End of London. This includes personnel and training, legal, finance and accounting, secretarial (company) and computing. These functions, excluding legal and secretarial, have some presence at plant level and act as advisors to the other divisions.

The design team is a separate entity based near the site of the first factory in north London. Clearly its responsibility is for research and development and product design. The production side covers all purchasing, raw materials, stock, physical manufacturing, distribution and quality, while the retail side includes marketing and marketing research as well as the outlets.

Each division has a general manager who is on the board. Communications between the units are excellent and informal.

The retail and marketing side of the business is very successful. All the outlets have an old-world charm akin to a Victorian Christmas card with stage-coach and horses in the snow. Electronic point-of-sale allows for daily analysis of sales and helps stock control, purchasing and marketing efforts.

Promotion tends to be through local and national press advertising with features in women's magazines, particularly at the time of the new collections. There is some advertising through the marketing statements of the major credit cards. A new in-store credit card is now being floated and appears to be quite promising.

As for the future, the firm is committed to the market-place. Good management controls aided by information technology are all linked to the central computing system. The stock, re-ordering and marketing areas are assisted by this computerization while Ray Wing's computer-aided design continues to be excellent. Computerization has enabled the company to act as one unit, all operating on the same data, and this has contributed to its success.

1 Identify the primary and support activities of the value chain of The Designer Company.
2 Describe and analyse the links between the activities.
3 Explain the importance of the links.

Resources and the value chain

The resources of a business are distributed among the activities it performs and are part of the value chain. There are four groups of resources:

1 **Physical resources** such as buildings, materials, plant and equipment, products and so on, and their age, condition and location.

2 **Human resources**: the number of employees, their adaptability, ages, location, skills and so on.

3 **Financial resources** such as cash flow, investment, sources and uses of money, control and so on.

4 **Intangibles** such as brands, contacts, designs, 'goodwill', image, logos, patents and reputation.

These resources and activities are organized into systems which produce the products or services for the business. In order to record the primary activities and resources of a business we can complete the charts in figures 3.15, 3.16, 3.17 and 3.18. These combine the primary activities and the associated resources for each of the support activities. Each support activity

Support activity: Procurement					
	Inbound logistics	**Operations**	**Outbound logistics**	**Marketing and sales**	**Service**
Typical procurement resources	Transport Warehouse Capital	Machines Consumables	Transport Warehouse	Product patents brands research	Credit facility
Physical resources					
Human resources					
Financial resources					
Intangibles					

Figure 3.15 Chart to record the primary activities and resources required in the procurement activities of the business.

Support activity: Technology development					
	Inbound logistics	**Operations**	**Outbound logistics**	**Marketing and sales**	**Service**
Typical technical resources	Know-how Design R&D	Process development	IT network	IT network	Fault diagnosis
Physical resources					
Human resources					
Financial resources					
Intangibles					

Figure 3.16 Chart to record the primary activities and resources required in the development of technology in the business.

Support activity: Human resource management					
	Inbound logistics	**Operations**	**Outbound logistics**	**Marketing and sales**	**Service**
Typical human resources	Recruitment Shareholders Creditors	Team spirit Job satisfaction	Sub-contractors	Agents Sales Distribution	After-sales reputation
Physical resources					
Human resources					
Financial resources					
Intangibles					

Figure 3.17 Chart to record the primary activities and resources required in the management of human resources in the business.

Support activity: Management systems					
	Inbound logistics	**Operations**	**Outbound logistics**	**Marketing and sales**	**Service**
Typical management resources	Purchasing Materials handling Scheduling	Planning Quality Cash and stock control	Delivery	Orders and debtor control	Service system
Physical resources					
Human resources					
Financial resources					
Intangibles					

Figure 3.18 Chart to record the primary activities and resources required in the management systems of a business.

indicates the typical resources associated with it. Others can be added as necessary. When completed, these charts should be analysed to identify the key linkages or the linkages which can be developed to provide a competitive advantage.

There are several sources of competitive advantage:

■ Business image or culture
■ Business systems such as quality control
■ Innovation
■ Flexibility
■ Uniqueness such as brands and patents

The main objective in going through this process of identifying the value chain is to develop a competitive edge which is sustainable. This means that the overriding objective of a business should be to stay ahead of the competition. For this we also require cash flow, investment and ideas.

The resources themselves need to be measured in terms of efficiency and effectiveness:

Efficiency   The key measurements are: profitability, labour productivity, yield, capacity fill, working capital and production systems. Efficiency is important for those businesses competing on the basis of cost.

Effectiveness This measures the use of: people, capital, marketing, distribution, resources, research knowledge, production systems and the exploitation of intangibles. Effectiveness is important for businesses that compete by differentiating themselves from competitors.

The extent to which resources are controlled is also important. Look for evidence of the way managers control their business in the following areas:

■ Costs
■ Intangibles
■ Losses
■ Outlets
■ Quality
■ Personnel
■ Production
■ Stock

A functional approach to competitive advantage

Another approach is to consider the five functional areas of the business and identify the strengths and weaknesses in each. Look for sustainable competitive advantages in them. Jauch and Glueck[12] suggest preparing a strategic advantage profile for your business (see figure 3.19).

Functional areas	Competitive strengths or weaknesses
Marketing	
R&D	
Production	
Management	
Finance	

Figure 3.19 A strategic advantage profile.

Source: Adapted from Jauch and Glueck, 1988.

To conclude this unit you should analyse Activity BP3.4. Apply any of the analysis techniques in the unit that you think are relevant. You may also wish to consult Box BP3.7.

BOX BP3.7

A policy – based on price?

A policy based on cheap prices may not be sustainable for ever. In the UK, Tesco, a major food retailer, had a principle of 'stack 'em high, sell 'em cheap'. It worked. Now Tesco has moved more towards a qualitative approach to its market while still remaining reasonably price-sensitive.

Kwik Save has now moved into Tesco's original position. At the time of writing, it has proved quite successful, with sales up more than 14 per cent on the previous year's equivalent period and profits up 19.1 per cent. The sales growth in existing outlets has been some 8 per cent (allowing for new store openings).

If Kwik Save can follow Tesco's well-trodden path, others can follow Kwik Save. Shoprite, Netto and Aldi are also in the discount business. A limited number of lines, low prices and high-volume sales seem to be the formula in the current recession.

Branding and 'own labels' allied to a wider range of lines may put off the evil day but price is not sufficient as a policy in the long term and it will be interesting to see whether Kwik Save goes more upmarket like Tesco or attempts even more price cuts in some trench warfare with the newer discount stores.

ACTIVITY BP3.4

THE QUALITY FOOD STORE AND INDUSTRY STRUCTURE

Activity code
- ✓ Self-development
- ✓ Teamwork
- ✓ Communications
- ☐ Numeracy/IT
- ✓ Decisions

The Quality Food Store was being challenged by The Northern Stores and by The Southern Stores. The Syndicate Stores were now losing market share because of the lower prices of the other three firms' large outlets. Buy Them Stores was also a rival as it bought up every small (under 20,000 ft²) retail food store or company which came onto the market. The amalgamation of Economic and Cheepo Stores had proved almost unworkable and this debt-ridden outfit was no longer a serious challenger to the other leading stores. Indeed, Buy Them Stores was probably looking at Economic and Cheepo Stores at this very moment with a view to a rescue plan. Other smaller stores were not really operating at a national level.

Pricing, good distribution, a range of products, quality and customer service seemed to be the industry features which offered competitive success. Perhaps size and buying power should be added to these criteria.

Barriers to entrants revolved around the cost of a site, distribution issues and reputation. On costs alone, a large operational site could cost some £3 million. The entrants tended to be small one-person businesses or small specialist chains dealing with 'European' or 'Indian' food ranges.

The supply chains tended to favour the big outfits owing to their bulk-buying capacity, which they tended to pass on to the customer, in part at least, with reduced prices compared to the smaller shops or chains.

Substitutes for food did not really apply, although many variations in taste had to be accounted for by the retailers. The customers had different motives for buying from one store rather than another but price, quality and convenience ranked quite highly. Demand increased on an annual basis although pure food demand was tapering off and was linked to demographics. There was little real product differentiation although 'own labels' gave some attempt at branding to differentiate one store from another. As a result of these 'own labels', customers receive a reasonable product at a cheaper price.

There was a geographical concentration in the South apart from the northern-based Syndicate Stores and The Northern Stores. Further, a concentration was also occurring in the industry with the major firms tending to get bigger at the expense of Syndicate Stores and the small corner shops.

The industry food boundaries tended to be horizontal in most cases with a range of fresh, canned, frozen, packaged and preserved goods in most organizations. One or two, Syndicate and Quality and, to a lesser extent, Buy Them, had some vertical boundaries in the sense that they had production and processing plants, freezing, distribution and wholesaling facilities. The others did not share this processing/production/freezing approach and increasingly they were all moving away from having their own distribution facilities owing to cost and possible labour relations difficulties. In addition to retail, some specialist firms dealt with wholesale and tended to deal with the smaller chains/one-person businesses.

Competitor behaviour can be summarized as follows:

- Quality and Southern were at each other's throats. Both were moving north into the territory of Northern and Syndicate. Both were buying up edge-of-town sites and building as though there was no tomorrow. Both knew that the market was not infinite, so share had to come off others. Price wars occasionally flared up between the rivals. Quality Stores had attempted to live up to its name while Southern had moved away from its cheaper-priced philosophy to embrace both price and quality.

- Syndicate was troubled and losing out to the others. Its rebuilding programme was slower and it was hampered by many small urban outlets which could not compete with the range or the prices of the major companies at the edge of the town. It tended to serve an older population compared to its southern rivals, who catered for all groups.

- Northern was a lively store but capital restrictions had limited growth opportunities. In the past it had been very aggressive and had tried to move south but its logistical lines were being stretched and its real focus still tended to be in its loyal north. It had a similar type of building programme but perhaps emphasized price rather than quality *per se.*

- Buy Them was a mixed company with quality stores acquired through purchase and, at the other end of the spectrum, rather dismal stores catering for a price-conscious clientèle with a limited product range. It did not have the common imagery of the other three giants as its market-place was clearly segmented and still being run as mini-companies under the umbrella of Buy Them.

- Economic and Cheepo Stores appeared to be in difficulty and a debt-ridden organization made trading on equal terms quite difficult.

- Specialists. There were other family 'chains' of up to ten stores, often small and usually localized. Specialist stores existed in the larger cities selling vegetarian and health food and catering for different cultural tastes. Often these stores opened all hours and stocked a wide range of articles in a bid to be convenience stores.

- Ultra-cheapos. A new trend was appearing whereby a restricted line of goods (no fancy labels or packaging) would be sold by comparatively new chains of small stores, often in urban areas. Price was their weapon against the giants.

1 Analyse the main themes of this food industry structure. You may wish to consider the following:
   (a) structure and success in that structure;
   (b) competition and competitive behaviour;
   (c) possible changes in the structure.
2 Note the factors which make for the intensity of competition within this industry.
3 From the details above, can you determine the possible successful firms and the also-rans in this scenario?
4 What policy would you now pursue if you were with The Quality Food Stores?

Unit Three has looked at the competitive environment and ways of gaining a sustainable competitive advantage. Unit Four will examine the business environment.

Notes

1 Quoted by Shadow Transport Secretary John Prescott, 'Airline affair more than a commercial dispute', discussing the British Airways/Virgin Atlantic scandal over competitive practices.
2 Peters and Waterman, *In Search of Excellence.*
3 McNamee, *Tolls and Techniques for Strategic Management.*
4 Kotler, *Marketing Management.*
5 Rowe et al., *Strategic Management: a methodological approach.*
6 Thompson and Strickland, *Strategic Management: concepts and cases.*
7 Porter, *Competitive Strategy.*
8 Ibid.
9 Thompson and Strickland, *Strategic Management: concepts and cases.*
10 Porter, *Competitive Strategy.*
11 Ibid.
12 Jauch and Glueck, *Business Policy and Strategic Management.*

Unit Four

The Business Environment

Learning Objectives

After studying this unit you should be able to:

- describe the Seven S Framework for any organization;
- understand and use the generic strategies;
- understand the functions of the structure of a business;
- identify the three key factors in business structures;
- analyse the information systems in your organization;
- apply the use of control systems;
- understand the concepts of decentralization;
- discern the various leadership and management styles;
- recognize the causes of business failure;
- understand the development of core competencies;
- understand the significance of Human Resource Management and the Four Cs;
- analyse the place of shared values and design in an organization;
- apply the generic skills.

Contents

Overview

Strategy

► Generic strategies for dealing with competitive forces

Low-cost leadership

Differentiation

The focus or niche approach

► Generic strategies for business development

► Variations of the generic strategies

Structure

► The key decisions

► The task environment

► Technological factors

Systems

► Information systems

► Management control systems

► Decentralization

The major forms of decentralization

Style

► Causes of business failure

Management skills

Financial management

Competitiveness

Comments

► Management style

Skills

► Competence and the value chain

Staff

Shared Values

► Culture

► Design and culture

Key Issues

Unit Four

" If you don't know where you are going then any road will do. "

Anon

Overview

So far we have looked at the environments in which the business operates. The next stage is to examine the internal environment of the business itself. The success of a business is determined by its ability to design, produce, market, deliver and support its products or services.

This unit is based primarily on the model for a business developed by Waterman et al.[1] The basic idea of the Seven S Framework is that organization effectiveness depends on seven factors which interact. These are shown in figure 4.1.

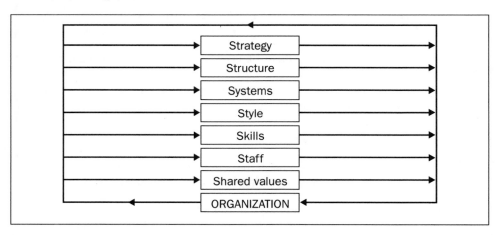

Figure 4.1 The Seven S Framework.

This system or framework illustrates several concepts:

- The capacity of a business to change depends on more than one factor.
- All of the factors are interconnected so that changing one will affect all of the others. Thus, to make progress, a manager has to pay attention to all of the Seven Ss.
- The factors are not hierarchical and there is no beginning or end. The driving force or factor for any business at any point in time will be controlled by the situation. In other words, there is no logical plan such that if you do A and B, C will happen. The key is to analyse the situation and develop the Seven Ss to meet the key issues identified.

123

The seven factors – Shared values, Structure, Strategy, Skills, Staff, Systems and Style – form the basis for an analysis of the internal business environment of the organization, and we will adopt this framework here. But first we need to comment further on the related work of Peters and Waterman (at this point, study and complete Activity BP4.1). In this Activity the principles of excellence are related to some of the key features of the Seven S vision.

ACTIVITY BP4.1

TOWARDS EXCELLENCE?

Activity code
- ✓ Self-development
- ✓ Teamwork
- ✓ Communications
- ☐ Numeracy/IT
- ✓ Decisions

Peters and Waterman seem to have caused a revolution in business policy. Their eight attributes of so-called excellence have been used as the criteria to gauge the relative success of an excellent company; these attributes are summarized below and then applied to a disguised company.

The eight attributes are:

1. *A bias for action* – an activity orientation rather than endless indecisive committees.
2. *Staying close to the customer* – a belief that the customer takes precedence.
3. *Autonomy and entrepreneurship* – a 'small-is-beautiful' syndrome with independent and competitive units.
4. *Productivity through people* – rewarding the best efforts of staff.
5. *Hands-on/value-driven* – keeping top management's fingers on the pulse of the core business.
6. *Stick to the knitting* – staying with what the company knows best.
7. *Simple form, lean staff* – few layers in the hierarchy and not top-heavy.
8. *Loose–tight properties* – a climate where the central values of the organization are combined with a tolerance to staff (who accept these values).

Midway Travel
A limited air travel market in this Middle East country in the 1960s meant that there was little internal competition. The internal competition that existed soon evaporated with a buy-out from the state which already owned Midway. The company was innovative (A), leasing a Comet 4C in the early 1960s and acquiring its own jet in 1964. Expansion (B) followed and the route map now included London.

Traffic increased, necessitating bigger aircraft. The first 707s were delivered in the late 1960s and, by 1978, the entire eight-strong fleet was comprised solely of 707s, the Comets and Tridents having been removed from service (C).

Wide-body planes now appeared and the 747s arrived. The routes expanded to Manila and New York, and the fleet was constantly being modernized. The Airbus 310s and A300-600s started to appear in the early 1980s and, by 1986, 767–200ERs had joined the wide-body fleet. By 1986, the annual freight traffic amounted to well over 50,000 tonnes and over 1.5 million passengers travelled to over 48 destinations in over 35 countries (D).

Government backing (E) assisted with capitalization and the source of money seemed inexhaustible, although it may have become more restricted since the recent troubles in the area.

Support services include engineering, training, reservation and catering (F).

Diversification (G) in the form of a helicopter project for a local company has occurred. Interest in this concept has also been indicated by various organizations, from road traffic reporting to fire fighting and rescue facilities.

Regular training (H) takes place. For example, the cockpit crews, often ex-airforce, have been regularly trained both overseas and in their own country. 'Traffic' courses exist for reservation staff, while technical courses are used for engineers and there is also a crew-training unit.

Technically, a sophisticated reservation system has been installed which is the envy of many airlines. This system is seen as a cost-effective method of communications and has also been marketed successfully to other countries.

Hotels overseas (I) followed as part of the plan, linked to a hotel in the company's own country to act as a stopover for passengers.

The senior management (J) are all nationals, and the chief executive reports to the state minister. There is a permanent advisory committee to give guidance to the chief executive. The departments are shown in the chart.

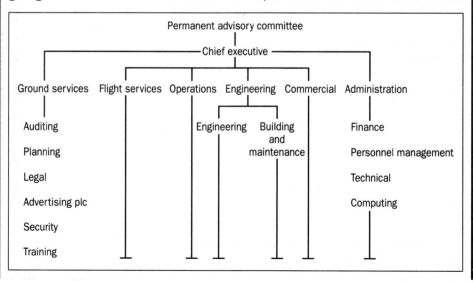

Performance management (K) is one of the firm's main principles. Planning is centralized but group discussion and execution are encouraged. Initiative is supposedly rewarded but 'scientific procedures' exist in manpower from selection to training. An established manpower/human resources plan exists with detailed job descriptions and elaborate performance schedules (L).

The company appears to be an integral part of the body politic (M) of the state and is committed to the goals of that state.

Now apply the eight-point formula to test the 'excellence' of Midway Travel.

1 Give example(s) if possible. Extrapolate from the known details if appropriate.
2 Make a comment on each of the eight attributes.
3 Conclude by noting the 'degree of excellence'.

The letters A–M in the text may help you to determine a given category, but you can add your own vision as well.

	Example	Comment
1 A bias for action		
2 Staying close to the customer		
3 Autonomy and entrepreneurship		
4 Productivity through people		
5 Hands-on/value-driven		
6 Stick to the knitting		
7 Simple form, lean staff		
8 Loose–tight properties		

Source: List adapted from Peters and Waterman, *In Search of Excellence*

The functional approach is a different vision of the business environment. We will use the Seven S approach but will make a parallel analysis from the functional perspective.

Strategy

Over the years businesses worldwide have tried numerous methods to beat their competitors. Porter[2] made a study of these approaches and proposed three generic strategies for dealing with the competitive forces in an industry.

Generic strategies for dealing with competitive forces

A generic strategy leads to a competitive advantage for a business. The choice of which generic strategy to use depends on the industry competitor analysis and the capabilities of the business. The defensive approach is not considered a strategy by Porter since it does not lead to a competitive advantage.

The three generic strategies Porter proposed are:

1 **Overall low-cost leadership** – overall low-cost producer in the industry.
2 **Product or service differentiation** – the differentiation of products and services from those of rivals.
3 **Focus or niche strategy** – either low-cost focus or differentiation focus.

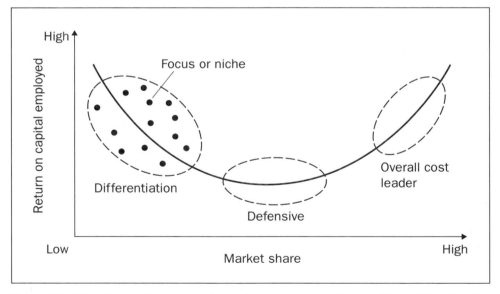

Figure 4.2 The return on investment/market share curve and the positions of the generic strategies on it.

Source: Adapted from Rowe et al., 1989.

Focus		**Differentiation**
Customers		Add value
Products/services		Uniqueness
Geographical markets		Marketing
Expand with care		Look for change
Defensive		**Low-cost leadership**
Strengthen position		Increase volume
Keep moving		Increase market share
Reduce costs		Economies of scale
Improve efficiency		
Increase cash flow		

Many / Few — Number of options

Low — Competitive strength — High

Figure 4.3 The generic strategies of Porter related to the number of options available and the competitive strength.

These result in the profit and market-share positions shown in figure 4.2. The various options available to managers are shown in figure 4.3 and Porter's three generic strategies are explained below.

Low-cost leadership

Low-cost leadership means becoming the overall low-cost producer in the industry. This is useful in markets where people base their decision to buy on price, i.e. where buyers are price-sensitive. The objectives are:

- To open up a sustainable cost advantage over competitors.
- To use low cost in order to underprice competitors and so gain market share or to increase profit margin at the going price. However, aggressive price cutting to gain market share can lead to reduced margins.

The aim should be to reduce costs below those of competitors and so make this the theme of the business. However, there is a limit to this since products or services can be produced so cheaply that they lose customer appeal.

In order to reduce costs the value chain must be examined in order to remove some of the cost-producing activities. No area should be overlooked and a cost-conscious culture should be developed, producing spartan facilities, reduced waste and employee participation in cost reduction, for instance.

In order to gain a cost advantage the costs across the value chain must be lower than the costs of competitors. This can be done by:

- improving efficiency and controlling costs throughout the current value chain, and/or
- changing the chain to bypass some cost-producing activities.

The drive for costs is reflected, for instance, in spartan facilities, no perks, no waste, tight budgets and employee participation in cost control. At the same time investment in cost-saving improvements is high. Cost drivers have to be identified and pushed down or eliminated year after year.

The low-cost producer sets the industry's price floor but still earns a profit. If price becomes a market force then the inefficient competitors suffer first. Thus a low-cost producer has a good defence against Porter's five competitive forces:

- **Buyers** – it is rare that powerful buyers will be able to bargain the price down past the next most cost-efficient producer.

- **Competitors** – the business will be able to set the price floor, win sales and market share on price, earn above-average profits and defend in a price war.

- **New entrants** – low prices should provide a barrier against new entrants.

- **Substitutes** – the business will be able to use price as a defence against substitutes.

- **Suppliers** – there will be greater protection against powerful suppliers if the cost advantage is due to greater efficiency. Now read Box BP4.1.

BOX BP4.1

The plus and minus of low-cost leadership approaches

Low-cost leadership is powerful if:

- Price competition is strong.
- The product or service is a standardized commodity type easily available from several competitors.
- It is difficult to differentiate the product or service.
- Price rather than features or quality is dominant.
- Customers have low switching costs.
- Customers are large with the power to bargain prices down.

There are also risks for the low-cost producer such as:

- A technological breakthrough may give a competitor an advantage.
- The low-cost methods may be easy to imitate.
- A management focusing on cost cutting may miss changes taking place in the market.
- Large investments in cost reduction may lock the business into its current strategy and technology.

Differentiation

Differentiation occurs when customer needs and preferences are so diverse that they cannot be satisfied by a standard product. A business that has skills and expertise which competitors cannot match can use them to differentiate its products or services from the competition. Such advantages are hard to copy quickly and profitably and are based on:

- Customer services
- Value for money
- Quality
- Technical superiority

The costs of producing the differentiation must be paid for out of the extra price the differentiated product or service warrants. These factors enable the business to:

- Charge a premium price
- Gain customer loyalty
- Sell more products or services

Profitability increases when the extra price charged is greater than the extra costs incurred in differentiating the products or services. As with low-cost production, differentiation can be developed anywhere in the value chain. Differentiation is best when products or services can be easily differentiated, the market is large with many different customers and there are few rivals. The best sources of differentiation are those based on competencies in the value chain. A long-lasting competitive edge is based on technical superiority, quality, customer support or value for money since they are difficult and expensive for rivals to copy.

Successful differentiation also provides a defence against the five competitive forces:

- **Buyers** find the products and services of competitors less attractive and so their bargaining power is reduced.
- **Competitors** are forced to fight over other parts of the market.
- **Entry barriers** of customer loyalty and uniqueness can be produced. This allows premium prices to be charged.
- **Substitutes** find it difficult to enter that market niche.
- **Suppliers** find it difficult to raise prices since the high margin enables the business to argue from a position of strength.

The problem with differentiation is that there is a tendency to increase costs. The trick is either to control costs or to offset lower profits by increased volume. In other words, the unit costs must not be allowed to get out of line with the competition.

Before continuing with the focus approach, please read Box BP4.2.

BOX BP4.2

Value for money

If a manager can combine a low-cost with a differentiation approach, the business can give more value for money. In other words, the objective of the business is to exceed the expectations of the customer on features, quality, performance, price and service. Thus managers can position their products or services in the market-place in any of the following ways:

- Cheap basic products or services at low cost.
- Medium-quality products or services at below-average prices.
- Very good products or services at an average price.
- Expensive products or services distinctly differentiated.

If your products are equal to rivals on quality, service, features and performance, the firm with the lowest cost base will have the competitive advantage. This is an attempt to provide value for money. The objective is to produce a medium-quality product at a below-average price or a very good product at a medium price. Most people, in an affluent society, will prefer a middle-range product to the basic cheap product of the low-cost producer or the expensive product of the exclusive producer.

The focus or niche approach
The **focus or niche approach** identifies a market niche where customers have a distinct preference or requirement. There are various ways of determining a niche:

- The geography or the location of the market.
- The specialized needs of the customer.
- The special attributes of the product or service.

A manager who focuses on a niche market can apply a low-cost or a differentiated approach or both, as described earlier. Focusing is the approach to use when:

- The niche is large enough to be profitable, has growth potential and is not necessary for the success of large competitors.
- The business has no resources and skills to service the niche effectively.
- The business has superior customer goodwill and service abilities.
- The customer requires specialist expertise or customized products.
- No other competitor is in the niche.
- The business does not have enough resources to obtain a wider market.
- A market has many different niches, thus allowing a business to choose a niche to match its strengths and abilities.

An example of niche marketing can be seen in Box BP4.3.

BOX BP4.3

A policy of niche marketing

One of the things that strikes most parents is that children are becoming increasingly selective in what they wear at a much earlier age. The marketeers with their branding and special labels have saturated the communications mix and have linked in to pop music and traditional children's television to produce pre-teenage teenagers.

The research done by Adams, a UK retailer of children's wear, may have reached a similar conclusion. The company has deliberately positioned itself to appeal to an age group up to eight years old when perhaps parents still have a significant input into the purchasing decision, although children of that age are also a key part of the purchase.

Of course, a revamped product range, good sites for outlets, heavy investment, point-of-sale equipment, a streamlined distribution system, a better stock control process and the financial clout of Sears all help, but the niche market policy seems to be crucial in the challenge against established stores such as Mothercare.

Source: Adapted from Thornhill, 'Why eight is a lucky number'

Again, the special skills of the business provide a basis for defending against the five forces:

- **Buyers** find difficulty in switching to competitors.
- **Competitors** find it difficult or costly to serve the same niche.
- **Entry barriers** are provided by the specialized skills or expertise.
- **Substitutes** find difficulty in overcoming the specialized skills or expertise.
- **Suppliers** have limited outlets for their products or services.

Generic strategies for business development

Much of the discussion in textbooks is about business growth but many businesses, either by choice or circumstances, do not have growth as their main objective – for example, survival is sometimes the overriding objective. Therefore, a business must change in order to survive and a business may need to develop rather than grow in order to adapt to change.

Two basic questions managers have to answer in any business are: (1) what business are we in? and (2) why are we in business? The first question provides the mission statement and the second involves setting the objectives.

This approach is developed by Jauch and Glueck[3] who believe that the first question to be asked needs to clarify the products or services provided, the markets served and the functions performed. Then managers should decide how they can develop the business. These authors identify four generic methods for developing a business – stability, expansion, retrenchment and combination. The generic methods are based on answers to the following questions.

1 What is our business? What should it be? What business should we be in five years from now? In ten years?

2 Should we stay in the same business(es) with a similar level of effort?(*Stability*)

3 Should we get out of the business entirely or some parts of it? (*Retrenchment*)

4 Should we expand into new business areas by adding new functions, products and/or markets? (*Expansion*)

5 Should we carry out alternatives 3 and 4, 2 and 4, or 2 and 3? Simultaneously or sequentially? (*Combination*)

The business may decide to change its functions, markets or products under its current generic position or it may decide to change the effort it is putting into its generic position (see figure 4.4).

	Expand	**Retrench**	**Stabilize**	**Combine**
Products	Add new products or develop new ones	Drop old products or reduce product development	No change except for packaging or quality improvements	Drop old products while adding new ones
Markets	Find new territories or penetrate markets	Drop distribution channels and reduce market share	No change but protect market share and focus on market niches	Drop old customers while adding new ones
Functions	Develop vertical integration and/or increase capacity	Sell to one customer and/ or decrease R&D, marketing etc. or lay off employees	No change but improve production efficiency	Increase capacity and improve efficiency

Figure 4.4 Some of the ways in which a firm may change its products, markets or functions according to whether management decides to expand, retrench, stabilize or use a combination of these.

Source: Adapted from Jauch and Glueck, 1988.

Stability is not a 'do nothing' approach, nor are goals such as profits or cash flow abandoned. Little change is made to the products, markets or functions but efforts are concentrated on maintaining or increasing profits and efficiency and reducing costs. In order to achieve such objectives a competitive strategy may be used involving prices, packaging, differentiating products and segmenting markets.

Businesses in a mature industry or with mature products or services often pursue a policy of stability. Small businesses also frequently adopt this position and sometimes businesses which are performing erratically often decide to follow the stability approach for a while.

Expansion occurs when a business decides to add new products or markets or perhaps integrate backwards and make its own products. Also, the business may increase its efforts to gain market share and expand facilities. High investment and risk taking is implied.

However, increased assets or size may lead to increased return on investment (ROI) but inefficiencies may result. In fact, expansion can be desirable or undesirable, since an expanding business can be inefficient.

There is a general belief that rapid change in the environment demands expansion which in turn leads to improved performance. This is not always the case, as expansion can lead to inefficiencies because the attention of managers is diverted from running the business.

Retrenchment occurs when a business has to reduce its products, services, markets or functions and so reduce any negative cash flows. The business often divests itself of products, services, businesses or markets, reduces functions or focuses on fewer customers by withdrawing from distribution. In extreme cases it may be necessary to write off losses, go bankrupt or realize assets.

Retrenchment is often reserved for dealing with a crisis and involves abandoning markets, reducing costs and assets, cutting products and increasing cash flow. Such approaches are often useful during the decline stage of a business or industry.

However, although perhaps regarded as an admission of failure, a retrenchment approach can be used to reverse negative trends and set the stage for further development of the business. Therefore, it can be part of a periodic reassessment of the business. Now read Box BP4.4.

The example in Box BP4.5 may not be pure retrenchment but it does break down the existing business unit.

Combination occurs when a business uses the previous methods – stability, expansion and retrenchment – at the same time or sequentially. Jauch and Glueck believe this approach is not easy to operate and is more common in large, multi-business organizations during periods of change.

BOX BP4.4

Retrenchment – or keeping your head low

The construction sector is a good barometer of national economic success or failure. The example of the UK construction group Mowlem is an interesting case in point. Mowlem is involved in large capital construction, from hospitals to office blocks.

Recession has severely affected many firms in this sector. Bad debts at Canary Wharf, London, losses at London City Airport and a poorer showing by SGB scaffolding have meant considerable suffering for Mowlem as well. Its worth has fallen from a high of around £400 million to less than £100 million.

A policy of retrenchment or survival has been taking place at Mowlem. Tightening up on costs, cutting back to the basic operations, and not taking business for its own sake – irrespective of the margins – have all helped.

Debt reduction has also occurred through selling off the HSS hire shop which was outside the core business. Times are still hard for many, but the leaner outfits who 'stick to the knitting' may have greater chance of surviving recessionary times.

BOX BP4.5

Demerger: breaking up is not so hard to do

The chemical giant ICI successfully fought off the Hanson interest in 1991. By 1993, demerger was the policy adopted by the senior management of ICI, with a heavy chemicals side and the Zeneca division.

In essence the business has become two large units; arguably, a corporate focus may be lost while predators may be more able to kill a young animal than a mature adult.

A policy of 'centralized decentralization' would have been another structural variant; this would have retained the central corporate focus and allowed greater local flexibility.

Variations of the generic strategies

There are several ways in which the generic methods can be carried out – internally or externally, related or unrelated development, by vertical integration and either offensively or defensively. The way chosen will depend on the internal strengths and weaknesses of the business, the opportunities and threats offered by the environment and the preferences of the management. These methods are summarized in figure 4.5.

Methods	Expansion	Retrenchment	Stabilize	Combine
Internal	Penetrate existing markets. Add new products. Add new markets.	Reduce costs, and assets. Drop products, markets and functions.	Seek production and marketing efficiency. Reorganize.	Subcontract.
External	Acquisitions. Mergers.	Divest SBUs. Liquidate. Declare bankrupt.	Maintain market share.	Cross-licence. Joint venture.
Related	Seek synergy from new products, markets, functions.	Eliminate related products, markets or functions.	Improve products.	
Unrelated	Conglomerate diversification in products, markets, functions.	Eliminate unrelated products, markets or functions.		
Vertical	Add new functions.	Reduce functions.		
Offensive	Innovative, entrepreneurial moves.			Grow to sell off.
Defensive	Imitate in R&D and new products.	Reactive defence of position.		

Figure 4.5 The various options available for carrying out the generic strategies.

Source: Adapted from Jauch and Glueck, 1988.

The 'tight ship' philosophy is very much part of recessionary times and an example of this can be seen in the case of Storehouse (Box BP4.6), which is probably retrenchment/internal according to figure 4.5.

The word 'diversification' often arises when considering the development of a business. Diversification changes the basic nature of the business in some way, for example, by acquiring new businesses in related or unrelated areas or by investing in new ventures. There are the added

---

BOX BP4.6

Getting smaller is beautiful!

The case of Storehouse is an example of a UK company that has got smaller as a deliberate policy in order to pull itself back from the effects of expansionist plans over the last 25 years.

The core BHS and Mothercare shops remain alongside Blazer, a menswear chain. The removal of Habitat and Richards has trimmed the cloth of this retail giant. It now looks as if the organization has become more manageable and sales in BHS and Mothercare are certainly moving in the right direction. Perhaps if Blazer goes as well the ship will be a lot tighter.

---

complications of operating in new and unfamiliar areas but the risk may be justified for those firms limited by strong competition or restricted markets or who have uncertainties in their supply and distribution channels.

Structure

Chandler[4] made a study of 70 large corporations in the USA and found that the structure of a corporation often changes with its growth strategy. However, he found that the change does not usually occur until inefficiency and operating problems trigger the structural changes. In fact there was a consistent sequence of:

> development → new strategy → new administrative problems
> → decline in profitability and performance → change to a
> more appropriate organization structure → recovery

This sequence could be repeated several times during the lifetime of the corporation. In other words, in this study the choice of organization structure does make a difference to the performance of a business. Therefore, any change in strategy may also involve a change in the organization structure. The structure is the means for organizing people and co-ordinating tasks efficiently and effectively.

A business often expands from being a small single business to a complex vertically integrated business. Geographic expansion then causes product or market divisions. At the same time management changes from owner-manager to functional departments to divisions to decentralized business units. Single business units usually have a centralized functional structure. The change from one type of structure to another can take short or long periods of time and can be smooth or traumatic.

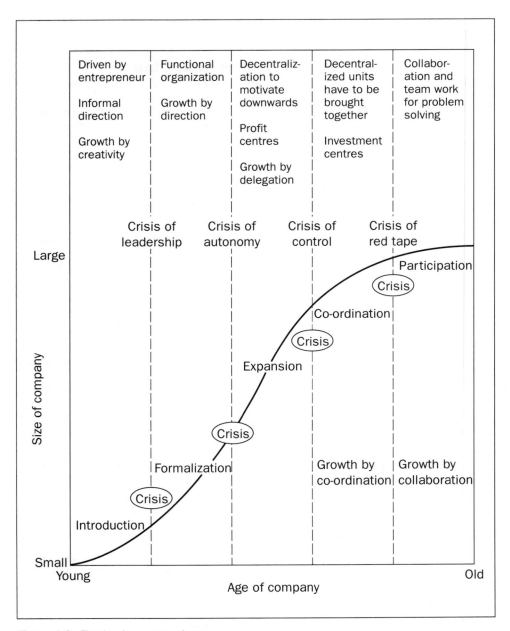

Figure 4.6 The business growth curve.

Source: Adapted from Greiner, 1972.

Greiner[5] identified five phases in the growth curve of a business. Each phase ends in a crisis that can only be resolved by a change in the form of management or organization structure. Figure 4.6 shows a typical organization growth curve.

The first phase is characterized by an entrepreneurial management style and the business is quite small. The main emphasis is on creating a product and a market and the organization structure is informal. As the business grows, the founder is unable to control the business as skills are required in the functional areas and this leads to a crisis of direction.

The second phase shows an increase in efficiency with the improvement in management until managers become restricted by the centralized control. The bureaucratic structure and the analytic and directive top management begin to restrict the operations of creative middle managers. There is a crisis of autonomy. Is there a case for decentralization?

The third phase sees decentralization and the establishment of a divisional structure based on geography or products which leads to strong market expansion for the business. Another crisis develops when the top management begin to realize they are losing control over the business.

The fourth phase illustrates how top management develop the strategic business unit or product group structure. This ensures that the autonomous managers have to co-operate with the rest of the group in order to co-ordinate plans, money, technology and human resources.

The fifth though not necessarily the final phase occurs as the need to adapt to change becomes the key to survival. This means that organizations need to be adaptive, with rapidly changing systems that perhaps are arranged around problems.

It is obvious that each phase requires a different style of leadership and the crisis often lasts until the top management is replaced by one more suitable for the current situation. The phases and the crisis periods often last several years.

It is also obvious that within large organizations individual units at various stages on the growth curve may be found.

The **structure** of a business links the common elements that characterize the business by identifying the relationships between the people, tasks and technology. Within the structure managers use information and control processes to transform inputs into outputs. Essentially the structure performs three functions:

1 Defines authority and responsibility.
2 Facilitates the flow of information.
3 Creates integration between separate entities.

When considering the structure of their business, managers should consider the following factors:

- their key decisions;
- the task environment;
- the technology.

The key decisions

The **key decisions** managers make affect the structure they choose for their business. The decisions include:

- Product or service to be offered – how many, quality, number of models.
- Managers' values and philosophy – centralization, quality, people, service.
- Types of customer served – government, industrial, residential.
- Where to market the products or services – locally, regionally or globally.

A change in one of these decisions may require a change in structure. If that change is not made, the business will struggle for years, possibly until at last change does occur. For instance, a small business gradually develops into a functionally organized business until the number of products becomes too large or too diverse to control. Then there is the change to a divisional structure, perhaps based on products. If the business then begins to expand globally there may be a case for a divisional structure based on the different markets.

Superimposed on these structures are the concepts of centralization and decentralization. How much control does management need and what kind of control should it be? It depends as usual on the situation. A structure which is working well with one set of contingencies may not work with another. Businesses can often take years to adjust to new situations or sometimes they pass through a traumatic experience by changing very quickly. This often occurs when managers do not adjust to change continuously.

The task environment

The **task environment** includes the stakeholders and the knowledge and technology involved in the business. The study by Burns and Stalker[6] of about 20 British industrial firms in the 1950s is a landmark in the study of organization design. They concluded that environmental forces are felt directly by the business and that the structure of a business varies according to the environment. Unstable environments mean rapid changes in competitors, economic conditions, markets, products and technology.

Burns and Stalker discovered that there are two major types of structure which are effective in different environments: (1) mechanistic (bureaucratic) structures which are effective in stable environments and (2) organic (adaptive) structures which are effective in unstable environments. These are illustrated in figure 4.7.

This concept has been developed further in recent years because environments can be described in terms of their stability and complexity. This is illustrated in figure 4.8.

Simple environments have few competitors, one market and little government regulation, such as the environment of a village shop.

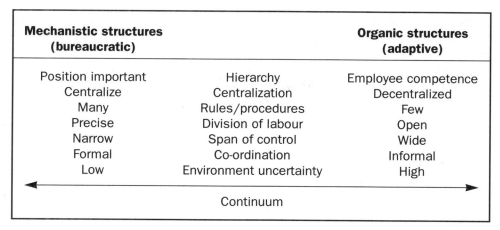

Figure 4.7 The continuum between mechanistic and organic structures.

Stable	
Low uncertainty	**Moderate uncertainty**
Few environmental factors exist	Many environmental factors exist
Factors are similar to each other	Factors are not similar to each other
Factors remain basically the same	Factors remain basically the same
Use: Simple mechanistic structures	**Use:** Mechanistic structures that emphasize high levels of differentiation and formal integration
Examples: Salt manufacturers Printing firms	**Examples:** University Registrar's Offices Petrol refining/ distribution firms
Moderate uncertainty	**High uncertainty**
Many environmental factors exist	Many environmental factors exist
Factors are similar to each other	Factors are not similar to each other
Factors are continually changing	Factors are continually changing
Use: Organic structures with informal horizontal integration and low levels of differentiation	**Use:** Organic structures that emphasize both differentiation and high levels of horizontal integration
Examples: Fast food firms Consumer products firms	**Examples:** Telecommunications firms Biotechnology firms

Stability of environment (left axis, Stable at top, Unstable at bottom)

Simple ——— **Degree of complexity** ——— Complex

Figure 4.8 The various types of task environment.

Source: Adapted from Hellriegal et al., 1989.

Complex environments have strong competition, many customers and suppliers, geographical diversity and high government regulation, such as the environment of a High Street bank.

Stable environments show little or no change over time and any change can generally be predicted, such as the environment of many commodity producers.

Unstable environments show rapid, unpredictable change owing to rapid product innovation, changes in demand, market changes, competitors entering and leaving the industry and changes in government regulations, such as the environment of the computer industry.

Now read Box BP4.7.

BOX BP4.7

Specialization and integration

Lawrence and Lorsch studied three different industry groups as representatives of environments in which change and environmental uncertainty appeared to be high, intermediate and low. The industries were plastics manufacturing, package foods and standardized containers. They identified businesses in each industry that were high and low performers. Then they assessed the level and nature of specialization and integration in each business.

They discovered that successful businesses in the rapidly changing plastics industry were more highly specialized than unsuccessful businesses. They were also more specialized than successful businesses in the food and container industries. Successful plastics businesses also used more integrating and informal procedures.

The successful package food businesses were also more specialized than unsuccessful ones with higher integration.

The businesses in the container industry all had similar levels of specialization but the more successful businesses were more highly integrated.

This study showed that specialization is necessary and can even be found in stable environments. Also, successful businesses in all the industries are well integrated. The results are summarized below:

Environment	Structure	Industry
Predictable	Mechanistic	Containers
Moderately certain	Organized with integration	Foods
Uncertain	Organized with formal integration	Plastics

A criticism of this work is that the structure may be characteristic of part of the business only, other parts of the business having different types of structure.

Source: Adapted from Lawrence and Lorsch, *Organisation and Environment*

Technological factors

Technology is normally associated with the nature of the equipment used to complete the tasks of the business. However, in this case technology refers to the science of applying information and knowledge to solving problems, that is, technology as a technique.

Three technological factors influence the number of departments in a business, the delegation of authority and responsibility and the need for a formal integrating mechanism. These are the work flow uncertainty, the task uncertainty and the task interdependency.

Work flow uncertainty is the degree of knowledge in a department about when inputs can be expected for processing. It is low when a department has little discretion to decide which, when or where tasks can be performed.

Task uncertainty is the degree of well-defined knowledge in a department regarding the performance of tasks assigned to it. It is low when members of the department know how to perform the desired tasks and high when members of the department have to use experience, judgement and intuition to solve problems.

Task interdependence is the degree to which decision making and co-operation are necessary to perform a task and can be classified into three types – (1) pooled, (2) sequential and (3) reciprocal.

1 **Pooled** occurs when each employee or department is not required to interact with others to complete a task, for example, mailing brochures or the sales office of a large business.

2 **Sequential** occurs when each employee or department must complete certain tasks before other employees can perform their tasks, such as in mass production.

3 **Reciprocal** occurs when outputs from one employee or department become inputs for others and vice versa, such as can be found in a family or team. This may involve collaboration, communication and group decision making.

The importance of the structure as it relates to technology is illustrated by the classic work of Woodward (see Box BP4.8).

BOX BP4.8

Structure and technology

Woodward decided to find out whether there was 'one best way' to organize a business. She studied 100 businesses in south-east England that employed more than 100 employees. Woodward found that there was no clear relation-ship between the size of a business, type of industry, profitability and the structure of the business. However, a relationship was found between the structure of the business and the manufacturing technology.

Woodward identified three types of technology which increased in technical complexity:

1 small batch or unit production such as furniture or scientific instrument making;
2 large batch and mass production such as car manufacturing;
3 continuous processing such as in an oil refinery.

At the same time, the number of management levels and the span of control for senior managers also increased. However, supervisors in small batch or unit production had the smallest spans of management.

The large batch or mass production businesses had the largest number of rules and controls, rigid chains of command, and inflexible job specifications and employer–employee relationships.

The successful structures can be summarized below:

Technology	Successful structure
Small batch/unit production	Organic
Large batch/mass production	Mechanistic
Continuous process production	Organic

Woodward's conclusions indicate that instead of searching for 'one best way' to organize a business, managers should link the structure of the business to the production technology.

This was a major piece of work but, with hindsight, other non-technological variables will also have an impact on a contingency approach to organization structure.

Source: Adapted from Woodward, *Industrial Organisation*

Technology in the service sector:

- focuses the efforts of people with special expertise, such as doctors or teachers, onto the needs of the clients;
- links together people needing a mutually beneficial exchange such as buyers and sellers;
- passes a client from one point to another for various aspects of the service, such as in a self-service restaurant.

The structure of the business must reflect the congruence of the tasks, people, technology and the information and control processes. Therefore in analysing a case or a business one can think about the structure of the business along the lines indicated in this section. At this point, see Box BP4.9.

BOX BP4.9

Checklist on structure

Key decisions	What key decisions have been/need to be made?
Task environment	Degree of complexity and stability?
Technology	Production method – is it unit or small batch, large batch or mass production or a continuous process?
	For a service – does it focus efforts, link people or pass people?
Structure	Is it mechanistic or organic?
People	Examine the job design, skills, selection, leadership, motivation, rewards etc.
	Do they fit together or are they pulling in all directions?
	Do they or will they fit the structure at present or in the future?

Systems

The value chain described in Unit Three is seen here as the key to deciding the systems required in a business. This is because the value chain identifies the key activities both inside and outside the business which are essential to its success. To control any part of the value chain managers need information. Therefore, the information system is the key to the development and control of a business.

Information systems

Information systems are now almost indispensable for planning, decision making and controlling a business. The speed and accuracy of the information about what is going right or wrong in a business determines the performance of the business. Therefore, managers have to be comfortable with computers at all levels of management.

Management information represents the key features of a situation which require action and it should be accurate, relevant and timely. The information has to be developed from raw data and put into a form that managers can use to make decisions. Data are a collection of unorganized facts, opinions, statistics or predictions. When data mean something to someone so that they can be used for decision making, they become information. In order to be used as information, data should have many of the following properties: accuracy, availability, comprehensibility, consistency, relevance, reliability, timeliness and usefulness.

Information systems provide major benefits by:

- allowing routine tasks, such as stock control and recording transactions, to be performed faster or more cheaply;
- helping people in business make better decisions;
- improving customer service;
- improving old or creating new products;
- changing the basis of competition;
- adapting quickly to change, taking advantage of short product life cycles and exploring niche markets.

There are five general areas where control is required – (1) finance, (2) organization, (3) production, (4) quality and (5) stock:

1 **Financial control** is carried out using budgets, analysis of the accounting statements and ratio analysis.
2 **Organization control** includes the organization structure and its planning and decision-making systems together with the control of employees.
3 **Production control** is the routing, scheduling, and timing of a product, service or project.
4 **Quality control** maintains the quality of products or services.
5 **Stock control** is focused on raw materials, work in progress, finished goods and warehousing.

Many controls which should increase motivation are very often threatening to employees. Therefore, the goals of the business and the objectives on which the standards are based should be explained to them. Employees who develop the necessary standards also have a commitment to meet the controls. The standards should be relevant and appropriate. Therefore, the clear communication of goals and standards, realistic appraisal, timely feedback and employee participation create confidence in the control system.

If employees believe the standards are more important than the business objectives on which they are based, **goal displacement** occurs. For example, emphasis on profits can decrease long-term investment and the future of the business.

Overcontrol can lead to sub-optimal results. For example, reducing costs in one part of the value chain may increase costs in another and even increase the total costs. Therefore, consideration of the value chain is important at all times.

Overcontrol can also be used to gain power and may lead to higher costs, increased labour turnover, low morale and reduced production.

Management control systems

These systems guide and motivate managers to attain the business goals and to correct ineffective and inefficient performance. All management control systems have the following features:

- A focus both on activities to achieve goals and on responsibility centres. An activity such as a product line may involve several responsibility centres.
- The process involves two types of information: planned data (budgets and standards) and actual data (what has actually happened in a business or externally).
- The process co-ordinates and optimizes all parts of a business and therefore has to be an integrated system.
- It tends to focus on financial controls.
- The process involves periodic planning and feedback.

The management control system includes both formal and informal controls. The informal controls are part of the business culture.

The overall goals of a business tend to be timeless and set the overall guidelines for management control which in turn sets the guidelines for task control.

Management control generally controls people and is used to control the whole business. It ensures that the business achieves its goals, whereas task control ensures that tasks are completed efficiently and effectively and are designed specifically for a particular task.

Task control generally controls things and is more precise than management control in that it is based on a set of rules and procedures and normally provides precise numerical standards for evaluating performance.

If a system is a set of interrelated parts or a structure that functions as one unit, then a management control system is based on the parts of the business – its structure – and the information flows between the parts. The process is what the managers do with the information.

Controls ensure desired results are obtained. First, managers should determine the **key activities** which must function effectively for the business to be successful. At the same time, it is important to identify **key control points** where monitoring and collecting information should occur. These are usually at points of change.

Decentralization

The issue of decentralization is concerned with the extent to which power is devolved in the business. **Centralization** is the degree to which authority is concentrated at the top of the business, whereas **decentralization** is the delegation of power, authority and responsibility to the lower levels of the business. This often has the effect of producing small self-contained business units.

What is meant by power? It means power to take decisions over operational issues such as production or recruitment, or power to take decisions about the future of the business, for example new plant or diversification. In fact decentralization can mean operational decentralization, strategic decentralization or both.

There is a tendency to think of functionally organized businesses as centralized and divisionally organized businesses as decentralized. However, a divisionally organized business can be centralized or decentralized.

The advantages of decentralization are believed to be: the release of pressure on top managers; better decisions because they are made closer to the action; better training, morale and initiative at lower levels; faster decisions and more flexibility in changing environments.

Centralization is often seen in negative terms and decentralization as positive, but decentralization with no co-ordination and leadership is undesirable. Therefore, it is the extent or degree of decentralization that is important. This depends on the contingencies which influence the extent of the decentralization at the time, such as:

- External environment – market, competition, raw materials, technology and so forth.

- Size and growth rate of the business.

- The characteristics of the business such as costs, propensity for risk, the preference of managers to become involved, organization culture and the abilities of the lower-level managers.

The major forms of decentralization

In order to operate successfully a business is built up from a responsibility centre or centres and each responsibility centre has a manager responsible for its performance.

Control operates at all levels in a business. In a small business all the control may be in the hands of the owner, whereas in a large corporation there may be a large number of managers involved at any level. Thus in order to control a business as it grows it is necessary to create **responsibility centres** to control **expenses**, **revenues**, **profits** and **investments**. Such centres are classified according to the way in which inputs and outputs are measured.

Expense centres have inputs measured in money, but the outputs are not. There are two types of expense centre: (1) engineered expense centres where costs are precise and (2) discretionary expense centres where expenses can be at the discretion of the manager. Some businesses have outputs which are not measurable in money terms, such as accountants, lawyers and research and development businesses. In these cases, the control can be expressed in expense terms only and budgets are used to control and motivate managers. There is no way of determining what is the correct amount of expense.

Usually, expense centre managers are also responsible for quality and production volume as well as efficiency. Engineered expenses should be kept as low as possible relative to the standards of quality and safety necessary in the business, whereas discretionary expenses may depend on the manager spending the agreed amount since reducing expenses may impair the long-term survival of the business. For example, a manager may improve current profits by cutting training expenses but the long-term future of the business may be put at risk.

In a **revenue centre** the outputs can be measured in money terms. Expenses are only measured for the centre itself and there is no attempt to relate inputs or expenses to outputs. Revenue centres are usually found in marketing businesses and are based on budgets or sales quotas.

In **profit centres** the measurement of profit provides an incentive to maximize profits rather than minimize costs. Both revenues and expenses are measured and matched to determine the profit and this motivates managers to balance increased expenses against an increased contribution from higher sales.

Generally, responsibility is delegated to the lowest level in the business where the necessary information for control is available. This leads to speed in decision making, since the necessary information is close to the activity and decisions need not be based solely on the analysis of data.

Manufacturing and service businesses are sometimes profit centres. However, when there is more than one profit centre there can be problems in measuring profits, owing to transfer prices between centres, common revenues and common costs.

In **investment centres** both the profit and the investment – capital – used in producing it are measured, that is, the profit is compared to the assets employed in earning it. This is an important concept because a business manager has two important responsibilities:

1 To generate adequate profits from the resources available.
2 To invest in additional resources only when they will produce an adequate return on the investment. This also implies disinvesting if the return is not there.

The return on capital employed (ROCE) is often used as the ratio for comparing businesses and measuring performance. However, **residual income** is a money figure, not a ratio, and is a superior concept (see the section on finance in Unit Six).

The residual income is found from the profit before interest and tax (PBIT) less a capital charge. The capital charge is derived from the total assets obtained from the balance sheet multiplied by a rate (%). The rate can be based on the weighted average cost of capital (WACC) for the whole business. It can be either raised or lowered according to the risk of the part of the business under consideration.

Residual income $=$ PBIT $-$ capital charge

Capital charge $\quad=$ total assets $\times$ WACC

Therefore:

Residual income $=$ PBIT $-$ (total assets $\times$ WACC)

However, the use of investment centres has to take into account the problems of fixed asset accounting. Do you use gross book value, net book value or annuity depreciation? One way to overcome such problems is to regard the investment in fixed assets as sunk costs and only use the **controllable assets** which are receivables and stock.

Style

Management involves planning, organizing, leading and controlling. Carrying out these activities involves managers in a pattern of actions. These actions communicate priorities to employees much more effectively than words alone and can profoundly influence performance. Thus managers indicate by their actions the factors they consider are important for the organization.

The way managers communicate can be by leading, by the decisions they make, by personal relationships, their values, attitudes and the way they use power, by the degree to which they focus on tasks or people and by the way they direct, support, set goals and standards and involve others. Thus managers give signals to their employees and so communicate values and objectives in order to reach organization goals.

Much also depends on the situational contingencies such as the characteristics of:

■ subordinates – abilities, experience, independence, needs and skills;

■ work environment – rewards, structure, work group and tasks (routine/non-routine, simple/complex, feedback and intrinsic satisfaction);

■ organization systems – clarity of plans, policies and rules, size and influence of the staff functions.

Managers are expected to apply these ideas through a series of tasks and/or interactions with people. This is called **transactional leadership**.

At the same time, managers are expected to influence the beliefs, values and goals of their employees and cause them to achieve almost impossible objectives. They transform people into high performers using inspiration and personality. Such managers show **transformational leadership** and have vision, integrity and charisma. They use symbols and empowerment and provide intellectual stimulation.

Managers develop a personal style of management. This style may be suitable or otherwise for their organization at any particular time. It may also be successful for a while but, unless the manager adapts to changes in the business and the environment, a mismatch will eventually develop and both manager and business will begin to fail. In fact, the manager will probably be the one to fail as organizational style is far more deeply entrenched than personal approaches.

A number of management styles have been identified:

- task oriented
- people oriented
- autocratic
- consultative
- group oriented
- directive
- supportive
- participative
- achievement oriented

Does a manager use one style all the time or change from one style to another as the need arises? To what extent does change in the business and its environment affect the management style? There is no ideal answer to these questions; it is possible to say only that management style and successful businesses tend to be matched for a particular environmental situation. When the situation changes, most managers find it difficult to change their style to match the new environment.

The question is: how is it possible to choose managers who can adapt to change or, put another way, how can managers be changed or replaced before they damage the business? To determine the need for style flexibility, we must determine the potential symptoms of business decline which trigger the need for change. These triggers may require altering the style of management but other issues may also be involved; at this point, read Box BP4.10.

BOX BP4.10

Symptoms of malaise

Ansoff provides a manager profile with ten attributes which can be applied at various levels of environmental turbulence.[1]

For the small business and owner-manager, the key people are often unaware of what is going wrong at any particular time whereas, in larger businesses, pressure to replace the failing manager builds up. However, this may be after much damage has already been done to the business.

Symptoms of decline indicate that a business may be heading for trouble. Argenti analysed 40 UK businesses that were in the process of decline and found ten major symptoms:[2]

1 Falling profitability
2 Reduced dividends
3 Falling sales
4 Increased debt
5 Decreasing liquidity
6 Delays in publishing financial results
7 Reduced market share
8 High turnover of management
9 Fear
10 Lack of clear direction

Sources:
1   Ansoff and McDonnell, *Implanting Strategic Management*
2   Argenti, *Corporate Collapse*

Causes of business failure

What causes a business to fail? According to Slatter, the causal factors may be classified under three headings: management skills, financial management and competitiveness.[7]

Management skills
- The business may be dominated by one person whose objectives or style create problems and lead to poor performance.
- New strategies, products or services are not developed quickly enough as current ones go into decline.
- Weak managers may support the dominant leader or weak non-executive directors may encourage tunnel vision.
- Key issues may be ignored if managers are too functionally oriented. Businesses dominated by accountants or engineers may not pay sufficient attention to the market.
- A business undergoing rapid change or diversification may ignore its core business.
- Acquisitions may fail to meet expectations and may have cost too much in the first place.

- Large projects may be badly managed due to:
  - underestimating capital requirements
  - design changes during production
  - development time longer than intended
  - unforeseen start-up difficulties
  - market entry more expensive than expected

Financial management
- Poor financial control indicated by cash flow and over-trading.
- Poor costing systems which do not differentiate between the products and services provided so that, if the mix changes, a loss can occur.
- High fixed costs may make the business volume-sensitive.
- Poor budgets and lack of attention to what the variances are telling managers.
- Economies of scale and experience can give cost advantages.
- The business structure and product variety can give both advantages and disadvantages. For example, the overhead costs of an expensive head office may disadvantage a large business against a small one.
- Costs may be increased owing to poor operating management.
- The debt ratio must be used carefully so that in times of low profit a business can still invest for the future. Conservatism can lead to cash reserves and no loans but no investment either.

Competitiveness
- Failure to maintain clear differentiation.
- Increased costs of reserves and fluctuations in the currency markets can cause problems.
- Poor marketing.
- Environmental forces.

Comments
The causes of a decline in a business may be due to a number of the above factors which are interlinked. For example, a business losing sales and therefore suffering a reduction in profits may have high costs or lack differentiation of its products from its competitors. This could be due to poor managers who failed to control costs or create sustainable competitive advantage, or it could be due to external competitive forces which are outside management control.

Managers have to be able to separate the symptoms of a decline from the underlying causes. Both need attention and action. In the example above, the reduction in sales and profits may be symptoms but the causes could be the fault of management or the external environment or both. Now read Box BP4.11 and Box BP4.12.

BOX BP4.11

The Z Factor

Altman developed a useful predictor for the bankruptcy of manufacturing businesses. He uses the Z Factor, which is a discriminant function with five significant ratios.

$$Z = 1.2A + 1.4B + 3.3C + 0.6D + E$$

where:

A = working capital/total assets

B = retained earnings/total assets

C = EBIT/total assets

D = market value of equity/book value of total debt

E = sales/total assets

and

working capital = current assets − current liabilities

total assets = fixed assets + current assets

retained earnings = accumulated profits

market value of equity = (number of ordinary shares × current market price) + value of preference shares

book value of total debt = long-term + medium-term + short-term loans + overdraft

For businesses in the UK with a Z value of less than 1.5, bankruptcy is fairly certain, whereas businesses with a Z Factor of more than 2.0 are almost certain not to go bankrupt. Z Factors of between 1.5 and 2.0 give cause for concern only if they recur over several periods. In order to compare businesses, the Z Factor is best used for those which are in the same industry and phase of the organization life cycle.

Source: Adapted from Altman, 'Financial ratios, discriminant analysis and the prediction of corporate bankruptcy'

BOX BP4.12

Good housekeeping or relative decline?

Competition abounds and the term 'competitive advantage' is heard in every sector. Some organizations have favoured a policy of cost cutting in order to remain competitive.

There is a parallel in sport: if we adopt a policy of defence (cost cutting), it may make it difficult for the opposition to win, but it may also prevent us from winning (maximizing profit).

Hoover's retreat to Scotland from France to utilize cheap(er) labour can be cited as an example. Similarly, the Vespa scooter manufacturer Piaggio's planned development of the Mezzogiorno, south of Naples, with potential state aid, can also be seen as a move to cut costs. Thus both companies have taken steps to reduce costs – particularly labour costs – in Dijon and Pontedera respectively, by reducing labour charges through cheap(er) labour.

Costs must be contained for business efficiency, but we cannot help feeling that sometimes this moving or trimming back of labour is almost an end in itself.

Management style

Management style will vary with the situation but it essentially revolves around the following tasks:

1 Knowing what is happening and how well things are going.
2 Developing a supportive climate and culture to achieve and perform to high standards.
3 Responding to change, being alert to new opportunities and generating new ideas.
4 Building a consensus and dealing with company politics.
5 Developing ethical standards.
6 Taking corrective action as necessary.

These are explained as follows:

(1) In order to know how well a business is doing, managers must develop a network of formal and informal contacts and sources of information. As information passes through a business to managers it gets filtered, so that managers must guard against surprises. To this end, accurate information and a 'feel' for the business are important. Management by walking about (MBWA) is used by many managers to keep contact with the business.[8] There are many styles of MBWA and it is up to individual managers to develop their own style, for example getting to know employees by using first names, visiting them at work, working on the line, sitting with a driver on a journey, joining the night shift, taking snacks to share during a break, and so on; finding out what attitudes, ideas, observations and problems employees have, and what they need to do a good job.

(2) The development of a supportive climate is a part of MBWA – both words and deeds play a part in this. What a manager says can inspire, set norms and values, provide reasons for change and new viewpoints and priorities. Managers can also increase commitment and confidence. The things managers do adds credibility to what is said, creates symbols and provides examples of the behaviour expected of the employees. Attention

to detail, quality, costs and idea generation can be focused by managers drawing attention to such concepts in symbolic ways, for example, picking up litter, commenting on quality or standards or asking for help.

(3) Every idea for something new or different should have a volunteer champion who will be committed, competitive, fanatic, persistent and tenacious about seeing it through successfully. In order to create conditions where champions can thrive managers should:

- Encourage individuals and groups to put their ideas forward and take the initiative.
- Generate tolerance for new ideas and experiments.
- Generate tolerance for mistakes and failures so that learning can occur.
- Allow ad hoc organizations to develop as necessary.
- Provide large, visible and immediate rewards for successful champions.

(4) A consensus should be developed over the business structure, staffing and budgets. Therefore, political skills and knowledge of and influence on the power structure are necessary skills. The support of key people or groups needs to be attracted so that a broad consensus occurs.

(5) Ethical behaviour must be a commitment of every manager. Words and deeds are again important in symbolizing this commitment. Managers should set an example by their own behaviour and take a strong stand on ethical issues. Ethical education should be continuous throughout the business and it should be easy to raise and discuss ethical issues. Managers should be prepared to act swiftly and decisively in cases of misconduct since a failure to do so is always interpreted as a lack of commitment. Managers should develop a programme to ensure ethical standards in a business.

(6) Corrective adjustments can be both reactive and proactive to situations. This involves both monitoring the situation and actively looking for ways of improving performance. Managers have to creatively adapt and reshape their ideas as time goes by. They must use their skills to align the activities both inside and outside the business with the overall objectives of the business.

Skills

Until recently the best way of examining the skills and capabilities of a business was through its functional areas – finance, human resource management, marketing and operations. This is demonstrated in Box BP4.13, which gives a review of the internal analysis from the perspective of the disciplines and skills of management. Please study this box next and then complete Activity BP4.2.

BOX BP4.13

The internal environment – a functional checklist

An internal scan of your organization is critical. Not only does this activity focus on the resources of the firm, the supply side of the equation, but it highlights what we can and cannot do. Christensen et al. note four key components of policy:

- market opportunity;
- corporate competence and resources;
- personal (leaders') values and aspirations;
- obligations to other segments of society and not only to shareholders.

This internal environment deals with three of these four factors and corporate competence and the harnessing of resources to these abilities must be the hallmark of success.

A functional analysis does help us to pull together our diverse strands in order to determine our unique competence. It also highlights weaknesses, of course, which can be either marginalized or tackled. However, we should major on our strengths for, if we score five goals, we can win as long as we concede only four. Again, a functional analysis is artificial, for it has to be synthesized to make one; it has to have some real synergy to be effective rather than adopting a mechanistic approach to the four main functional areas of management.

Finance and profitability

- How well are existing assets being used?
- Is the value of the enterprise actually increasing?
- What is the profitability track record?
- How is the cash flow?
- Is there an investment policy?
- What about external funding for projects – how available or accessible are these monies?
- What about the gearing (relative percentage of debt and equity financing)?
- What major resource allocation decisions have been made in the last three years?
- What of the investment analysis of new or proposed programmes?
- What of the history of profits and their forecasts?
- What percentage of dividends are retained?
- What reinvestment is being made?
- How do the capital costs affect any investment policy?
- What is the current market value?
- Is this actual or representative of reality?
- What is the earnings potential of the firm?
- Can you fight off acquisitions?

Marketing and sales

■ Is the marketing concept prevalent across the whole organization?
■ Is there a marketing plan?
■ The marketing mix needs to be seen in the light of the plan.
■ Intelligence and consumer/client information need to be researched on an ongoing basis – is this the case?
■ What segmentation policies are applied?
■ Is there a form of competitor monitoring?
■ What is the status of your product portfolio (e.g. life cycle)?
■ What new products are planned?
■ Outline the 4Ps tactics to meet the overall plan.

Operations/production

■ What products are being designed?
■ What is the adequacy of your present equipment?
■ Are major technological advances (e.g. new technology) being made in your sector which have an impact on the operations?
■ Are you happy with the standards of quality control and assurance?
■ Is your stock rotating?
■ Are the raw materials cost-effective?
■ What 'added value' are you giving to the initial product or service?
■ What of downtime, maintenance and overall production efficiency?
■ Is the best use being made of machinery and layout?
■ What about productivity levels?
■ Are there sufficient controls?

People/organization

The organization can include systems and information processes, or these can be dealt with under operations/production.

On organization matters:

■ What is the span of control?
■ What type of structure do you have? Does it meet your objectives (e.g. closeness to the customer)?
■ What is the span of control?
■ Do people know their job responsibilities?
■ How 'open' are these jobs and responsibilities?
■ Do people have performance targets linked to the needs of the overall plan(s)?

On systems and information processes:

■ Do the existing systems meet your needs? Consider all systems – from accounting to production control, goods inwards and outwards, banking, invoicing etc.
■ Are the employees trained in the documentation?
■ Is the information being utilized (e.g. customer database to sales reporting)?

People are *the* most important asset:

- Do you have a manpower plan?
- Is the manpower plan related to the business plan?
- Are the following sub-functions operating: recruitment and selection, training, compensation and benefits, welfare, development and labour relations?
- How adaptable are your staff?
- Do you have a 'lean machine'?
- Are the communication processes within the firm open?
- Do you have a commitment to all your staff and do they know it?
- Do you ask the staff's views on the business and its policies?

Any of these functional strengths can contribute to the core competence of the organization. The issue is to highlight your distinctive competence and align it to marketing opportunities.

Sources: The four components are noted by Christensen, Andrews, Bower, Hamermesh and Porter, *Business Policy – Text and Cases*

ACTIVITY BP4.2

THE PAPER MILL: AN INTERNAL ANALYSIS

Activity code
- ✓ Self-development
- ✓ Teamwork
- ✓ Communications
- ✓ Numeracy/IT
- ✓ Decisions

The company's managing director, Bill Smythe, was very concerned about the recent training report produced by the training officer, Jim McDonald. The report had used a functional type of analysis. Smythe knew this affected the capability analysis of the firm. Its distinctive competence as well as its ability and willingness to do its specific task all rested with this internal analysis. He commissioned a planner to review McDonald's earlier findings and to take an outsider's view of the business and its internal competence.

The first part of the report gives an overview; the second part gives more of a summary of potential. From the report, compile your own views and report on the strengths and weaknesses of The Paper Mill.

OVERVIEW

The company

The company in question is an independent manufacturer of paper and board, based in Donside, Aberdeenshire. The paper is not high quality and is used for the packaging industry. The board, or chipboard, is predominantly used for the building industry. The firm employs some 400 people on a continuous shift system (6a.m.–2p.m., 2p.m.–10p.m. and 10p.m.–6a.m.) and works all year round, apart from three weeks' maintenance closure in July which coincides with the main vacation of the nearby town. It is an old plant, founded in the late eighteenth century, but with considerable modern machinery recently imported from Germany. There are two board machines and two paper machines with approximately 100 employees to each. In addition, there is a staff of white-collar administrative and commercial group of ninety-two.

The market

Although it is well established, the board market is quite fickle, as it is dependent primarily on the building industry – itself a good indicator of the economic wellbeing of the country. The packaging industry is less fickle and is expanding, although there is competition from the plastics industry. However, from milk cartons to chocolate eggs, the company has a growing presence in this market sphere.

Production

Production is a continuous flow process, with the raw materials (which are increasing in cost) being mixed at the wet end of the machine and appearing at the dry end as almost the finished product. Printing and coating as necessary are done in the finishing department. Breakages of paper flow through the machine are quite frequent.

Finance

The company is still family owned but increasingly it has opened up to take professional managers in to run the firm. It is highly profitable and much of the money has been ploughed back over the last ten years (at least) to buy more modern machinery. This has trebled the potential output, although the plant is running at only 68 per cent capacity. There are no cash-flow problems, although an over-reliance on the building industry in the past has caused difficulties, particularly over the winter months owing to the construction slump then. Reserves and borrowing power are strong.

Organization structure and personnel

The chart opposite shows the structure. The rest of the employees are employed in production, catering, finishing and as 'outside' staff. There is an external security firm (400 people).

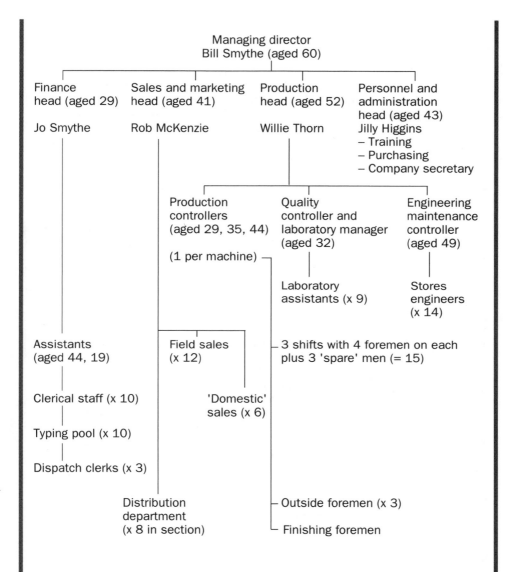

Managing director
Bill Smythe (aged 60)

Finance head (aged 29)	Sales and marketing head (aged 41)	Production head (aged 52)	Personnel and administration head (aged 43)
Jo Smythe	Rob McKenzie	Willie Thorn	Jilly Higgins – Training – Purchasing – Company secretary

Production
controllers
(aged 29, 35, 44)

(1 per machine)

Quality
controller and
laboratory manager
(aged 32)

Engineering
maintenance
controller
(aged 49)

Laboratory
assistants (x 9)

Stores
engineers
(x 14)

Assistants
(aged 44, 19)

Field sales
(x 12)

3 shifts with 4 foremen on each
plus 3 'spare' men (= 15)

Clerical staff (x 10)

'Domestic'
sales (x 6)

Typing pool (x 10)

Dispatch clerks (x 3)

Distribution
department
(x 8 in section)

Outside foremen (x 3)

Finishing foremen

POTENTIAL

Marketing

- There is a lack of market research in the firm.
- There is a strong division of opinion between the production people and their product orientation and the marketing and sales people.
- All the products are profitable.
- The company is price-sensitive in the packaging area but less so in the board and building area as it is believed the latter sector can take the weight.
- The ratio between estimates given and accepted has been rising over the last two years.

- The delivery dates for longer runs are usually met but are more problematic for shorter runs.
- The building company McSweeney is a key account for this firm, alongside Porter Brothers. It could be that too much reliance is placed on these firms as in winter construction declines as does the production of board.
- The packaging market is growing but the company focus is still on board (five years ago 70 per cent of the profit came from board; now it is 53 per cent).
- The products are generally regarded as well designed and well made by customers. The product range has been in existence for some time.
- Advertising is light.
- Promotion is very much geared to the sales team and direct selling.
- Distribution is not difficult in spite of the plant's geographical position, as road and rail networks are very good.
- Creating new business does not account for much of the sales reps' time, as their job is to take and follow up orders with most customers.
- The new product development emanates from the production and engineering departments owing to the technical nature of the products.

Production
- The costs of stopping or starting are high in this ongoing continuous process.
- The firm appears to be production-oriented.
- The plant and equipment machinery (4 main machines) are relatively new (three under 20 years old, one under 40 years old).
- There is a view, pushed by the production staff, that a new German machine is needed for board making (cost £2 million).
- Spoilage and board waste are high but most can be repulped. This means that the machines break down as a result of splits in the paper or board, which both inconveniences management throughput and adversely affects the employees' bonus.
- Stock levels look high as the entire raw material stock clutters the place while overruns of the finished product also exist. The board is expensive and a considerable quantity of goods (100 rolls) awaits pickup in Shed 3 for the construction industry at any one time.
- Quality checks linked to the lab are quite sound.
- Quality standards are widely known and respected.
- Much of the breakage comes from the old board machine (hence the desire to replace it).
- The stock record systems are operational.
- The flow of work looks well organized.
- Some labour difficulties and unrest exists (see below).
- The R&D is ongoing and has been written up in specialist journals.
- The engineering and laboratories are seen as a supportive strength of production.

Personnel
- According to the training manager, the employees are not necessarily the most skilled people around, but this is being rectified.
- An 'old guard' versus 'new guard' mentality exists among junior management and administrative staff.

- Labour relations difficulties dominate the entire company. Labour turnover and absence is high and productivity could be higher. The past strike record is not too impressive, either.
- The style of management is very task-oriented in the production area and (too?) relaxed in the sales and marketing areas. Incentive difficulties exist.

Finance
- The attached figures are not dazzling, but there are no real problems over the one year. (Ratio analysis on profitability/liquidity/performance can be extrapolated in your own time.)
- However, sales last year were around £23 million and the cost of materials was nearer £8 million. There is a significant jump in raw material prices.
- The wage bill looks somewhat excessive as well (an average of £25,000 including employer costs looks far too high). The balance sheets look reasonable but not inspired.

Balance sheet:

Fixed assets:	6,552,600
Shareholders' funds:	5,138,800
Capital employed:	11,307,100
Total assets:	14,039,100
Current assets:	7,486,500
Current liabilities:	2,732,000
Working capital:	4,754,500
Trade debtors:	4,161,100
Trade creditors:	2,233,800
Liquid assets:	4,164,000

Profit and loss:

Sales	24,132,600
Purchases/materials:	10,404,900
Direct wages, salaries, etc.	9,756,000
Net profit pre-tax	3,971,700
Number employed = 400	

Use appropriate ratio analysis to determine profitability, liquidity and performance indicators.

Management and organization
- The calibre of the senior team looks good.
- The next tier down looks lighter.
- The shift structure of 6a.m.–2p.m., 2p.m.–10p.m., 10p.m.–6a.m. could be examined for alternatives as this probably adds to labour costs (overtime at the weekend) and also to alienation of employees as well as straining co-ordination by the management.

A functional analysis is clearly a useful approach for analysing the internal environment. We will now return to the value chain which is a more recent approach for identifying internal competencies.

Regardless of managers' ability to develop a superior strategy compared to their competitors, they must be better at carrying the strategy out. A business has to develop the skills and capabilities needed to gain a competitive advantage. A core competence is something the business does particularly well compared to its competitors and is therefore a source of competitive strength.[9] This strength can be in research and development, a technical process, manufacturing, distribution, sales, response rates, cost leadership, customer service and quality and so on. The value chain is probably the best basis for identifying competencies.

Once the key parts of the value chain have been identified, managers have to build critical mass in these areas by:

■ finding and supporting critical tasks and activities;
■ staffing these areas with high-calibre managers and technical talent;
■ developing high quality and high standards;
■ rewarding effort and success.

Distinctive core competencies are not easily copied by competitors. Therefore, any competitive advantage gained should be sustainable over time and lead to above-average performance. Whether an advantage is sustainable or not depends on price, aesthetics, function, availability, visibility, service, quality and uniqueness.

Opportunities can be provided by working conditions, image (reputation, consumer awareness and trust), uniqueness (patents, licences and regulations), capability for innovation, flexibility and adaptability.

Investment in R&D, product development, performance, advertising, response to customer needs, delivery and service is necessary in order to sustain competitive advantage. Now read Box BP4.14.

BOX BP4.14

R&D and competitive advantage

The aerospace industry has suffered from the so-called 'peace dividend'. In the UK, it is also suffering from a lack of investment in research and development.

Current government funding is around £25 million per annum, but the sector feels that four times this amount would be required to keep abreast of the competition and to become involved in joint international projects.

The failure to invest in this capital-intensive sector could lead not only to the industry's marginalization in the UK, but ultimately to its demise.

Quality is increasingly important in both manufacturing and service industries and Garvin identifies eight standards for product quality in terms of customer preferences:[10]

1 aesthetics

2 conformity to standards

3 durability

4 features

5 perceived quality

6 performance

7 reliability

8 serviceability

The business should aim at least to maintain market share and profitability and focus on, monitor and update those activities which will sustain its competitive edge.

Competence and the value chain

The generic strategies of cost leadership and differentiation are the basis for business competence or skills. For instance, in order to manage costs effectively it is important to know which cost drivers influence the value chain. Porter identifies the following:[11]

- economies of scale, experience and learning curve benefits;
- capacity utilization and product control;
- links or liaisons;
- interrelationships and shared activities;
- vertical integration;
- timing of buying and selling;
- standards for procurement and production;
- issues of location;
- institutional factors.

The cost advantage gained is always relative to the competition. Since competitors generally improve, it is usually difficult to catch up once you are behind.

There are opportunities for differentiation in all parts of the value chain, both inside and outside the business; for example, read Box BP4.15.

It is important to isolate the key success factors as far as the customers are concerned.

It is also important to allocate costs to the value chain and to evaluate whether costs can be saved or additional investment is required to gain additional benefits. Can you add value that the customer will pay for? However, there may be difficulties in allocating costs which have to be addressed in any particular case.

BOX BP4.15

Value chains – opportunities for differentiation

Primary activities:

Inbound logistics	wastage and timing
Operations	quality, output and delivery
Outbound logistics	distribution and quick delivery
Marketing and sales	advertising, research, sales force, technical information
Service	installation, service, repairs, spare parts

Support activities:

Procurement	quality, speed
Technology development	innovation, information technology, production methods
Human resource development	quality, rewards, training
Firm's infrastructure	management systems, support and investment

---

Managers must recognize that the business is primarily there to serve customer needs and not to beat the competition. Concentration on the competition may cause management to miss significant changes in the market-place.

Staff

Successful businesses manage people in the same way they manage other resources. In other words, people are resources that have to be allocated, developed, guarded and nurtured just like money or equipment. Traditionally, human resource management is seen as the process of keeping a business supplied with the right kind of people in the right place at the right time.

The process consists of a series of steps:

- **Human resource planning** which is based on the analysis of internal factors, such as the current and expected skill needs, vacancies, expansion or reduction, and external factors such as the labour market. Such analysis enables both short-term and long-term plans to be developed for a business.

- **Recruitment** which develops a pool of candidates for the vacancies in the human resource plan.

- **Selection** which involves evaluating and choosing from the pool of candidates.

- **Socialization** which helps selected candidates fit smoothly into the business.
- **Training and development** which increases the skills of individuals and groups. Training increases the skills in the present job whereas development educates people beyond their current position so that they are ready for promotion or a change.
- **Performance appraisal** which compares a person's job performance against the standards or objectives developed for that role.
- **Internal movements** such as:
  - ◆ promotion which provides a major incentive and a way of recognizing superior performance; fairness and appropriateness are important;
  - ◆ transfers which give people a broader job experience and help to fill vacancies as they occur. They are used as part of the promotion ladder and to keep people interested in the business. However, inadequate performers may be moved to reduce harm to the business;
  - ◆ discipline, demotion and separation are other ways of controlling and moving people about in a business.

The narrow definition of human resource management (HRM) just described has been modified in recent years by a general recognition that HRM is also influenced by both the stakeholders and the situation. In other words, managers should also consider these aspects while developing their HRM policies and plans. In turn, the policies should be evaluated against the four Cs:[12]

- **Commitment** to work and the business.
- **Competence** of employees and the needs for training and development.
- **Congruence** between the philosophy and goals of the business and its employees and managers.
- **Cost-effectiveness** of the policies in terms of wages, benefits, turnover of employees and managers, absenteeism, strikes and so on.

We can usefully link HRM or personnel policies to the Four Cs to give a business a considerable edge over its competitors. This is a constructive use of human resources. Unfortunately, some firms do not seem to see people as a resource at all but as a mere cost – and a cost that can be cut; now read Box BP4.16.

BOX BP4.16

Labour and competitive advantage

Cheap labour can give an advantage over the competition, particularly as, in the UK, existing skills are not necessarily tapped appropriately. The failure of the Conservative government to ratify the Social Chapter of the Maastricht

Treaty, in particular as far as it relates to workers' rights, can be attributed to an ideological vision of the right; it can also be put down to the desire to provide cheap manpower for incoming businesses.

Labour flexibility can also give some competitive advantage. For example, the trend towards part-time employment, particularly amongst women, means not only greater flexibility for a firm but probably cheaper labour as well. Companies like Burton, BHS and British Airways are deliberately cutting full-time jobs in favour of part-time workers.

Labour costs can also be 'saved' by employers settling pay claims below the rate of inflation or, as in the case of 20 per cent of employers in the UK, by employers 'freezing' or 'deferring' pay.

A more positive approach to gaining competitive advantage is through training and development and by treating labour as a valuable and unique asset. For example, the National Training Awards illustrate the real benefits to both individuals and firms in meeting their objectives.[1]

A highly skilled and competent workforce with job security and job interest is probably one of the key aspects of any drive for competitive advantage.[2,3]

Sources:
1 Adapted from Anderson and Kyprianou, *Effective Organizational Behaviour*
2 Adapted from Anderson, *Effective Personnel Management*, and Anderson, *Effective Labour Relations*
3 Adapted from Anderson, *Successful Training Practice*

Shared Values

Shared values are the guiding concepts, values and aspirations that unite the business in its common purpose. They are usually expressed succinctly and provide a sense of purpose and stability as both the business and its environment change over time. These shared values and the drive to satisfy them often separate the successful business from its competitors. Please read the examples of guiding concepts in Box BP4.17.

Shared values identify who we are, what we do, where we are going and what we stand for. The term 'shared values' has been used in order to make the concept fit in with the Seven S Framework.

Culture

Essentially, we are concerned with the culture of the business which is a complex pattern of assumptions, attitudes, beliefs, expectations, ideologies, norms, philosophies and values. Schein believes culture includes all of the following factors to a greater or lesser extent:[13]

BOX BP4.17

The guiding concepts of a few firms

3M	Innovation
Avon Cosmetics	Distribution
Benetton	Rapid response to fashion
Hewlett-Packard	Concern, trust and respect
IBM	Customer service
McDonalds	Quality, service, cleanliness and value
Rolls Royce	Quality and image
Swissair	Service and reliability
YKK	Cycle of goodness

- Observed behavioural regularities when people interact, such as organizational rituals and ceremonies and the language commonly used.
- The norms shared by the working groups throughout the business, such as 'a fair day's work for a fair day's pay'.
- The dominant values held by the business, such as 'product quality' or 'price leadership'.
- The philosophy that guides the business's policy towards its employees and customers.
- The rules of the game for getting along in the business, or the 'ropes' that a newcomer must learn in order to become an accepted member.
- The feeling or climate conveyed in a business by the physical layout and the way in which its members interact with customers or outsiders.

Sathe simplifies this by limiting culture to 'important shared beliefs and expectations which generate shared goods and services, shared sayings, shared activities and shared feelings',[14] whereas Schein believes that the culture of a business can be reinforced or changed by the following:[15]

- The things managers pay attention to, measure and control. The things that managers notice and comment on are strong signals to employees about what is important and expected of them.
- A manager's reactions to critical incidents and business crises can reinforce the existing culture or change the culture in some way.
- Managerial role modelling, teaching and coaching are ways of communicating culture to employees.
- The criteria for the allocation of rewards and status convey the priorities, attitudes to risk, and values of the management to employees.

- The criteria for recruitment, selection, promotion and separation have a powerful influence on the culture and can be used to maintain or change it.
- The legends, business ceremonies and rites are often found to express the underlying beliefs and values of a culture.

The concept of culture is seen by some people to be the 'climate' of the whole enterprise; now read Box BP4.18.

BOX BP4.18

Culture and climate

Ansoff believes culture is a part of the will to respond or climate of a business. This will to respond or climate involves the following:

1 The attitude of the business to change – whether it is hostile, passive or predisposed to change.
2 The attitude of the business towards risk – whether managers avoid, tolerate or seek risks; whether managers are only comfortable with familiar risks or whether it seeks novel ones.
3 The time perspective in which management perceives its problems – whether it puts full reliance on past experience, prefers to deal with the present or puts emphasis on the future.
4 The action perspective – whether business attention and energies are focused on internal operations or on the external environment.
5 The goals of behaviour – whether it is stability, efficiency, effectiveness, growth or innovation.
6 The trigger of change – whether a crisis or accumulation of unsatisfactory performances are necessary or whether the business continuously seeks change.
7 The degree of initiative – from none to self-starting.
8 The degree of decentralization.

Each of these attributes can be measured in a business and the profile produced should match the turbulence of the environment. If it does not, Ansoff believes effort should be made to correct the situation. Ansoff provides pro-formas for this exercise.

Source: Ansoff and McDonnell, *Implanting Strategic Management*

Is it possible or necessary to change culture? Why not choose goals which match the current strategy rather than goals which cause a general upheaval of the business? On the other hand, much depends on whether the culture fits the current or future environment. Ansoff provides further discussion.

Design and culture

All businesses involve design in their products, packaging, work environments, buildings, stationery, literature and advertising. Design therefore appears at every contact between a business and its environment. Since design pervades the whole of a business it is a key feature of its culture and therefore a strategic resource to be nurtured and developed. Sir Ralph Halpern, Chairman of the Burton Group, once said: 'Design is not a smart word for appearance. It is integral to the generation of profit . . . Design is what differentiates a company from its competitors.'[16]

In our experience, the literature makes little attempt to explain what is good design. We believe good design of products and services is shown by their fitness for their purpose and their cost effectiveness; they should also be aesthetically pleasing and they should convey a message. Olins believes a designer's objective should be to make manifest the corporate strategy and corporate purposes to the communities with which the corporation deals.[17] These are its shareholders, its customers, its suppliers and its neighbourhoods. Gorb prefers to describe rather than define design as 'a planning process for artefacts' which is applied to designing products, environments, systems or strategies.[18]

These definitions of design indicate how design can be used to give organizations an identity of their own. A corporate identity, according to Topalian, expresses what the organization is, what it stands for and what it does and can be found in the physical, operational and human characteristics of the organization.[19] However, when people talk about corporate identity, more often than not they mean the visual schemes that designers use to portray their clients. In many cases company symbols and logotypes are expected to provide corporate identity. See Olins for further discussion.[20]

Worcester says that the 'corporate image' of a business is the profile – or sum of impressions and expectations of that business – built up in the minds of individuals who comprise its publics.[21] Thus the visual design of outputs is but one of the factors that contribute to a business's corporate image. A receptionist, service engineer or sales person may create just as good an impression of the business as the headed notepaper or the signs about the buildings.

Topalian believes that corporate identities are projected and are largely under the control of the host organizations, whereas corporate images are received by target audiences and can only be influenced by the host organizations.[22] The sources of the corporation's image are numerous and diverse and they are difficult to focus and control. Thus, few businesses set out to plan and co-ordinate the messages they transmit to their publics in order to influence their images in the market.

The visual identity of a business is projected by the appearance of products, printed materials, packaging, advertising and the interior and exterior of all the premises of the business. Every business tries to present a 'face' to its public. For some, this is clear and unambiguous whereas for others the identities are muddled. Efficient-looking businesses which are in fact disorganized are more disappointing to the public than the business which has a sloppy image and promises nothing. If the corporate identity of a business is not appropriate, there is nothing visual identity alone can do to improve matters.

Visual identity programmes are often the first stage in the movement of a business towards a consideration of design. Visual identity has to be based on a consideration of corporate identity and corporate image. Usually, a start is made with graphic design programmes which, with experience and success, develop into exhibition design, interior design and architecture. Corporate design programmes covering every aspect of design in a business are the end result of this developmental process.

Examples of the effective way in which design has been used in organizations are given in Boxes BP4.19 and BP4.20.

BOX BP4.19

WH Smith

In 1969, Sir Simon Hornby, then Buying Director of WH Smith, prepared a paper describing how the quality of design in the company had deteriorated. He recommended that a new visual identity should be developed to reflect the changes taking place in the company at the time. By 1971 Professor Richard Guyatt, Head of Graphics at the Royal College of Art, had been asked to carry out a thorough investigation of the company's design requirements. Two requirements were considered to be essential to this exercise: support for the design policy should come from the top and there should be an efficient design management structure with strict budgetary control.

The new visual identification system developed by Guyatt had the following elements:

- A symbol that could be combined to form attractive linear repeats, patterns, shapes and multiple textures.
- A rationalized name style 'WH Smith' designed into a stronger logotype.
- Two corporate colours, brown and orange, selected to blend with a broad range of environments.

Two committees were set up in 1972:

- Design Policy Committee – to make major decisions on design, oversee implementation and maintain design discipline.
- Design Administrative Committee – to carry out detailed work based on the former's decisions and directions. This was later replaced by the Design Review Body in 1973.

A WH Smith Corporate Identity Manual was produced in 1973 with ten sections covering corporate symbol, logotype and colours; packaging; marketing and point of sale; stationery and forms; communications; printed materials; shop and bookstall exteriors; vehicles; interiors; divisions and subsidiaries.

Unfortunately, the manual was not kept up to date and did not keep pace with trends and developments, both in the market-place and within the group. It ceased to be a meaningful vehicle for projecting a dynamic organization.

By 1986 it became increasingly apparent that the group, which had been growing and diversifying rapidly, had more complex design problems. Owing to decentralization, the role of design co-ordination needed to be filled by an experienced person with a higher status. David Clapp was appointed Design Manager with day-to-day responsibility for design in the group.

By 1988 design in the WH Smith Group was controlled by three bodies. The Design Policy Committee met four times a year and was responsible for the selection of designers, all major new design concepts, changes in design policy, new buildings and major alterations, and staff uniforms. A subcommittee, the Design Clinic, met monthly to give advice and help, approve minor design changes and establish a register of designers. The Design Review Body met six times a year to monitor graphic design in its widest sense.

The aims of WH Smith's co-ordinated design policy were to establish a contemporary image which reflected its quality to the public, staff and suppliers and also to increase efficiency. This policy was expected to grow out of the group's functional needs rather than be a 'glossy top coat'. It was also realized that there was little point getting the retail environment and graphics right without the right products.

Source: Adapted from Topalian, *Design Management at WH Smith Group PLC*

BOX BP4.20

Jaguar Cars

In the mid-1980s, Peter Battam was the manager of World Marketing Services and custodian of the image of the company and its products, i.e. its visual identification programme. The company did not differentiate between what it was as a business and how it presented itself. A comprehensive scheme was being developed in carefully planned stages across the world to ensure that Jaguar's visual identity was uniform and that it was presented in a manner which met the company's specifications. Jaguar had to symbolize an exclusive 'Englishness', accompanied by gentility, quality and success.

After privatization of the company in the early 1980s, Jaguar focused on the sales environment and rationalized its dealer network. To keep costs manageable, it upgraded its sales environment and practices in stages. The first stage was the introduction of strict rules followed by a strong external identification programme through consistent signing and fascia treatment. However, dealers were allowed some latitude to express their personalities. Upgrading of showroom interiors followed, and a Franchise Development Fund was set up whereby a 3.5 per cent margin off new car sales was withheld until dealers had implemented the first stage upgrade to their operations and facilities.

Once the sales environment had been upgraded, sales staff and reception-ists were required to attend week-long courses at the factory. Three levels of performance exist within Jaguar: minimum, operating and optimum. Most dealers in the UK operate at the optimum level.

At the same time, the reception lobby at the factory was refurbished and a modern, comprehensively equipped presentation theatre was built. Outside designers only were used for promotional material, exhibitions and confer-ences.

The Jaguar Identity Manual was published in 1984 for documentation, com-munication and control, and contains sections on basic elements, stationery, vehicle livery, distributor and dealer showroom and service signing, distributor and dealer showroom exteriors and interiors, dealer stationery, advertising and sales promotion.

A Jaguar Facilities Development Manual was produced to ensure that all new facility developments and redevelopments reflected the overall philos-ophy and operating standards. Jaguar aimed to learn from each project and so develop and benefit both the company and the franchisees.

No document listing Jaguar's principal design policies existed and there was nothing in writing about the styling department's mission other than the statement: 'to continue the tradition of producing beautiful, elegant cars'.

Peter Battam realized there was a major need for design awareness train-ing in relation to industrial design. He also recognized that design manage-ment skills training was important for Jaguar Cars, though no such training was taking place at that time.

Source: Adapted from Topalian, *Jaguar Cars Limited: upgrading the design and service of the dealership network*

Key Issues

Now that we have studied the external environment, the competitive environment and the business environment, we should be able to identify the key issues in any business situation.

By now you should also be able to identify the strengths and weaknesses from the business environment and the opportunities and threats from the external and competitive environments. A SWOT analysis is a good way to summarize these conclusions. However, we must be clear why activities or resources are strengths or weaknesses. At the same time you must ask yourself: 'Strength relative to what?' 'Weakness relative to what?' The key links in the value chains of the business should also be identified. This includes examining the value chains of suppliers, distributors and customers for strengths and weaknesses, opportunities and threats.

This unit has explored the business environment using the Seven S Framework which identifies the seven interlocking features of a business, all of which must be in tune for the business to be successful. There is no point designing a new structure for your company if your systems cannot cope and you do not have a succession of management planned to take over. Management must also share the same values, and so on through the framework. Each of the Seven Ss is linked with the others in order to create synergy or make the whole greater than the sum of its parts.

Activity BP4.3 is the final Activity in this unit. It is designed to integrate Units Two, Three and Four and should be completed before proceeding to the next unit, which will explore the various options for change that can be used to make your business successful. Study the case and make use of your general knowledge to complete the tasks.

ACTIVITY BP4.3

COSMOPOLITAN COSMETICS – A SPIN-OFF OF NATURAL BEAUTY?

Activity code
✓ Self-development
✓ Teamwork
✓ Communications
✓ Numeracy/IT
✓ Decisions

Natural Beauty PLC is a large American multinational firm specializing in beauty and skin care products. Currently, it has 182 outlets with 5,000 independent door-to-door agents, covering almost every European country and North America. It is a classic example of the 'American Dream' with a Scottish flavour.

The product range continued to expand. It includes:

Hair shampoo – coconut oil, primrose oil and Danzinc, a zinc pyrithione anti-dandruff agent

Hair conditioner – protein glycerine, hair conditioner and Dodgel, a unisex hair gel

Skin cleansing lotion – witch hazel with avocado oil for skin treatment and vitamin E. The beeswax formula for sun treatment continued to sell and was being used as a type of cleansing cream as well

Skin moisturizer – a lemon and glycerine compound and wheatgerm/vitamin E anti-wrinkle formulation

A new range of cosmetics from blushers to foundation creams was also being quite aggressively marketed. The fragrances of the old Scottish factory had been suitably and exotically updated to produce sophisticated perfume oils for the skin.

Wherever possible, natural elements were used in production and no animal testing was allowed in the product development. The market had also been segmented into men/women, babies, teenage girls, mature women and the 'older woman' range. Essentially this involved different packaging rather than material differences between the ranges.

Doddie's entrepreneurial management style, allied to the ruthlessness of Denis, with his OTC marketing background, proved a successful but demanding combination.

The Green family, husband and wife, worked for Natural Beauty. Lynn Green was a research chemist and Bob Green was in sales. They had both been working in industry for some time – even before they joined the senior ranks of Natural Beauty.

Lynn resigned from the company first and went to work for herself on new formulae for skin cream products. Natural Beauty was sad to lose her, but was unaware that she had set up on her own. She had no restrictive clause in her contract. Initially Bob stayed with Natural Beauty, but eventually left to join his wife.

The Greens' marketing strategy was to integrate skin care instruction with the direct sales approach developed from Natural Beauty. Consultants would arrange skin care classes for five or six 'guests' at the home of a 'hostess'.

Like Doddie of Natural Beauty, Lynn and Bob were active churchgoers. Unlike Doddie, they had a more democratic vision of Christianity which was reflected in their new Midland-based business, Cosmopolitan Cosmetics. They believed that people should have control over their own efforts and their own lives. There was no pressurized sales here – no sales quotas, few rules, flexible hours and an open style; interpersonal rivalry was discouraged.

First-year sales touched £100,000; the second-year figures edged nearer to £300,000. In 1993 the company achieved sales of almost £180 million. New distribution centres were opened in Australia, Canada and North America.

Success came as the firm filled a void in the sector by teaching skin care and make-up application; this was linked to the ability of the consultants to build up their 'own' businesses and at their own pace.

Major influences on demand in the cosmetics sector include consumer needs and wants, competition and the state of the economy. Unrelated businesses are now edging in on cosmetics and the market has lately been a little flat. A shake-out is occurring in the sector, particularly in the middle of the market. Population and social changes have an impact on the market. The population is getting older and the demand for anti-ageing products seems to be unfulfilled. For people out of work, cosmetics may also be perceived as something of a luxury.

However, more and more women in the UK in the 1990s are in work and the younger element has plenty of disposable cash for such cosmetics – particularly those who are married and either at work or at home with the family. These busy women like consultants calling on them at their homes to organize parties.

The products are subject to health regulations in most countries covering marketing, packaging, labelling, product content and the physical manufacture of the goods. Labour law varies from country to country, as do fiscal and customs and excise regulations. The environment is changing and is monitored on an ongoing basis by the firm. There is competition for agents from businesses selling plastic plates and utensils and from those selling lingerie, and these businesses encroach on the 'party selling' process.

Although the industry sector is really personal care, the firm is also involved in direct sales, so competition comes from both sectors; on the cosmetics side, competition is from Avon, Revlon, Kleen-e-ze Cosmetics, Estée Lauder, and so on, while Tupperware and Ann Summers are competitors on the party planning side. The cosmetics sector is mainly based on over-the-counter sales, but women are increasingly trading down owing to economic pressures.

The most important marketing resource is the distribution network. The firm 'employs' almost 100,000 consultants who operate as independent contractors. Products are distributed via the consultant, who buys them at wholesale prices from the firm and sells them on to the customer at retail prices. There are no designated territories and each consultant can sell whenever she wishes.

Advertising through women's magazines and general newspapers is set at 1.5 per cent of overall sales. With industry demand falling, this may have to move to 2 per cent.

Cosmopolitan Cosmetics' distribution network is probably one of the keys to its success. Sales managers are full-time paid employees of the firm and provide co-ordination and training. The best performing consultants have the opportunity to become sales managers. In turn, consultants get a fee for recruiting other consultants to sell the product range. They also receive a commission from the sales of the consultants they have been responsible for recruiting.

The products are not far removed from Doddie's products at Natural Beauty: skin care, glamour, body care and an increasing market in men's toiletries.

The consultants buy their supplies direct from the firm at wholesale prices and sell them with a mark-up of between 50 and 100 per cent, depending on the product. The average is 78 per cent mark-up for the standard 60 products. Consultants can stockpile if they have the facilities, but most carry just enough stock to fill orders at a party. Additional orders mean that the consultant pays the firm before delivery, which avoids bad debt for the firm. Each consultant pays £500 for a start-up pack. Sales kits, manuals, beauty profiles, training sessions and so on are co-ordinated by the sales managers.

Production has been contracted out to other firms. Quality is monitored, as are the rigid specifications, but the firm's real concern is warehousing, packaging and research and development. The firm has a keen interest in research into various skin conditions; it sponsors a chair at a university and funds a research team at college for this purpose. Feedback from customers is taken into account in the R&D plans. Much of the budget is spent on making continuous improvements.

The personnel side of the business is very much a personal one; networking and circles of friends are a critical component. Supportive training material and sales aids form the backbone of the firm. An open style of management prevails and the Greens like to think of the firm as their cosmopolitan family.

Make use of the skills you have developed by studying Units Two, Three and Four to answer the following questions:

1 Make a SWOT analysis of Cosmopolitan Cosmetics and discuss your conclusions.
2 Discuss the value chain for Cosmopolitan Cosmetics.
3 Discuss the competitive environment and say how you think it will influence the development of Cosmopolitan Cosmetics over the next five years.
4 How do you account for the success of Cosmopolitan Cosmetics? What were the key factors contributing to its success?
5 Write a report for the Board of Cosmopolitan Cosmetics indicating the way forward to the year 2000.
6 From the perspective of Natural Beauty, conduct a competitor analysis of Cosmopolitan Cosmetics.

Notes

1 Waterman et al., 'Structure is not organisation'.
2 Porter, *Competitive Strategy: techniques for analyzing industries and competitors*.
3 Jauch and Glueck, *Business Policy and Strategic Management*.
4 Chandler, *Strategy and Structure*.
5 Greiner, 'Evolution and revolution as organisations grow'.
6 Burns and Stalker, *The Management of Innovation*.
7 Slatter, *Corporate Recovery*.
8 Peters and Austin, *A Passion for Excellence*.
9 Prahalad and Hamel, 'The core competence of the corporation'.
10 Garvin, 'Competing on the eight dimensions of quality'.
11 Porter, *Competitive Strategy*.
12 Beer et al., *Human Resource Management*.
13 Schein, *Organisation, Culture and Leadership*.
14 Sathe, 'Implications of corporate culture'.
15 Schein, *Organisation, Culture and Leadership*.
16 Pilditch, *Talk about Design*.
17 Olins, *The Corporate Personality*.
18 Gorb, 'Design profitability and organisational outcomes'.
19 Topalian, 'Corporate identity'.
20 Olins, *The Wolff Olins Guide to Corporate Identity*.
21 Worcester, 'Research and the corporate image'.
22 Topalian, 'Corporate identity'.

Unit Five

Options for Change

Learning Objectives

After completing this unit you should be able to:

- develop mission and objectives statements for an organization;
- assess an organization and decide on the options for change;
- understand how to develop a portfolio of businesses;
- apply the generic skills.

Contents

Overview

The Vision or Mission Statement

Performance Objectives

Organization Assessment

Options for Change

► Expansion

► Acquisitions

► Offensive options

► Defensive options

► Vertical integration

► Diversification

   From competitive advantage to corporate strategy

► Three options for creating shareholder value

Portfolio Management

Unit Five

" Change is a phenomenon which cannot be restricted solely to the 'behavioural' aspects of management learning. It needs a perspective which can blend the behavioural with the economic, the historical with future-oriented decision making, and the political with the social and economic factors of change. "

D. C. Wilson, A Strategy of Change [1]

Overview

In the previous units we have identified the strengths and weaknesses of the business itself and the opportunities and threats from the external and competitive environments. Do the strengths of the organization as regards its skills and capabilities enable it to meet the opportunities and threats posed by the environment? Does the organization have weaknesses which have to be strengthened?

Managers prioritize issues based on this information and then choose options for change. These options can be operational, for improving the way the organization is running at the moment, or long-term, for promoting the organization's long-term sustainable future.

Managers are continually looking for competitive advantage, congruence between the parts of the organization and their objectives, profit, growth and stakeholder satisfaction.

Thompson and Strickland believe the five tasks of the manager are to:

1 develop a vision or mission for the organization;
2 convert the mission into specific performance objectives;
3 develop options for making the changes necessary to achieve the objectives;
4 implement the strategy efficiently and effectively;
5 evaluate performance and make corrections as necessary based on experience, changing conditions, new ideas or new opportunities. [2]

In this unit we shall be considering tasks 1, 2 and 3 and building on the generic strategies discussed in Unit Four. Unit Six will deal with tasks 4 and 5.

This unit begins with the development of a mission statement. This is then 'operationalized' and converted to a statement of objectives for managers to work towards. Managers have to make assessments of their organizations in order to decide on any changes that are planned or may have to be made because of the environment. The various options available

183

are then considered. Once the business grows into a portfolio of business units, ways of developing the business further are considered. This process is illustrated in figure 5.1.

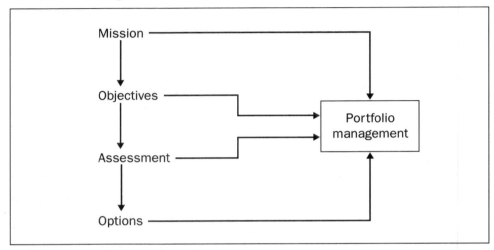

Figure 5.1 Chart to show the relationships between the topics covered in Unit Five.

The Vision or Mission Statement

The development of a strategic vision or mission statement is a creative act based on the analysis described in earlier units. Essentially, managers try to identify a new future that can be communicated both inside and outside the organization. The organization responds by developing its resources to achieve that vision. According to Rowe et al.,[3] in order to do this a vision statement needs to be:

- simple, clear and easily understood;
- sufficiently forward-looking to allow for dramatic changes, but close enough to attract commitment from employees;
- able to focus the organization on the right things at the right time;
- frequently articulated to gain a consensus that the vision is desirable and attainable.

The following definitions may be useful:

- **Vision** – a statement of where the organization is heading over the next five to ten years.
- **Mission** – the purpose of the organization, why it is in business, what it does and who it serves. Good mission statements enable employees to develop loyalty and direction from a common purpose.
- **Values** – the broad beliefs about what is or is not done in or by the organization. The corporate culture is the value system for the organization as a whole.

Now read Box BP5.1.

BOX BP5.1

People versus profit, or a hierarchy of goals?

England, writing in 1967, examined the goals of American managers.[1] The study rated profitability very highly as the main objective, followed by efficiency within the industrial sector. Sales and marketing objectives also ranked quite highly, although below the financial goals. These task-oriented or 'hard' goals took precedence over the people, or 'soft', goals of employee-related aims and those to do with wider social responsibility.

The Shetty study of 1979 is less black and white.[2] Profitability goals are still ranked highly, but greater marketing orientation or a toughening competitive situation is illustrated by the fact that sales and marketing are on a par with financial goals. Efficiency is still middle-ranking but employees are becoming more important – at least in the area of remuneration and benefits, so 'reward management' is on a par with profitability goals; indeed, it can be seen as a corollary of these goals. Job satisfaction and 'softer' people goals are still ranked quite low, while social responsibility, on paper at least, is in the same rank as profitability. Interestingly, a middle-ranking was given to other goals such as 'diversification', which may be illustrative of the period.

Sources:
1   Adapted from England, 'Organizational goals and expected behavior of American managers'
2   Adapted from Shetty, 'New look at corporate goals'

Useful topics for consideration are:

- commitment to quality
- commitment to innovation
- duty to and respect for employees
- duty to shareholders
- duty to suppliers
- importance of ethical standards
- importance of honesty and integrity
- importance of protecting the environment
- importance of corporate citizenship and social responsibility

A useful way forward is to study actual statements which reflect the views of various organizations. These formal statements have to become informal reality within the organizations concerned, and this represents a challenge for any management. Study Boxes BP5.2, BP5.3, BP5.4, BP5.5 and BP5.6.

BOX BP5.2

A health care firm's code of ethics and values

We believe our first responsibility is to the doctors, nurses and patients, to mothers and all others who use our products and services.

In meeting their needs, everything we do must be of high quality.

We must constantly strive to reduce our costs in order to maintain reasonable prices.

Customers' orders must be serviced promptly and accurately.

Our suppliers and distributors must have an opportunity to make a fair profit.

We are responsible to our employees, the men and women who work with us throughout the world.

Everyone must be considered as an individual.

We must respect individual dignity and recognize individual merit.

Employees must have a sense of security in their jobs.

Compensation must be fair and adequate, and working conditions clean, orderly and safe.

Employees must feel free to make suggestions and complaints.

There must be equal opportunity for employment, development and advancement for those qualified.

We must provide competent management, and management's actions must be just and ethical.

We are responsible to the communities in which we live and work and to the world community as well.

We must be good citizens – support good works and charities and bear our fair share of taxes.

We must encourage civic improvements and better health education.

We must maintain in good order the property we are privileged to use, protecting the environment and natural resources.

Our final responsibility is to our shareholders.

Business must make a sound profit.

We must experiment with new ideas.

Research must be carried on, innovative programmes developed and mistakes paid for.

New equipment must be purchased, new facilities provided and new products launched.

Reserves must be created to provide for adverse times.

When we operate according to these principles, the shareholders should realize a fair return.

Comment

In order for them to be implemented, such ethics and values must be:

■ incorporated into training and development programmes;

■ used in recruitment and selection;

■ endorsed and followed by all management, and procedures must be developed for handling violations.

BOX BP5.3

An engineering firm's vision, mission and principles

Vision
Dedicated to growth
Committed to quality

Mission
We are dedicated to growth through quality, innovation and profitable reinvestment.

Principles
Since we are responsible to our customers, shareholders and employees, we shall:

- provide our customers with innovative, functional and reliable products and services at a cost and quality consistent with their needs;
- concentrate on enhancing long-term shareholder value;
- actively pursue equal opportunity for all individuals and provide an environment which encourages open communications, personal growth and creativity;
- expect integrity and professional conduct from our employees in every aspect of our business;
- conduct our operations ethically and well within the framework of the law;
- actively contribute to the communities and industries in which we operate.

BOX BP5.4

A University

Values statement

Commitment to the principle of life-long learning and hence the provision of opportunities for personal development for all students and staff to enable them to achieve their maximum potential as individuals.

Development of a caring organization that emphasizes openness and co-operation and treats individuals solely according to ability, aptitude and experience.

Attainment of the highest standards of teaching, scholarship and research, and the pursuit of excellence in all aspects of the University's activities.

Protection of, and respect for, freedom of belief and expression and hence the encouragement of the acquisition of knowledge and the free expression of ideas without fear or hindrance.

Creation of a stimulating cultural and intellectual environment in which arts, humanities and sciences are maintained and flourish, both informally and formally.

Providing educational opportunities to all those who are capable of taking advantage of its academic programmes and, in particular, positive consideration towards those from groups traditionally under-represented in higher education.

Development of the University as a vital contributor to the community locally, nationally and internationally.

Recognition and encouragement of the diversity of cultures and traditions within the University and the broader community.

Offering opportunities for students and staff to gain international experience and understanding through study and working both in an international community within the University and other countries throughout the world.

Development of an academic programme that is relevant to the intellectual and vocational needs of individuals.

Commitment to the promotion and development of social, political and environmental responsibility.

Mission statement

The purpose of the University is to provide comprehensive opportunity for educational and personal development through a supportive learning environment in a multi-campus institution.

Vision statement

All students are provided with an experience which enables each to develop their full potential in a good, honest, open, supportive and exciting environment where people are accepted and valued, and they are happy to be, where ideals are discussed freely, and there is a sense of sharing in a continuing process of discovery and self-fulfilment.

All staff are respected and empowered and participate in the decision-making process. They work in an atmosphere of openness, mutual support and confidence which enables them to make their own best contributions to the provision of a stimulating educational environment.

The University will be an integral and supportive part of the community contributing extensively and in partnership with others to its educational, cultural and social life. In this the University will be nationally and internationally respected for its teaching and research.

BOX BP5.5

Corporate citizenship

We believe we should invest in the communities in which we work and we are committed to contribute accordingly. Our businesses around the world help local communities through charitable donations and appropriate sponsorships. It is our corporate policy to strive constantly to improve our environmental performance.

BOX BP5.6

Aims and values: a multinational

We aim to:

- provide our customers with high quality, competitively priced products and services;
- provide our shareholders with growing returns on their investments;
- continue to develop and grow the Group in its chosen business areas by acquisition and investment;
- provide our employees with job satisfaction and the opportunity for personal development;
- contribute to the communities and safeguard the environment in which the company operates;
- manage our business with integrity.

Values

- Quality is our first priority. We look for quality in products and services, in working practices and in human relationships, with customers and suppliers.
- Our employees are the Group's greatest strength. It is their vitality, commitment and skills which provide the foundations for continued success. The company will build on this strength by encouraging teamwork and employee involvement, and by providing opportunities for continuous learning and development matched to individual abilities and the needs of the Group's business.
- Wherever we are located in the world, we must understand the regulatory framework within which we work. Business ethics must never be compromised and the highest personal standards must be maintained by the employees.
- The financial wellbeing of the Group is a fundamental requirement. Profitability is a measure of success, both in meeting the needs of the customers and in the efficient management of the business. Profits are vital to development and growth, and to the increase in value of the shareholders' investment.

To decide on its vision and mission statements, the business and its products or services need to be assessed in terms of their potential on two counts:

1 Can the business, product or service be made more valuable to the customer (increase customer value)?

2 Can the business, product or service maintain its competitive cost advantage through system innovation?

These two questions form the basis for the corporate development matrix of Rowe et al. (see figure 5.2).[4] Depending on its position in the matrix, a business, product or service will be assigned a high or low priority in the organization. The priorities are:

- **Losers** – businesses, products or services with little potential for increased customer value or competitive cost advantage should be sold or closed.

- **Watch and wait** – these businesses, products or services need analysing further but in general may carve out a profitable niche. They are unable to establish a sustainable cost advantage because of the competitive position.

- **Unstable cash bonanza** – those businesses, products or services which are temporarily stable and very profitable have a high competitive cost advantage but little potential for a further increase in customer value. As the market matures, these businesses, products or services are vulnerable to severe margin and/or substitution pressures.
- **Winners** – these are businesses, products or services which have the potential for both continued increase in customer value and competitive cost advantages through system innovation.

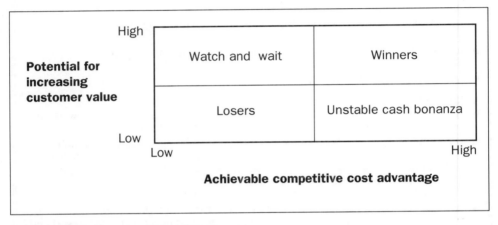

Figure 5.2 The corporate development matrix.

Source: Adapted from Rowe et al., 1989.

Increase in customer value depends on understanding a customer's needs and problems. In order to find out customers' present needs, research tools such as customer surveys, visits, panels and test marketing are often used. However, customers' future needs need to be determined, and this requires innovation and creativity. The key is to imagine oneself in the customer's position and increase the product's present value to the customer.

Often, customers have ideas about how value can be increased or the cost structure improved. Customers may simply need help in using the product or service more efficiently rather than using an improved product or service. The question to be asked is therefore: 'In what ways can we increase the value of our product or service in the customer's system?'

System innovation is the key to gaining a sustainable competitive cost advantage, according to Rowe et al.[5] In order to develop system innovation managers need the vision to:

- overcome functional specialization and look at the delivery system as a whole;
- consider quantum leaps, not just incremental improvements.

In order to do this three questions need to be answered.

1 What kinds of delivery system changes would be valuable to our customers?

2 What would it mean to our customers if delivery cycle times could be cut in half or if other performance criteria could be doubled?

3 What would a delivery system that could achieve these fundamental improvements look like?

Leading organizations demand continuous innovation from these systems because, by the time competitors are able to understand and imitate it, the organization has moved on to something new. In this way, managers and employees become accustomed to change, making the organization more competitive. The significance of the value chain mentioned in earlier units is important in this process.

Performance Objectives

> *When an organisation performs consistently at or near peak capability, the outcome is not only improved strategic success but also an organisational culture permeated with a spirit of high performance. This should not be confused with whether employees are 'happy' or 'satisfied', or 'get along well together'. An organisation with a spirit of high performance emphasizes achievement and excellence. Its culture is results orientated, and its management pursues policies and practices that inspire people to do their best.* [6]

The mission statement has to be converted into objectives while still taking into account the vision, values, ethics and culture of the organization discussed in Unit Four. Now read Box BP5.7 which provides a context for the economic and social objectives, then go on to Box BP5.8 which suggests a solution to the mix of social and economic goals.

Managers must care about *how* an organization does its business or they will put its reputation and ultimately the business at risk. Good value statements and practice enable stakeholders to gain an understanding of organization values and directions. Some organizations place value to a greater or lesser extent on aggressiveness, innovation, risk taking, quality, service, participation, flexibility, the environment and so on.

Performance objectives convert the mission statement into specific performance objectives and enable managers to evaluate performance. Objectives define what managers are committed to produce in a particular time period and so direct attention to what needs to be done. Objectives are required for two major types of key result area, financial and strategic.

BOX BP5.7

The four main internal constituents and social responsibility

---

The overall aims must cover the whole organization and not just key departments or sections. The aims can be implicit and can be derived from the behaviour of the leading actors, but this exercise can easily degenerate into a drifting, non-quantified scenario where the actual goals cannot be achieved. Equally as important as making the goals explicit is to make them dynamic, since they will have to be fine-tuned as new intelligence on the competition becomes available. These aims need to cover areas which influence survival, growth and profitability.

One approach to objectives that reflect the overall purpose of the organization is a functional one. A typical format might be as follows:

Financial	There is a 'hierarchy of objectives' in the firm and monetary matters tend to be at the apex. Quantification can include a range of measures which are required: return on capital employed; earnings per share; return on trading assets employed; return on shareholders' equity, and so on.
Market	As the customer is the business, this should define what market(s) the firm is actually competing in and to what extent it is putting in x level of effort. The market share, the piece of a segment, the potential for sales and the type(s) of target customers can be noted. Product development is marketing; operations and research and development are usually part of the operations and production facility. Either way, some commentary on such objectives is needed.
Operations	This can include the innovation and development noted above, the targets on production, the money prepared to be spent on development, the cost per unit of outputs and some commentary on productive capacity and productivity levels (machines, plant, capital, methods and people).
People	People are the organization, so the chart of authority and responsibilities by function, section and job can emanate from these overall objectives. Views on compensation, job satisfaction and the role(s) of management can be highlighted.
Social responsibility	The goals should not only reflect 'internal' responsibilities to people, but the wider community and suppliers, as well as the customers, need to be considered.

Financial objectives tend to be short-term and include revenue and earnings growth, dividend rates, profit margins, returns on investment, credit ratings, cash flow, share price and so on.

Strategic objectives tend to be long-term and include the following: market share, industry ranking, product or service quality, low relative

---

BOX BP5.8

Corporate objectives – a model?

Integrity and mutual respect between the key constituents are required and shareholders, consumers, suppliers, employees and the wider community must all be covered.

- To maximize shareholders' wealth through growth in real earnings per share and profitable expansion of the business.
- To meet the needs of the customers and build long-term relationships by offering a quality service at a value-for-money price.
- To maintain an ongoing relationship with suppliers and to ensure raw materials, goods or services are of the correct standard with prompt delivery and payment.
- To manage the staff in an open manner reflecting their skills and experience and to compensate them accordingly. Further, to develop the staff to sustain their individual needs and our long-term competitive strength.
- To conduct business in a socially responsible manner acceptable to the wider community.

---

costs, product line breadth and attractiveness, leadership in technology or innovation, ability to compete regionally, nationally or globally, and so on.

Which of these two groups of objectives takes priority? Perhaps the Japanese point the way when they gain market share at the expense of short-term profits, whereas Western firms have mainly pursued short-term profits and neglected the long-term future. On the other hand, letting your competitors know your objectives enables them to develop their objectives to defeat you.

Strategic objectives set out the organization's business position or strategic intent (see Hamel and Pralahad).[7] Most organizations that become successful set themselves strategic intentions which are out of all proportion to their current capability or market position. They pursue their long-term objectives relentlessly over perhaps ten or twenty years. Komatsu set out to beat Caterpillar, Canon to beat Xerox, Walmart to beat Sears and so on. Such long-term battle-cries can focus the efforts of the organization far better than detailed strategic plans coming out of ivory towers.

The objectives often result from the expectations and power of individuals, coalitions and stakeholders. Organizations require several objectives to satisfy their mission statement and these are often separated into **short- and long-term objectives**. Managers are often pressured into short-term objectives but these can have a severe impact on the long-term success or even survival of the organization.

Long-term objectives focus attention on what is required to be done *now* in order for them to be achieved. At the same time, managers are forced to examine their short-term objectives in order to determine what effect they will have on long-term performance. Short-term objectives should be stepping stones to long-term objectives.

Objectives also have to be prioritized and measured in terms of efficiency or effectiveness (efficiency is the ratio of inputs to outputs, whereas effectiveness is the degree of achievement of the objective relative to some standard). Sometimes there must be a trade-off between efficiency and effectiveness.

Objectives should be challenging but attainable and should cascade down through the organization in a way that ensures goal congruence between its various parts. Box BP5.9 gives a 'feel' for the actual objectives of an engineering firm.

Quite often there is a difference between **official** objectives and **actual** objectives. Official objectives are those that the organization says it seeks whereas actual objectives are those in which it invests its money and time. Managers should be aware of this dichotomy and the effect it may have on stakeholders.

Management by Objectives (MbO) can be used to develop an organization's philosophy to encourage managers to define their objectives in formal, specific, time-based, prioritized, measurable terms which are challenging but attainable.

Some managers tend to resist being specific about objectives since they claim that this reduces flexibility and prevents them from exploring new ideas.

BOX BP5.9

Organizational objectives

Financial objectives

We are committed to providing our shareholders with an attractive return on their investment, and our specific goals for doing so are to:

- achieve a minimum after-tax return on capital of 14 per cent;
- achieve a return on shareholders' equity through a capital structure including 25–35 per cent debt;
- achieve a minimum return on equity of 18 per cent;
- pay dividends equal to approximately 40 per cent of earnings;
- achieve average annual growth in earnings of at least 10 per cent.

Operating objectives

Market leadership

- Have a leading market-share position in our major markets.
- Be recognized as a leader in the application of technology to meet customer requirements.
- Be a 'best value' supplier throughout the world.
- Expand our international business to a level equalling 20–5 per cent of company sales.
- Invest in research and development at a rate of 4 per cent of sales as a means of achieving our market leadership objectives.

Employee development

- Encourage initiative, innovation and productivity by appropriately recognizing and rewarding employee performance.
- Invest in employee training and development at a rate of 2 per cent of payroll.
- Honestly and accurately appraise and evaluate the performance of each employee on at least an annual basis.
- Provide for orderly succession in management.
- Maintain a positive action programme and provide employees with the opportunity for advancement commensurate with their abilities.

Social and community responsibility

- Maintain a safe, clean and healthy environment for our employees and the communities in which we operate.
- Invest 1.5 per cent of net income in social, cultural, educational and charitable activities.
- Encourage appropriate employee involvement in community activities.

Organization Assessment

Essentially, an organization is striving to build and strengthen its long-term competitive position in the market-place. It does this by responding to changes in the political, economic, social and technical environments (PEST), and by developing its own future in a series of changes that will build a sustainable competitive environment. Essentially, it is the manager's job to manage change. This can be of two kinds – change imposed on the organization because of changes in the environment, or change chosen by the organization. This section of the book is concerned with the latter, and deals with the question: what changes should a manager make?

In order to decide what changes are required, you need to carry out both a PEST and a SWOT analysis (explained in Units Two and Four). In order to obtain an even better appreciation of the possibilities for change, Rowe et al. developed the Strategic Position and Action Evaluation approach (SPACE).[8] They identified four major characteristics of the business and its environment:

1 Strength of the industry.
2 Stability of the environment.
3 Competitive advantage of the organization.
4 Financial strength of the organization.

Financial strength and competitive advantage are the two major factors an organization's strategic position, while industry strength and environmental stability determine the strategic position of an industry.

Company assessment

Financial strength   Is this strong or weak? Why? What should you do about it?

Competitive advantage   Is this strong or weak?

Industry assessment

Environmental stability Is this stable or turbulent? What are the key characteristics? In what ways can you adjust to it?

Industry strength   Is this strong or weak? Why? What should you do?

Each of the four characteristics above can be made up of seven or eight factors which represent the essence of the characteristic. These factors are shown in figure 5.2 which can be used as a checklist for your organization.

A manager can assign numerical values to each factor. Rowe et al. rate 0–6 but our preference is for a rating of 0–5 or 0–10. The average for each characteristic can easily be worked out and their relative strengths appreciated. The reasons for the scores on the factors and the averages for the characteristics should be worked out. Special attention should be paid to scores which are out of line.

Managers should be able to make some decisions after examining figure 5.3. After studying how to use these charts we shall examine the various options for change.

There is very little one can do to change industry strength and environmental stability except adjust to them, whereas it is possible to increase the organization's financial strength and competitive advantage by the decisions you make.

Options for Change

To refresh your memory, read Boxes BP5.10, BP5.11 and BP5.12 before completing Activity BP5.1 on page 201.

Industry assessment

Factors determining environmental stability   Score

Technological changes
Rate of inflation
Demand variability
Price range of competing products
Barriers to entry into market
Competitive pressure
Price elasticity of demand
Other

                                Average = _____

Critical factors:

Comments:

Factors determining industry strength

Growth potential
Profit potential
Financial stability
Technological know-how
Resource utilization
Capital intensity
Ease of entry into market
Productivity, capacity utilization
Other

                                Average = _____

Critical factors:

Comments:

Company assessment

Factors determining competitive advantage   Score

Market share
Product quality
Product life cycle
Product replacement cycle
Customer loyalty
Competition's capacity utilization
Technological know-how
Vertical integration
Other

                                Average = _____

Critical factors:

Comments:

Factors determining financial strength

Return on investment
Leverage
Liquidity
Capital required/capital available
Cash flow
Ease of exit from market
Risk involved in business
Other

                                Average = _____

Critical factors:

Comments:

Figure 5.3 Chart for organization assessment.

Source: Adapted from Rowe et al., 1989.

BOX BP5.10

Some policy options

We will ignore any 'combination' strategies that borrow from several of the categories.

Stability
Essentially a maintenance approach of holding on to what you've got. It is a risk-reduction tactic as 'no change' is seen as 'no risk'. It is not quite so, of course, as others are changing and the market-place may be quite fluid, so you may be in relative decline if all the others around you are changing and you remain static.

Focus
This gives specialization. It is particularly important for a smaller organization to follow this strategy as it will otherwise be overstretched, although it carries the risk of leaving no other option to fall back on if a crash occurs.

Innovation
Development may be one of the keys to success. Product life maturity and the ageing process will certainly demand repackaging as a minimum position, while in some sectors, such as consumer electronics, it really is a case of innovate or die.

Turnarounds
Also called internal retrenchment. Internal efficiency and savage cost cutting (often labour) are the hallmarks of this option which often occurs under new management in troubled times.

Retrenchment – divestment

A merger reverse in times of over-expansion and a large firm pulling back or a larger unit hitting hard times. It may be an attempt to readjust the core strategy back to the basics.

Retrenchment – liquidation

One of the growth industries in the 1990s depression in the UK. This is a slightly better option than bankruptcy, as you may get some money back, but not to be recommended.

Integration

Horizontal integration involves acquisition or merger with a competitor in a similar market-place. Vertical integration involves going backwards in the supply chain, e.g. a newspaper acquires a paper factory. This option may be cumbersome, with duplication of resources (at least initially) in the horizontal format; the vertical format may give cheaper raw materials but it may be a different business altogether – in spite of the initial synergy.

Diversification

Moving into new fields through merger or acquisition may be involved or the existing portfolio may be so fundamentally altered that the firm becomes diversified. Conglomerates may result from such diversification.

BOX BP5.11

Courtaulds and Hoechst in joint venture

Recently Courtaulds announced the effective takeover of the German chemical group Hoechst. It was called a joint venture, but Courtaulds indicated it would have a substantial majority of the shares in the combined business. Courtaulds would also be the larger partner as far as sales were concerned and might eventually buy out Hoechst. No cash changed hands and Hoechst got shares in the new fibre company.

According to chief executive Sipko Huismans, this deal would make Courtaulds the leading European player in the viscose market, as it already was in the United States, and so make it one of the leaders in the industry.

At the end of the last year Courtaulds had a net debt of £222 million, which was £11 million below the previous year end and represented 40 per cent of shareholders' funds.

Cash flow was helped by a cut in capital spending but the group continues to invest heavily and well in excess of the depreciation charge.

Courtaulds is no longer a textile company since it demerged its textile interests. Now it is a collection of specialist chemical businesses producing viscose fibre and film, paints and other materials.

BOX BP5.12

Philip Morris and diversification

In 1847 Philip Morris founded a tobacconist's shop in Bond Street in the West End of London. His customers included Cecil Rhodes and members of the Royal Family. However, by 1992, Philip Morris was, in revenue terms, the world's largest consumer package goods company with $59 billion sales, 170,000 employees and over 3,000 products.

Philip Morris has used its cash flow to fund diversification into food (about $30 billion in recent years) and build up its cigarette business. It now has critical mass in dairy products, coffee and chocolate.

Over the next five years Philip Morris will have free cash flow (after dividends and investment in current business) of $20 billion to spend on acquisitions.

ACTIVITY BP5.1

THE DETERMINATION OF POLICY OPTIONS

Activity code

- ✓ Self-development
- ✓ Teamwork
- ✓ Communications
- ✓ Numeracy/IT
- ✓ Decisions

Following on from Box BP5.10 on policy options, identify and classify current examples of each of the policy options. This can be done through a close examination of the business press. Comment critically on each of your examples, noting your views on the relevance and potential success of the option invoked.

Expansion

In this unit, expansion will be developed further since it includes a number of fundamental concepts which are important for managers to understand. The drive for growth appears to be inevitable but Boxes BP5.13 and BP5.14 give different perspectives on the policy of expansion. In order to get a stronger feel for expansion, complete Activity BP5.2 on page 203.

BOX BP5.13

Sales or margins?

Sales expansion and a knock-on effect on profitability through volume increases has a nice ring to it. In some cases, though, the policy may be sales expansion at the expense of margins. The case of Kingfisher illustrates the point.

B&Q, the Do-It-Yourself offshoot of parent company Kingfisher, is currently involved in what could be termed a price war. Yet it is also a long-term policy and not just another short-term promotion.

The policy reads thus: reduce costs, reduce the gross margin (buy and sell difference), get more customers in and sell more goods. The policy really is one of 'pile 'em high, sell 'em cheap'.

The problems with price cutting are that it can not only trigger retaliation but lead to an almost suicidal approach to the whole business; it is dependent on rigorous cost control and bulk buying where suppliers can be squeezed and it needs the volume throughput of customers in order to be viable.

To what extent it is a long-term policy may be more debatable.

BOX BP5.14

Going for growth

Ask a student of business about the core objectives of an enterprise and aspiration towards growth will almost inevitably surface.

The Bank of Scotland provides a good example of this policy of growth, but some of the negative side-effects are also worth noting.

The bank's traditional base by definition lies in Scotland and this was the case up until the late 1970s/early 1980s. Like so many Scots, the bank began to move south and, by the early 1990s, the southern business had overtaken the share of business in the north. Its share of the UK market has risen accordingly from 2 per cent to nearer 7 per cent in this period – a phenomenal growth policy.

The drive for growth has not been smooth. Coupled with recession and business failures, such phenomenal growth, even for a 'canny' Scottish bank, cannot be risk-free. Consequently, bad debt mounted to almost £372 million in 1992–3.

The motor behind the growth has been tight cost control within the organization and, above all, higher output and productivity by the staff. The staff and their productivity seem to be the key elements behind this growth policy.

ACTIVITY BP5.2

GROWTH OPTIONS FOR AREN DESIGNS

Activity code
- ✓ Self-development
- ✓ Teamwork
- ✓ Communications
- ☐ Numeracy/IT
- ✓ Decisions

Policy decisions will be affected by the organization and its strengths interacting with market possibilities in a competitive environment. However, it may be useful to relate several growth options to the Aren Designs case and to examine these options in their own right in the context of the known facts of the case. Proceed to do this, making comments on each option as it relates to the case at this particular time.

Aren Designs, owned by the Patel family, started its commercial life in the humble street markets of Hendon, north London, and Hitchin, Hertfordshire. The name Aren was derived from the two brand names – Karen and Daren, respectively geared for females and males. The market-place for Aren Designs was based on casual clothes – mainly jeans, skirts and jackets with denim as the common denominator.

The street market meant no till receipts, creative accounting practices, few (if any) overheads and a steady clientèle. Unlike many others, the Patel brothers reinvested surplus monies into the business. With a mark-up of up to 100 per cent on the goods, a nominal rent for the stall (seven days a week), 60 days' credit from suppliers and creative practices on sales turnover, the firm blossomed.

More members of the Patel family joined the firm. The stalls spread up the A1 trunkroad from Hendon to Hitchin, an hour's van drive from London. After three years the firm commanded nine stalls on a daily basis. On an average daily turnover of around £300, excluding Christmas and summer rushes, each stall provided approximately £2,000 per week. On an annual basis, this amounted to £100,000 per stall. With the summer rush and pre-Christmas buying, a turnover of £1 million was reached after the fourth year of operation.

The basis of the firm's success had been structured on good, cheap buying (usually from the Far East and the Indian subcontinent), a quality service (all goods could be returned 'without a quibble'), good sales techniques and the right pitch on pricing (not too dear, but dear enough to separate them from the inferior quality goods sold by their competitors on the market and well under the price of the large retail clothing chains).

The Patels had ambitions to develop new projects as well as maintaining their presence on the market stalls. Ready-made garments were fine for the street markets but the firm wanted a 'classier' image. Retail was fine as well, but the exclusion of non-family members (the employees they had were always under the control of the extended family, from nieces to grandparents) and a desire to 'trade up' pushed them into different directions. Retail shops in established shopping centres held no appeal – costs would spiral and control would be lost. They preferred to go into the wholesale market. Their Far East contacts could supply higher quality garments – at a price – and to a tighter design specification, and a new designer was recruited with considerable experience in textiles and fabrics.

A new shop was opened in the Seven Sisters Road area of north London. This was to be a wholesale venture rather than a retail outlet. The wholesale trade seemed to beckon to them, and they gradually moved out of direct retailing. Aren Designs was born, although the brothers kept a personal financial interest in the street markets which they handed over or sold to the rest of the extended family. The final move up-market was an address in London's exclusive Bond Street.

The Patels wanted rapid growth of their new wholesale venture and they reviewed the traditional policies of 'forced growth'. Acquisition of competing firms appeared to be an interesting proposition. This would be cost-effective and they could pick up cheap import and export wholesalers, who abounded in the old area of the business. Often these firms were on the verge of bankruptcy and acquisition could be a saving grace for them.

Perhaps they could move out of their area of textiles and into related or unrelated areas; wholesale was wholesale, after all. On the other hand, if they stuck with what they knew, they would have better market penetration for their products.

Geographical expansion had helped them in the past. Their humble beginnings in the street market had expanded thanks to geography. The domestic market could be given an international dimension with their export prowess and they could re-export as well, particularly to Europe.

Diversification

Some of their cash surplus could be pushed into unrelated areas such as housing and property, or they could opt for new products in an unrelated industry such as food wholesale or bric-à-brac imported from the Indian subcontinent and sold on to pottery shops and so on. They had the channels for bringing in cheap goods, from carpets to pots, and they could redistribute accordingly. They even had a friend in Kenya who could forward frozen prawns and lobsters to them.

Integration

This could also be an option and they could start to buy up the producers of their material in India for a very reasonable price. This would help quality control but it would mean a presence and time in India. They could also step up the retail side once again.

Commentary

Benefits/drawbacks

Acquisition

Geographical expansion

Diversification

Integration

Other options?

Acquisitions

A business normally expands through acquisitions, mergers, joint ventures or internal development. Mergers or acquisitions are often chosen as the routes to expansion but more than half are unsuccessful. This is usually because of the high premiums, the debt incurred to fund the purchase and the failure to produce synergy. Let us now examine some of the reasons for these failures.

When you buy another business you are making an investment and the basic principles of capital investment decisions apply.[9] This means that you should proceed only if the purchase makes a net contribution to shareholders' wealth. Many managers find this is a difficult decision because:

- benefits and costs are difficult to define;
- tax, legal and accounting issues must be taken into account;
- few managers understand the purpose of mergers or acquisitions and who gains and loses by them.

In order to measure the worth of an investment, we need to consider the value of the current and future benefits arising from the investment. If at all possible, these benefits should be expressed in terms of cash flows. However, the present value of cash flows in the future must be less than the same cash flows today. Therefore, the cash flows must be multiplied by a discount factor or rate of return (often known as the discount rate, hurdle rate or opportunity cost of capital).

An investment must make a **net** contribution to value, therefore the net present value (NPV) is found by subtracting the investment required from the present value (PV):

$$\text{VAN} = \text{NPV} = \text{PV} - \text{investment}$$

In this assessment we must also take account of risk. Some investments are riskier than others. Therefore, you should use a discount rate which also reflects the riskiness of the investment. This discount rate is often known as the opportunity cost of capital because it is the return forgone by your investment. You could instead, perhaps, invest in the stock market, if that is of equivalent risk. In that case your opportunity cost of capital will be equivalent to the average return you would get by investing in a portfolio of stocks in similar businesses.

There are two rules for investments.

1 The net present value rule – only make investments that have positive net present values.

2 The rate of return rule – only make investments that offer rates of return in excess of their opportunity costs of capital.

Let us take a very simple case and suppose that you are the manager of firm A and you wish to buy firm B. Will there be any economic gain from the purchase? There will only be a gain if the firms are worth more together than apart, that is, gain = present value (A + B) – present value A + present value B, expressed as:

$$\text{gain} = \text{PVAB} - (\text{PVA} + \text{PVB}) \tag{1}$$

However, there will also be a cost for the purchase which will depend on how the purchase is financed. Let us suppose the purchase is made using cash:

$$\text{cost} = \text{cash} - \text{PVB} \tag{2}$$

The net present value (NPV) of A purchasing B is measured by the difference between the gain and the cost:

$$
\begin{aligned}
\text{NPV} &= \text{gain} - \text{cost} \\
&= \text{PVAB} - (\text{PVA} + \text{PVB}) - (\text{cash} - \text{PVB}) \tag{3}
\end{aligned}
$$

You should only go ahead with the purchase if the NPV is positive.

For example, firm A has a present value of £1,000,000 and firm B a present value of £200,000. The purchase of firm B would result in cost savings for the combined business of a present value of £150,000.

Therefore, using equation 1:

$$\text{PVAB} = \text{gain} + \text{PVA} + \text{PVB}$$
$$= £150,000 + £1,000,000 + £200,000$$
$$= £1,350,000$$

Now suppose B is bought for £250,000 cash and we use equation 2:

$$\text{cost} = \text{cash} - \text{PVB}$$
$$= £250,000 - £200,000$$
$$= £50,000$$

This shows that the shareholders in B have gained £50,000, and *their gain is your cost*. They have gained £50,000 of the £150,000 purchase gain. In other words, your gain is only £100,000, not £150,000 as you expected earlier.

This can be confirmed using equation 3:

$$\text{NPV} = \text{gain} - \text{cost}$$
$$= \text{PVAB} - (\text{PVA} + \text{PVB}) - (\text{cash} - \text{PVB})$$
$$= £1,350,000 - (£1,000,000 + £200,000)$$
$$\quad - (£250,000 - £200,000)$$
$$= £100,000$$

Brealey and Myers explore this approach in some detail.[10]

If both A and B were public companies quoted on the Stock Exchange and investors had not anticipated the purchase of B by A, then the announcement of the purchase would cause the value of B's shares to rise by £50,000. This means B is now valued at £250,000 – a rise of 25 per cent.

If investors share the management's assessment of the purchase then the market value of A's shares will increase by £100,000, or 10 per cent.

From this example it appears that sellers normally gain from a purchase, whereas buyers may not gain very much relative to the costs and effort required to make the purchase. Therefore, it pays to observe what the investors think will be the gains or costs of the purchase. If the share price of the buyer does not change or falls, then investors either believe the benefits of the purchase are doubtful or the buyer is paying too much.

When you estimate the benefits of a purchase, do not discount the cash flows of the combined firm to give an estimate of PVAB. Instead, concentrate on the *changes in cash flow* as a result of the purchase. In other words, you must be able to demonstrate why the two businesses are worth more together than apart.

When you are selling a business, think about why you are selling it. For instance, if you think it is unprofitable and should be sold then, unless a buyer can run the business better than you can yourself, the price you receive will reflect the poor prospects of that business. No doubt these are already reflected in your share price.

Following on from this, some managers only buy into firms that are selling below book value. However, unless the buyer can somehow add value by giving that firm a competitive edge then the buyer will lose money.

You must also think about the implications when firms bid against one another for a target firm. Will the target be worth more to you or to the other bidders? If the answer is no then don't bid. Even if you won such a contest you would have paid too much and if you lost you would have wasted time and money preparing for it.

Several reasons can be given for buying another business or corporation, such as economics of scale, economics of vertical or horizontal integration, unused tax shields, combined complementary resources, as a use for surplus funds, to improve operations, to improve cash flow or to exploit unused debt capacity.

There are also several reasons which do not always result in increasing shareholder value. For instance, diversification is easier and cheaper for the shareholder than the corporation, as indicated earlier.

Increasing earnings per share (EPS) is often given as a reason for a merger or acquisition. A high EPS may indicate that investors believe that the firm has good growth prospects or that its earnings are low. A low EPS value means the opposite.

However, EPS values depend on what the firm means by earnings, since these are book or accounting figures and, as such, reflect accounting procedures which are not standard. These include the treatment of depreciation, valuation of stock, the way the accounts of merged firms are combined, the way research and development is capitalized or charged for, or the way tax liabilities are reported. All of these have an impact on the reported earnings of a business and can seriously affect the EPS values.

It should also be noted that EPS ignores both cash flow and risk, both of which are important in assessing whether a business will increase shareholder value.

Following on from this, suppose your business has a high price/earnings ratio because investors believe your business will have rapid growth in future earnings. You could satisfy these expectations, for example, by capital investment, product improvement or increased operating efficiency. However, instead, you might decide to grow by buying companies. If you were to buy slow-growing firms with low price/earnings ratios your EPS would increase in the short term but, in the long term, growth would slow down and earnings drop. See figure 5.4.

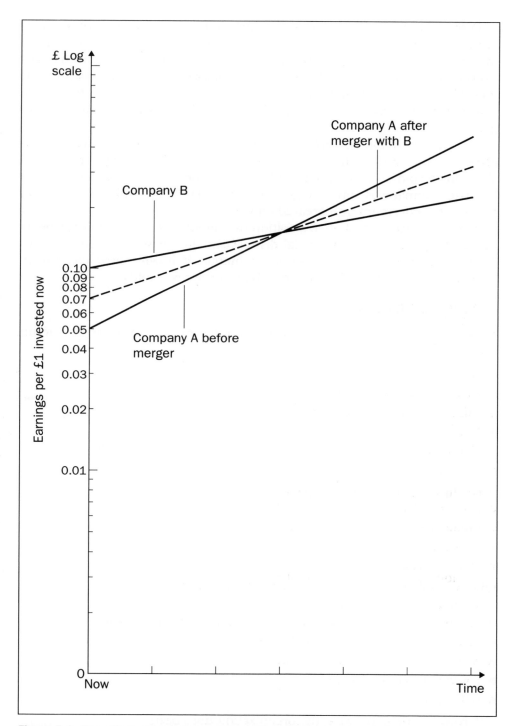

Figure 5.4 The effect of buying companies with low price/earnings ratios.

Source: Adapted from Brealey and Myers, 1988.

Before company A merges with company B, 100p invested in company A produced 5p of earnings and rapid growth prospects. However, 100p invested in company B before the merger produced 10p of earnings but slower growth prospects. The growth is shown by the steepness of the graph lines. If the total market value is not altered by the merger then 100p invested in the merged company produces 7p of earnings but slower growth.

In order to maintain growth, company A has to keep buying slow-growing companies with low price/earnings ratios. Eventually, growth will slow down and stop, earnings will fall and company A will fail. This is because company A has not grown, for instance by capital investment, product improvement or increased efficiency.

Another advantage of an acquisition or merger is that, other things being equal, the probability of financial distress should decrease. There will also be a net gain from an acquisition or merger if it will allow increase in borrowing and increased value from the interest tax shields.

Offensive options

According to Thompson and Strickland, there are six ways to mount offensives:[11]

1 Attack competitors' strengths.

2 Attack competitors' weaknesses.

3 Attacks on many fronts simultaneously.

4 First-mover offensives.

5 Guerrilla attacks.

6 Pre-emptive strikes.

Who should you attack?
- market leaders
- runner-up firms
- struggling firms
- small local and regional firms

Offensives depend on competitive advantages such as:
- lower-cost products
- changes in production that lower costs or enhance differentiation
- superior performance or lower user costs
- more responsive after-sales support
- a new distribution channel
- selling direct to user

Offensives depend on what the organization does best:
- its competitive strengths and capabilities
- key skills or strong functional competencies (the value chain is important here too)

The timing of offensives is just as important to success as the move itself. Making the first move is best when:

- it builds image and reputation;
- there are early commitments to raw materials, new technology, distribution channels etc. which can provide a cost advantage;
- first-time customers can remain loyal to pioneering firms when making repeat purchases;
- it is a pre-emptive strike which makes imitation hard or unlikely.

The disadvantages for the first mover are:

- pioneering leadership can be costly and the experience curve effects negligible;
- technological change is so rapid that early investments are soon obsolete;
- customer loyalty to pioneering firms can be weak;
- skills and know-how developed by pioneers can be easily copied by late movers.

Defensive options

Thompson and Strickland believe defensive moves lower the risk of being attacked, weaken the impact of an attack when it occurs and cause potential attackers to choose someone else.[12] Such options may not increase a firm's competitive advantage but they do help to sustain and strengthen those it has.

An organization can protect its competitive position by doing the following:

- Blocking any possibilities of being attacked by presenting a moving target rather than protecting the status quo. A good defence involves adjusting quickly to changing industry conditions and being the first mover in any situation.
- Signalling that you will retaliate strongly if attacked. This dissuades attackers from attacking or diverts them to attack other competitors.
- Reducing margins or using accounting methods that do not expose your profitability.

Vertical integration

The objective of vertical integration, according to Thompson and Strickland, is to strengthen an organization's competitive position.[13] Vertical integration must produce cost savings or a competitive advantage to justify the extra investment. Integration can be backwards towards the source of raw materials or forwards towards the customer. Backward integration only generates cost savings when the production volume is big enough to capture economies of scale or production efficiency which are the same as or better than those of competitors.

The value chain concept (see Unit Three) and the opportunity to differentiate products and services are important considerations.

The disadvantages of vertical integration are:

■ it uses capital which could be better used elsewhere;

■ it increases risks;

■ integrated firms are often vulnerable to new technologies and products since change requires capital investment. The high cost of replacing technology may cause a reliance on obsolete technology;

■ it is difficult to balance capacity at each stage of the production chain and this leads to inefficiencies.

Now complete Activity BP5.3.

ACTIVITY BP5.3

AApma

Activity code
☑ Self-development
☑ Teamwork
☑ Communications
☑ Numeracy/IT
☑ Decisions

The Andersons, husband and wife, started a consultancy firm in 1982. Both had considerable administrative and managerial expertise and were well qualified for the task ahead. The plan to go it alone had been in gestation for some time. A disillusionment with the restrictions of large bureaucratic organizations and, more importantly, a strong entrepreneurial feel meant that they were psychologically prepared for such a move.

The state of the marketplace was well researched, too. While in his job as a senior manager in personnel development, on behalf of the large bureaucracy, the husband had contacted every single known UK consultancy firm in the area of human resource management. The big name of the firm pulled in an overwhelming response. Fees, format, unique selling points, distinctive approach and expertise were all collated for the large bureaucracy. The research would do no harm to the husband-and-wife team either.

Their core expertise lay in human resource/personnel and general management. The research showed that the work of the competitors tended to be in recruitment, selection, salary administration, benefits, training, development and general personnel management. Some specialists existed as well in less mainstream areas, such as health and safety, counselling, welfare and employee communications. Labour relations seemed to be represented only by a minority. Both the Andersons had internal organizational perspectives from the public and private sectors, so they were aware of the buying process and the needs of the client.

The market was decided as being small businesses, recruitment, selection, training and development. The niche was seen as small to medium-sized firms without specialist personnel help on site. A retainer would apply rather than a daily rate, for this would give security to the firm and financial stability to the consultancy. The recruitment and selection would be aimed at management and would dovetail into the needs of the clients of these small to medium-sized businesses. Other research had noted the absence of personnel specialists in firms of fewer than 200 people. The training and development, although management-oriented, could include all staff from clerks to technicians in the needs analysis, and others would be brought in for the 'delivery' aspect.

The market was to be attacked with this three-pronged offensive. Considerable advertising was done, and much time and effort (and money) were spent contacting and visiting local firms in Cambridgeshire, Hertfordshire, Bedfordshire and north London. There were also mailshots and visits. The 'small to medium-sized business' approach was not working. Both the Andersons agreed that marketing and business policy with some finance might be the order of the day, but state aid and local government initiatives as well as expertise prevented entry into such markets. Maureen said, 'The fact that these people haven't got a personnel department in the first place shows that it is not a niche market at all. There is no such market, because they don't recognize the importance of personnel management. We either try bigger firms or stop throwing good money at it.' The big firms were sophisticated and had resources which the consultancy could not match. The personnel side of things was slowed down and the emphasis went elsewhere.

The recruitment and selection side of things looked attractive. Experience with a city head hunter had given keen insight into the mechanics of such work. The specialist knowledge again lay in the management side of things. Competition was ruthless. 'Agencies' chased up every advertisement in the press and bombarded personnel officers with neatly packaged but unwanted cvs. The 'temporary' market was a growth area. A survey showed sales of some £400 million, with a split between permanent placements and temps of some 10:90 per cent, within these agencies, a considerable market. The return on capital of a typical agency was considerable: on sales of £2,400,000 in the first year an expected loss of c.£30,000 could be reversed the following year. After some four or five years of operation such an agency would have a turnover of c.£4,700,000 with c.£300,000 net pre-tax profit. The company did not move into this segment, however, as it looked crowded. Instead it moved into management search and selection.

It had three arrows to its recruitment and selection bow: search, recruitment advertising and a contingency register. The company's leaflet describes these:

Overview

High-calibre managers are critical to the success of organizations. The selection of effective managers, although time-consuming, has to be right as it has serious consequences both for the individual and the organization.

Through executive search or advertising, or a combination of both, we provide an impartial assessment and shortlist of external candidates for the client. We are involved also in the internal assessment of management, development programmes and personnel consultancy. Our services are completely confidential to both our clients and candidates.

The services

1 Executive search and selection

Search, finding management without recourse to advertising, can be very useful when the job is specialized or where confidentiality dictates a discreet approach. Perhaps above all, search finds managers who are not actively job hunting. We have adapted the process to finding both senior and middle management:

■ *Client briefing:* the initial discussion centres on the client's specific needs. Full account is taken of our potential conflicts of interest with existing clients before undertaking an assignment.

■ *Profiles: job and person:* an exact definition of the appointment is discussed with the client, and a person specification of the ideal candidate is derived. This specification, once agreed, forms our working brief for the assignment.

■ *Search:* by means of an original search plan, applied research and a wide network of contacts, we call forward potential candidates for initial interview.

■ *Shortlist:* after in-depth interviews, qualitative reports and background checks are forwarded to the client on shortlisted candidates.

■ *Guarantees:* existing clients are strictly 'off limits' for the purpose of search. If the individual leaves within an agreed time, we do the search again without any additional fees being incurred.

2 Management selection – advertising

Where a wider range of individuals can be considered, advertising can be effective. A wider range of candidates can mean higher response rates to advertisements, with subsequent time, money and management effort being spent on the assessment process.

Our service frees client management from this time-consuming process and, by advertising or by a combination of advertising and search, we provide the important shortlist for the client's final selection.

Our recruitment service starts with drawing up a comprehensive brief and recruitment plan. Once agreed with the client, advertisements are inserted in the appropriate media. We review applications, invite people to the initial interview and reject unsuitable candidates. In-depth interviews are held and detailed candidates' reports are prepared for the shortlist.

If required, we have a testing facility. Background checks are made on shortlisted candidates. We continue to work with the selected candidate and client to bring about a successful and early conclusion.

3 Personnel Management – advisory service

Unlike many recruitment advisors, we are personnel consultants advising on organizational reviews, compensation programmes, personnel strategy and management development:

■ *Organizational reviews:* We audit the quality and performance of the management team and advise on the structure best suited to the needs of the organization.

■ *Compensation:* salary and benefit packages and structures are developed by the consultancy for individual organizations.

■ *Strategy:* we review the present practices and advise on the scope and application of personnel strategy.

■ *Management development:* the planning, resourcing and assessment of management form the basis of the design of our development and training programmes.

The search side is extremely lucrative. The industry trend is some 30–5 per cent fee retainer based on the initial remuneration of the executive. On average a job with a £30,000 salary would be filled in a company and a retainer of £10,000 would apply. The Andersons thought this was expensive, so their fee was 25 per cent, and they notified the licensing authority accordingly. On recruitment advertising, the fee norm was c. 18–20 per cent plus the full cost of the advertisement. The husband-and-wife team went for 16 per cent. The contingency register with people writing in would give a commission of 10 per cent – this is instead of $12^1/_2$ per cent used by the other firms. On price they could beat the competition and on quality they could more than match the expertise of most firms, which tended to employ sales people as consultants rather than personnel specialists.

Although the rewards are lucrative the business is time-consuming, with initial meetings, specification taking, writing up, clearing, agreeing, recruiting, searching and interviewing, with heavy reports on the candidates. More importantly, the work is fickle – the economic downturn of the late 1980s and early 1990s has destroyed many of the competitors who were in the market in the early 1980s.

It was agreed not to push this area given the depressed market. Instead a focus on overseas shorter-term assignments was instigated with a pro forma for organizations and one for potential or actual expatriates. Keeping track of these expatriates on contract proved to be a headache, and keeping up to date on their availability was difficult. However, it is working, and working quite well, with clients from engineers to managers and from petrochemical plants to catering institutions.

Assuming that if it worked for abroad it should work here, they designed a format for organizations in the UK and their firm AApma receives cvs on a daily basis. Companies are still tight on labour but the firm has stuck with permanent managerial jobs in the UK, and some come through the register. The process is shown in the flowchart overleaf.

The growth area which has been less dependent on the depressed economy has been training and development. Designing and developing programmes with potential links to managerial qualifications is one route. The

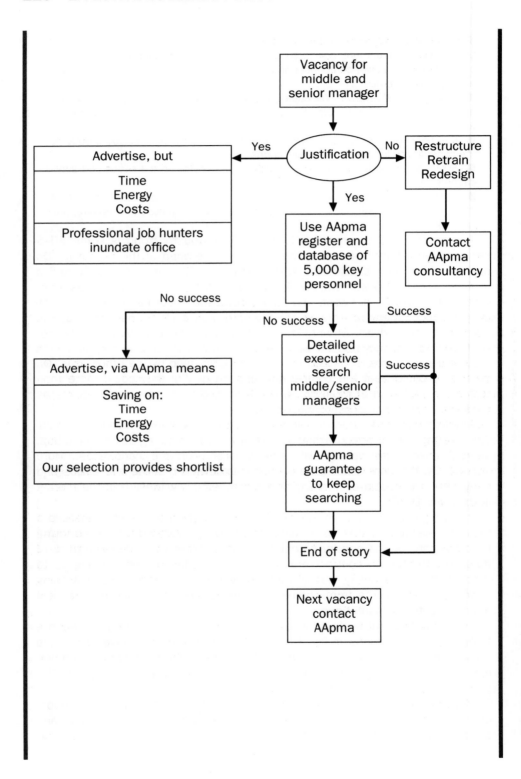

analysis of needs using a unique MPF technique based on competency, managerial areas, people areas and functional expertise has proved to be popular. The delivery aspect has been restricted to human resource and management, although other associates can be called in to deliver management training in finance, operations and project management, and sales and marketing. The work is best summarized in the following extract:

Development
- Build on your existing modules
- Integrate with an educational programme for management qualifications

Consultancy
- Needs analysis
- Surveys
- Evaluation/audits
- MPF technique

Management training and development

Design
- Tailor-made programmes
- Customized short course modules

Delivery
- Team building
- Leadership
- Interpersonal skills
- Appraisal
- Management of change, etc.

1 *Introduction*
While the customer may be the business, the organization's ability to adapt to the customer is really a human resource issue. It is the personnel and management in particular of the organization that forms a critical aspect of its internal competency.
Following careers in industry and commerce, we established a small specialized consultancy in human resource management (HRM) in 1982. Our emphasis is on management competency, involving selection and search, business and HRM policy, training and development. These notes are concerned with management training and development.

2 *Why bother with management training and development?*
We improve the competency of your managers. From planning to co-ordinating, from motivating to controlling, from leading to decision making, we assist in enhancing the individual's knowledge, skills and attitudes. Ultimately, this results in more fulfilled individuals, a more effective team and a more profitable enterprise.

3 *How does this relate to your own internal resources?*
Management training and development must remain your 'property'. Our tailor-made approach complements your own resources. We provide an expertise in

very specific areas; your managerial time and effort can be saved by using our services; as independent advisors, we give you an objective analysis and input; and human resource management by definition tends to be a sensitive area, so we provide a safe learning environment allied to complete confidentiality.

This assistance can range from:

Planning	Policy setting to a training plan
Designing	Establishing an appraisal scheme to developing training modules
Diagnosing	Training needs analysis to management audit and assessment
Facilitating and advising	Delivery of training modules to evaluation of existing management development schemes

4 *What are our core activities?*

Approach

The work is based on a systematic approach to training for the present, and development for the future. It can be summarized as follows:

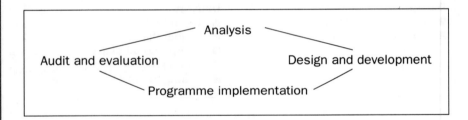

Levels

Our work can operate at various levels.

Core skills	Based upon the essential skill areas of management.
Individual manager	Role and functional analysis leads to specific self-development programmes.
Team or department	Group dynamics and effective team building enhance cohesion and reduce conflicts.
Organization	Change programmes can occur based upon a strategic analysis with implications for style and climate.

Style

- All programmes are developed for your requirements: we do not have 'packages'.
- The work is in-house only with no 'open' courses.
- The advisors are all practical managers as well as specialist consultants.
- The analysis and inputs are totally objective.
- All projects are completely confidential: we do not discuss your situation with other clients.
- Finally, the fee structure is cost effective.

5 What specific things do we do?
Some examples of the work include:

Attitude surveys
Employee communications audits
Assessment of management
Audit of appraisal schemes
Design and development of appraisal schemes
Training needs analysis
Training plans
Course design and development
General management course
Management of people course
Modules: selection, appraisal, communications, interpersonal skills, negotiation,
    group dynamics and leadership
Human resource management course
Evaluation of development and training
Human resource policies and strategic management

The training and development work is profitable. With daily fees of up to £600 per consultant and in-house courses of some £100 per person, weekly sessions can come to between £5,000 and £10,000, depending upon the numbers. The latest innovation has been to publish books through Blackwell Publishers of Oxford which can accompany the courses and which can also be linked to educational courses of established organizations. The firm is aiming to consolidate its position and is seeking a growth strategy for the next five years. So we need to determine their business plan with special reference to their 'products' and to environmental and competitor scans. Equally, they are in the market of establishing assessment centres which bridge the selection and training work and can call in the able assistance of Dr Jack Lane. An assessment centre programme also needs to be constructed.

1 Critically appraise the policy to date.
2 Construct a plan of action for the firm's policy for the next five years.

Diversification

Up to now the changes which a manager can make in a single business unit have been discussed. However, once a business becomes a collection of single business units, decision making and change become more difficult.

When the growth potential of a single business unit begins to wane the options for change are either to become more aggressive and take market share away from competitors or to diversify into other lines of business. This was mentioned in Unit Four.

The objective of diversification is not simply to diversify the business risk by investing in more than one industry but to **build shareholder value**. This is because shareholders can diversify their risk more easily by buying shares in businesses in different industries without paying a premium.

The premium paid in acquiring a business can have a crippling effect on the company taking over. For example, let us assume company A is making £150,000 profit after tax on a capital of £1 million, i.e. 15 per cent. Suppose company B has to pay £2 million to buy company A. This means that company B will have to make £300,000 on its investment of £2 million in company A in order to justify its investment. This is very difficult unless drastic changes are made to company A and the industry is growing strongly.

From competitive advantage to corporate strategy

Porter studied the track record of 33 corporations with a reputation for good management between 1950 and 1986 and found that most of them had divested themselves of more acquisitions than they had kept.[14] Each corporation entered on average 80 new industries and 27 new fields; 70 per cent were acquisitions, 22 per cent start-ups and 8 per cent joint ventures. On average, the corporations divested more than 50 per cent of their acquisitions in new industries and 60 per cent of their acquisitions in new fields. Thus even these successful corporations have dissipated rather than created shareholder value.

Porter believes there are certain premises which must be followed for successful diversification.

- **Competition occurs at the business unit level**. Diversified companies do not compete but their business units do. Successful corporations grow out of and nurture competitive business units.

- **Diversification inevitably adds costs and constraints to business**. Corporate overheads are obvious, but what about the effort spent explaining and complying with corporate systems, amongst other things?

- **Shareholders can easily diversify themselves** more cheaply than a corporation which has usually to pay a premium for an acquisition. Thus a corporation cannot be successful unless it adds value to business units *and* to shareholders.

In order to decide whether a diversification will increase shareholder value Porter applies three tests:

(1) **The attractiveness test** The industry chosen must produce consistently good returns on investment, have favourable competitive conditions and a market environment conducive to long-term profitability. Early growth does not mean long-term profit potential.

(2) **The cost of entry test** The cost of entry must not be so high as to erode profitability. Philip Morris is reputed to have paid four times the book value for Seven Up and ultimately had to sell it because they could not make the investment pay.

(3) **The better-off test** The diversifying firm must bring some advantage to the business it buys or the new business must offer some extra competitive advantage to the firm. There should be an opportunity to create a sustainable competitive advantage where none existed before and so increase profitability and shareholder value. Diversifying corporate risk does not satisfy the better-off test since shareholders can normally diversify more cheaply themselves.

Diversifications must satisfy *all three tests* in order for them to build shareholder value over the long term.

Three options for creating shareholder value [15]

(1) **Restructuring** seeks out undeveloped, sick or threatened businesses or industries on the threshold of significant change. Restructuring passes the three tests of successful diversification. Cost of entry is met by the types of company bought. The better-off test is clearly met and businesses are only bought if the industry is structurally attractive.

(2) **Transferring skills**. The value chain is useful for identifying an activity which creates synergy. This is the ability to transfer skills or expertise among similar value chains. Even though the units operate separately the similarities in the value chains allow sharing of knowledge and skills.

Three conditions must be satisfied in order for the transference of skills to lead to competitive advantage: (1) the business activities are so similar that sharing expertise is meaningful; (2) the transfer of skills involves activities which are important for competitive advantage; and (3) the skills transferred provide a significant competitive advantage for the receiving business.

The idea is to satisfy two of the diversification tests by offsetting the acquisition premium and/or lowering the cost of overcoming entry barriers. The attractiveness test must still be strictly adhered to in order to ensure success.

The transfer of skills should be ongoing, but if the transfer of skills is one time only, then the acquired business should be sold on.

(3) **Sharing activities**. Another source of synergy which can be defined by the value chain is the sharing of activities between business units, such as the sharing of distribution channels or research and development. The sharing of activities leads to competitive advantage by lowering costs or enhancing differentiation. Sharing activities, however, also involves the costs of managing them and the compromises needed to enable the activities to be shared.

In order for this approach to be successful the corporation must have:

- a strong sense of corporate identity;
- a clear mission statement that emphasizes the integration of business units;
- an incentive system that rewards more than just business unit results;
- cross-unit task forces;
- other methods of integrating.

Shared activities clearly meet two of the tests for creating shareholder value. These are: the better-off test because the units gain tangible advantages from one another, and the cost of entry test by reducing the barriers to entry. The attractiveness test must still be strictly adhered to in order to be sure of success.

The secret of the success of Porter's research is that a corporation can employ a restructuring policy at the same time as it transfers skills and/or shares activities. This means they are not mutually exclusive activities but reinforce one another.

Porter found that successful corporations had a very low percentage of unrelated acquisitions. Unrelated means that there is little or no opportunity to transfer skills or share key activities. Thus successful corporations diversify into areas which are related and synergy develops by transferring skills and sharing activities.

Successful corporations also have good records for start-ups and joint ventures. This is probably because of the high costs of integration. The Japanese normally diversify by start-up or joint venture. Building on a core business can be seen in Box BP5.15.

BOX BP5.15

Acquisition – a core business formula

Compass, the contract contractors, paid some £72 million to acquire the airport restaurant and contract catering business, Scandinavian SAS Service Partner.

The deal was financed by a new rights issue (six new shares for 19 existing) at 420p per share (price 528p).

Not only does this give the firm a step into continental Europe, it also builds on existing know-how and experience in a similar field of operations.

The research also indicates that none of the three options for creating shareholder value will work unless the structure of the industry and the implementation are good.

Porter provides the following action plan for a corporation.

- Identify the interrelationships among the current businesses.
- Select the core businesses and identify the corporate theme.

BOX BP5.16

Acquisition

The McKinsey formula for successful acquisitions based on post-acquisition returns on equity and assets and the cost of the capital acquisition can be cited:

- Stay with your core business.
- Tend to buy good local performers with a strong market presence unless buying in for technology or skills etc.
- Extend to the new acquisition the core competitive advantage of the acquirer.
- Use key managers to 'transfer skills' into the new acquisition.
- Evolution not revolution with gradual change to operating systems is advocated.
- Prior experience or a track record in acquisitions could only be an advantage to the acquirer.

Source: Adapted from *McKinsey Quarterly,* No. 3

- Create horizontal organization mechanisms to facilitate interrelationships among the core businesses and lay the groundwork for future related diversification.
- Pursue diversifications that allow shared activities.
- Pursue diversifications that allow the transfer of skills.
- Pursue restructuring if this fits the skills of management or if no good opportunities exist for forging corporate interrelationships.
- Pay dividends so that shareholders can be the portfolio managers.

An alternative approach, the McKinsey formula, can be seen in Box BP5.16.

Portfolio Management

Porter does not believe that portfolio management will create or enhance shareholder value because portfolios are not sources of competitive advantages.[16] The autonomy given to business units and their independence may actually reduce performance. At the same time the sheer complexity of the task of supervising numerous disparate units has defeated even the best portfolio managers.

In this article, Porter seems to be using the term 'portfolio' as synonymous with 'conglomerate' whereas, in this section, we hope to show how you can use the portfolio as a tool for developing your corporation.

Let us assume you have built up a portfolio of businesses which increase shareholder value as Porter suggests. How can you make decisions about what to do next?

		Strong	Average	Weak
	High	1	1	2
Long-term industry attractiveness	Medium	1	2	3
	Low	2	3	3

Competitive position

Figure 5.5 General Electric's industry attractiveness and competitive position matrix.

The portfolio approach is an aid to thinking and is based on the premise that each business unit generates or requires cash according to its position in the industry life cycle. The cash generators of a mature industry, for example, can provide cash for the business units in the developing and growth stages. Therefore, the portfolio helps in the allocation of investment in business units to satisfy the corporate mission.

McKinsey and Co. helped General Electric (GE) to produce a nine-cell matrix in order to analyse the GE portfolio (see figure 5.5).[17,18] The nine-cell matrix is based on the two dimensions of long-term industry attractiveness and the competitive position of the business. The positions in the matrix suggest possible options.

1 Increase market share by growing, dominating and investing, or defend market share by segmenting, investing and avoiding weakness.

2 Select opportunities to invest, hold position or find growth segments, or consolidate by producing specialized products, finding niches, investing selectively and improving management.

3 Minimize losses by finding niches, specialized products, minimizing cash outlays and planning an exit.

This nine-cell matrix defines the positions of businesses in the matrix at a particular time but does not identify a business which is about to become very attractive or about to enter the decline stage. In order to overcome these defects, Hofer and Schendel developed a 15-cell matrix based on the five stages of industry evolution and three levels of competitive position (see figure 5.6).[19] Circles represent the size of the industry and the pie slices the market share of the business. The same factors for competitive position are used in order to facilitate comparison with the General Electric matrix.

Since several factors are involved in determining the position on each axis, a method for determining quantitative measures for each axis is required (see figure 5.7). The chosen factors are assigned **weights** based on their importance to the corporate management. The sum of the weights

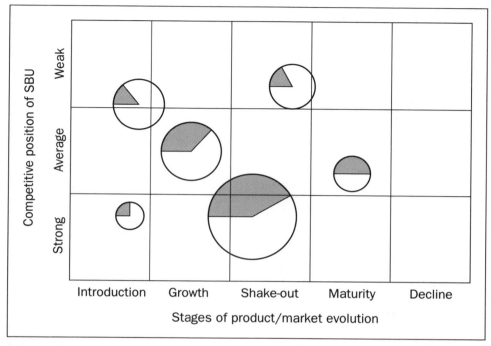

Figure 5.6 The product/market evolution portfolio matrix.

Source: Adapted from Hofer and Schendel, 1978.

must add up to ten. The industry is **rated** out of ten for each factor where ten is high and one low. The weight is then multiplied by the rating to give a weighted industry rating. For example, a rating of 5 with a weight of 3 gives a weighted industry rating of 15. The total of the weighted industry ratings will give the long-term attractiveness rating. These ratings, together with the competitive advantage ratings calculated in the same way, are calculated for each industry in the portfolio and plotted on a matrix as in figure 5.6. The area of the circle for each industry is proportional to the size of the industry and the pie slices represent the market share of the particular business.

The power of the life cycle matrix is the opportunity it offers to view all parts of the business at the same time and in a consistent framework. It provides managers with an idea of the contribution of each business to the portfolio both now and in the future.

The position of the businesses in the matrix will indicate the current approach to competition – expansionist, risk averse or risk taker.

The core business of the portfolio will generally determine whether the portfolio as a whole will perform strongly or weakly. Non-core businesses with poor competitive advantage, poor industry attractiveness and few prospects are candidates for divesting.

Industry attractiveness factors	Weight	Rating	Weighted industry rating
Market size and projected growth	1	5	5
Industry profitability	1	6	6
Intensity of competition	2	4	8
Seasonal and cyclical influences	0.5	7	3.5
Technological considerations	1	2	2
Capital requirements	2	3	6
Social, political, environmental	1	8	8
Emerging opportunities and threats	1	9	9
Barriers to entry and exit	0.5	1	0.5
Total	10		48

Industry attractiveness rating = 48

Competitive position factors	Weight	Rating	Weighted industry rating
Relative market share	1	6	6
Desirable core competencies	1	5	5
Profit margins relative to competitors	2	5	10
Product quality and service	1	4	4
Relative cost position	2	7	14
Knowledge of customers and market	1	6	6
Technological capability	1	8	8
Management capability	1	9	9
Total	10		62

Competitive position rating = 62

Figure 5.7 How to use weighting factors in order to determine the industry attractiveness and competitive position ratings.

Source: Adapted from Thompson and Strickland, 1992.

Questions about the portfolio need to be asked.
- Are there enough businesses in attractive industries?
- Are there too many problem businesses or mature or declining businesses?
- Are there enough cash producers to finance new developers?
- Is the portfolio vulnerable in any way?
- Does the portfolio put the corporation in a good position for the future?

The aim should be to build strong competitive positions and increase market share in order to capitalize on the portfolio. This can be done by moving the strategic business units (SBUs) from weak to average to strong competitive positions. A mix of SBUs should be developed in order to ensure continuity of profits into the future. The ones in the growth stage must be strong enough to fund those businesses in the development stage and also any business in the decline stage that needs help in refocusing.

If the SBUs are clustered in areas of the product or market cycle where profit is maximized, the corporation is obviously focused on profit making. SBUs clustered in particular stages, such as the growth stage, are emphasizing growth.

Risk preference is a significant factor in the choice of options for a business. There is considerable uncertainty about the viability of a product and its market in the development stage and later as the product or market moves into decline. Uncertainty also exists in the middle stages but it is not about the viability of the product and its market. This uncertainty is about the competition, products and the ability to build and sustain market share.

Therefore, the risk-averse manager can be expected to engage in businesses in the growth stage in which the market viability is clear and predictable. The manager will gain market share quickly and as the market approaches the decline stage the manager will divest the SBU. The risk-averse manager will therefore concentrate his or her businesses in the middle three cells of the 'Strong' column in figure 5.6.

The effective manager who is a risk taker will maintain a mixed portfolio based on a stable base of cash-generating businesses. There are then two opportunities, depending on the capabilities of the management of the businesses. On the one hand, skills in taking development risks in R&D will lead to developing the portfolio in the early stages, whereas skills in cost control and managing businesses in decline could lead to a portfolio in the later stages of the cycle. Much depends on the skills of the managers and their attitudes to risk.

In order to integrate some of the concepts in this unit, complete Activity BP5.4.

ACTIVITY BP5.4

CATIM

Activity code
✓ Self-development
✓ Teamwork
✓ Communications
✓ Numeracy/IT
✓ Decisions

CATIM stands for Consultancy and Training in Management. It is based at 49 Longton Grove, Sydenham, London SE26 6QQ. Its managing director is Abbas Baba BEng, MSc (Systems Analysis), MBIM and MIMC. Founded in

1980, the firm is a member of both the British Management Training Export Council and the Institute of Management Consultants (UK).

CATIM specializes in management consultancy for Europe and the Middle East. Prior to starting this business, Abbas Ridha Mohammad Baba had worked in a national centre for management development in the Middle East, with a specific remit on organization development, management development and performance and appraisal systems. Experience followed in London and Saudi Arabia in organization and methods, project management, systems, organization and performance management as both an in-house consultant and an external management consultant. Language and communication skills were in great demand when allied to this expertise, so lecturing and interpreting projects also followed. By December 1980 all of these skills and knowledge came together and CATIM was founded.

Since its inception, CATIM has followed a clear philosophy and specific objectives. It follows a strict code of ethics and fully adheres to the code of practice set by the Institute of Management Consultants. Indeed, Abbas Baba has been and is active in the institute and is both a fellow and a member of its committee on developing countries. He is also a member of the UK-based Institute of Training and Development, and the firm follows the good practice of that institute. The firm aims 'to provide the highest possible standard of consultancy and training services in Arabic and English to any organization at the lowest possible cost'.

The quality programmes are realistically costed and use is made of able sole practitioners and small specialist consultancy firms. Low overhead expenses result. The 'norm' of consultancy profit of some 10–15 per cent is easily met due to pricing policy and overhead cost control. The firm has links, both formal and informal, with a range of experts (some 3,000 in the Institute of Management Consultants alone) including leading business schools, management institutes and experts in training, development and consultancy.

The firm, unlike many, offers a free initial service for in-house research and consultancy. This problem-solving exercise allows a formal proposal to be drawn up. Apart from travel and accommodation charges (given the geographical spread of the firm), the service is free. Many projects have emanated from this policy.

In the early 1980s, CATIM began running a series of open courses in London for international managers. A range of courses of one or two weeks' duration was established as a summer school at London University:

Seminar number and title	Duration (weeks)
1 Human Resource Management and Development Seminar	2
2 Manpower Planning Seminar	1
3 Career Planning Seminar	1
4 Communication and Interpersonal Skills Seminar	2
5 Training for Trainers and Training Managers Seminar	2
6 Essentials of Management Seminar (suitable for Engineers)	2
7 Financial Planning and Control of Projects Seminar (including Economic Feasibility of Projects)	2
8 Techniques of Financial Analysis Seminar	1

By the mid-1980s, some seventy-five different courses had been prepared and ran for different organizations on an in-house basis. A specific example of one of the courses offered can be seen in the following extract:

The Skill of Effective Leadership Seminar (for top management)

Introduction
Every manager needs to acquire or develop the skills of leadership because these skills are essential for successful management.

Course objectives
To provide the participants with guidance to acquire or develop the necessary leadership skills.

Course participants
Presidents, director-generals and directors.

Course syllabus
- The nature of leadership.
- Types of leaders and their management styles.
- Leadership selection.
- Developing leadership.
- The nature of thinking.
- Problem solving.
- Decision making.
- Creative thinking.
- Communication.
- Effective speaking.
- Better listening.
- Clear writing.
- Meetings: the leader as chairperson.

Other non-training initiatives, from manpower analysis to research, are detailed below:

As CATIM makes use of the expertise of a large number of professional Arab, British and international individuals and organizations, its services cover most fields of management, including the management of social services. These services include, but are not limited to:

1 Consultancy and Training
- Organization and methods.
- Work study.
- Organization structure to determine authorities, responsibilities and lines of communications.
- Organization development.
- Stores, warehouse and inventory management.
- Work methods improvement and simplification.
- Systems analysis and design (manual and computerized):
  - inventory and purchasing systems
  - accounting systems
  - management information systems.
- Incentive systems.
- Personnel management.

- Manpower planning and development.
- Resource allocation.
- Performance appraisal.
- Job description and evaluation.
- Training of trainers.
- Training of consultants.
- Production and industrial management.
- Marketing.
- Financial and management accounting.
- Electronic data processing/computer and microfilm services.
- Customs and excise administration.
- Design of factories (in engineering and pharmaceutical fields).
- Recruitment services.
- Airlines management.
- Management of municipalities and urban development.
- Hospital management.
- Bank management.
- Petroleum management.
- University administration.

2 Research
- Design and execution of scientific research on:
  - Manpower
  - Manpower movement in Arab countries
  - 'Brain drain' from Arab countries
  - Influence of international variables on Arab situations.
- Design and execution of studies concerning Arab public opinion with respect to important current affairs.
- Design and execution of studies concerning identification of scientific criteria for optimum resource allocation for five-yearly development plans.

With an expertise in the Middle East and with many contact points in major corporations, the firm has come together with AApma (see Activity BP5.3) for a joint initiative on expatriate recruitment and selection for managers, engineers etc., and to run a new series of twelve one-week courses (at this stage) based on this *Effective Management* series from Blackwell Publishers.

Develop a detailed business policy integrating the work of AApma, CATIM and these two new initiatives (see AApma case study in Activity BP5.3).

This unit has examined the many options for change which a manager can consider when looking for the long-term success of a business. It began with the vision, mission and objectives followed by a consideration of the ways in which a business can be assessed additional to those in Unit Four. This was followed by an explanation of the options available and the development of a corporate portfolio.

The implementation and evaluation of the options for change will be discussed in Unit Six.

Notes

1 Wilson, *A Strategy of Change*.
2 Thompson and Strickland, *Strategic Management: concepts and cases*.
3 Rowe et al., *Strategic Management: a methodological approach*.
4 Ibid.
5 Ibid.
6 Thompson and Strickland, *Strategic Management: concepts and cases*.
7 Hamel and Pralahad, 'Strategic intent'.
8 Rowe et al., *Strategic Management: a methodological approach*.
9 Brealey and Myers, *Principles of Corporate Finance*.
10 Ibid.
11 Thompson and Strickland, *Strategic Management: concepts and cases*.
12 Ibid.
13 Ibid.
14 This section is based on the work of Porter, 'From competitive advantage to corporate strategy', winner of the McKinsey Prize for the best article in the Harvard Business Review in 1987.
15 Ibid.
16 Ibid.
17 Hax and Majluf, *Strategic Management: an integrative perspective*.
18 Allen, 'Diagramming GE's Planning for What's WATT'.
19 Hofer and Schendel, *Strategy Formulation: analytical concepts*.

Unit Six

Implementation and Evaluation

Learning Objectives

After completing this unit you should be able to:

- determine the responsiveness of both management and organization to change;

- determine the key activities and competencies of the organization;

- understand the social aspects of change and the principles of non-economic decision making;

- understand how to overcome resistance to change;

- understand the various concepts of control and how they work;

- understand and use both quantitative and qualitative criteria of evaluation;

- apply the generic skills.

Contents

Overview

Organization Capability

▶ Functional capability

▶ Management capability

▶ Organization responsiveness

▶ Key activities

▶ Key competencies

The Change Process

▶ Social aspects

▶ The social change model

▶ Principles of non-economic decision making

▶ Constraints on implementing change

▶ The management of change

▶ Pressure for change

▶ Resistance to change

▶ Overcoming resistance to change

Control and Evaluation

▶ Criteria for evaluation

▶ Qualitative criteria

▶ Quantitative criteria

  Ratio analysis

  Cash flow

▶ Other measures of performance

Unit Six

Overview

In previous units we have analysed the external environment, the competitive environment and the business environment and, in Unit Five, some of the options for change. When you have made a decision about your objectives for the future you need to implement those decisions. This involves management effectiveness or capability. It is no good having grandiose schemes for the future if it is not possible to put them into operation successfully. Implementation implies management which involves planning, organizing, leading and controlling and all in the context of the business environment. Other books in this series deal with these topics so in this unit we shall introduce some of the concepts which will help you to manage change in your business.

Western managers place a premium on decisiveness and those who negotiate with Japanese businesses are often frustrated by the long period taken by the Japanese to come to a decision. In the West, the speed of decision making often leads to resistance against the plans made, frustration and delays. Altogether, the time taken to get plans operating successfully is generally longer and this approach leads to an escalation in costs and delivery/reliability problems.

The Japanese take longer to come to a decision because they gain early acceptance for the decision, which therefore meets less resistance and is more easily implemented. Frequently, implementation plans have already been started before the decision is made. They gain the benefit of a shorter action cycle, the implementation is quicker and smoother and costs are more predictable.

Perhaps we can learn from this experience by gaining acceptance for change before implementation and starting implementation and planning activities in parallel. Now read Box BP6.1.

BOX BP6.1

Planning and implementation – a fusion

Ansoff proposed the following activities for building implementation into planning for change:

- Involve the managers who will be involved in the implementation as well as those who are involved in the decision process.
- Encourage discussion of the reasons for change and the possible outcomes.
- Provide education and training as necessary before implementation.
- Remember that planning is problem solving not form filling.
- Keep problem-solving techniques simple.
- The participants should be planning tasks which have an impact on their own jobs.
- Consideration of implementation is begun before the plan is completed and approved.
- The change or plan may be broken down into manageable chunks that can be put into operation before the plan is completed. Progressive decision making and early implementation provide valuable feedback.

Source: Ansoff and McDonnell, *Implanting Strategic Management*

So far in this book we have analysed our business in detail. We know its strengths and weaknesses and its opportunities and threats. We know how it works and the way in which the Seven Ss are linked. We have probably made decisions about opportunities to be exploited and threats to be dealt with, about competitive advantages, key competencies and key activities. We have decided on and prioritized our objectives and now we intend to implement them. How do we do this?

Organization Capability

Once a decision to adapt to change or deliberately change a business in some way has been made the effect is reflected either in the operational plans, if the change is relatively small, or in the project plans if the change is large (see Unit One, figure 1.1). Either way, change will affect the functional areas: research and development, production and operations, marketing, finance and human resources. Therefore, plans will be required to make the change occur in each area. These plans will be detailed and have relatively short time horizons. The plans for the functional areas must be co-ordinated in order to move the business towards its goals.

Each functional area has different priorities. For instance, marketing might like high stock levels in order to supply customers quickly, whereas finance would prefer stock to be kept low in order to reduce costs and release cash. Such disputes need to be resolved.

Operational plans involve annual objectives in order to clarify management tasks and roles and also to provide motivation. At the same time they provide a quantitative basis for monitoring performance, i.e. objectives must be measurable. This is easy in functions like production or finance but more difficult, perhaps, in human resources. Obviously, objectives must also be realistic and accepted by managers and employees. Finally, the objectives of the functional areas must be co-ordinated, contradictions resolved and priorities set.

Most books explain this process as an administrative one, with various tasks to be performed in the functional areas such as finance, marketing, production and operations, research and development, and human resources.

Others break the process down into key tasks associated with the Seven Ss such as: creating the correct organization structure; developing skills and core competencies; selecting top management and providing leadership; producing a budget for change; cost control; developing administrative, operating and information systems; creating rewards and incentives; developing a culture with shared values, ethical standards, a supportive environment and high performance.

The decision to change, whether it is a decision to decentralize at one extreme or produce a new product at the other, depends on management skills such as entrepreneurship, market analysis and vision, whereas, once the decision for change has been made, the implementation of change depends on a different set of skills such as working through others, planning, organizing, leading and controlling, i.e. management. In general it is much easier to decide on change than it is to make it happen successfully.

Functional capability

According to Ansoff, the capability profile of a business is composed of the functional capabilities – finance, human resources, marketing, production and operations, research and development – together with management know-how.[2]

The building blocks of each function are similar in that they use equipment, facilities, know-how, shared knowledge, skills and technology. In order for the function to operate, it possesses certain properties:

- The way in which the tasks are subdivided in each function – highly subdivided tasks are efficient but rigid whereas loosely defined tasks are creative but inefficient.

- The way in which the tasks in each function are related – partitioned tasks produce stability whereas coupled tasks produce flexibility.

- The culture of the function – a culture hostile to change contributes to efficiency but reduces flexibility.
- The power structure within and among functions – an autocratic structure leads to stability and efficiency whereas shared power enables change at the expense of efficiency.

Management capability[3]

Each of the functional areas will have a manager but since they are so diverse, with different objectives, it is necessary to integrate, co-ordinate and direct the functions towards common goals. This is the task of the general manager. General management has responsibility for the overall performance of the business. The capability of management is its responsiveness to changes in the environment and can be described by three capability attributes – climate, competence and capacity:

- **Climate** is the propensity of management to welcome, control or reject change.
- **Competence** is management's ability to respond.
- **Capacity** is management's capacity for work.

The overall capability of general management is only as strong as the weakest attribute.

Organization responsiveness[4]

Just as general management capability is indicated by its responsiveness to change, so the capability of the organization itself can also be described by its responsiveness to change. There are five types of responsiveness which serve various goals of the business:

1 Operating responsiveness – minimizes the operating costs.
2 Competitive responsiveness – optimizes the profits.
3 Innovative responsiveness – develops the short-term profits.
4 Entrepreneurial responsiveness – develops long-term profits.

In order for these four types of responsiveness to operate successfully a fifth type of responsiveness is required:

5 Administrative responsiveness, the capability for supporting the other types of responsiveness and adapting to change.

Operating and competitive responsiveness ensure the profitability of the firm's present products in its present markets, whereas innovative and entrepreneurial responsiveness develop the potential for the future profitability of the business. The administrative response must be anticipatory, dynamic, complex and flexible. The use of computers now enables these demands to be met.

Whereas profit centres tend to be responsible for the short-term performance of a business – the operating and competitive responsiveness

– the strategic business unit (SBU) is responsible for both short-term and long-term performance – organization capability.

Mention of the SBU makes it necessary to differentiate it from a similar concept – the strategic business area (SBA). Read Box BP6.2.

BOX BP6.2

SBAs and SBUs

The strategic business area (SBA) is a distinct part of the environment in which the firm does or may wish to do business. It has distinct trends, threats and opportunities.

Most managers view their business environment from the point of view of their current products or services and the ways they can sell them into that environment. However, managers should really think of the business environment as a field of future needs which any competitor can address – the SBA.

An SBA can be described by identifying:

- the need for products or services;
- the technology to serve the need;
- the type of customer which has the need;
- the geographical region in which the need will be served.

In order to be able to compare SBAs, we need to know for each one:

- the growth prospects;
- the profitability prospects;
- the expected turbulence;
- the success factors.

In order to make use of this concept the first step is to identify one or more SBAs in which your business might be interested. Compare their growth, profitability, turbulence and technology prospects. This should enable you to make three decisions:

1 In which SBA should you do business?
2 What competitive position should the business occupy in each SBA?
3 Which competitive strategy should the business follow in order to gain that position?

A strategic business unit (SBU) could be responsible for one or more SBAs so that a business could have a portfolio of SBAs. It seems sensible for a business to develop a portfolio of SBAs in order to spread risk both at the present time and into the future.

SBAs have a life cycle in the same way that products and technology do, therefore a portfolio should contain SBAs at different stages in their life cycles in order to ensure growth and continuity. At the same time involvement in different SBAs spreads the risk of threats from the environment.

Ansoff believes there are three ways of managing a portfolio of SBAs:

1 By exception – only when results are unsatisfactory does the chief executive officer interfere by using firm controls, replacing managers or divesting the SBA.

2 By portfolio balancing, using matrices of various kinds. The BCG matrix and the nine-cell Shell matrix, for instance, have been modified by Ansoff.

3 By portfolio optimizing – using the historical SBA portfolio as a start for designing a different future for the business, whereas both 1 and 2 use the historical portfolio as the basic core for the future business. Ansoff suggests a method for optimizing a portfolio of SBAs.

Source: Adapted from Ansoff and McDonnell, *Implanting Strategic Management*

Key activities

Key activities were first mentioned in Unit Four in connection with the value chain. As you are aware, in any business some activities and skills are more critical for success than others. For instance, much of the work in a business is routine, e.g. the payroll, stock control, distribution and production, whereas other activities are support functions such as accounting, data processing and training. In any particular business some of these activities need to be done exceedingly well in order for the business to be successful. For instance, a business with low margins needs tight cost control. A jewellery manufacturer will require high-quality craftsmen and designers. A high-technology business will require high research and development and innovative skills. Thus the critical activities of a business will vary with the business and the market and also from time to time as conditions change.

According to Drucker, managers have to decide which activities have to be performed exceedingly well and which parts of the business would be worst affected if performance in any area dropped.[5]

The activities performed in a business need to be related in some way – look for locations, sequences, types of customer, distribution or technology used, need for co-ordination, and so on. These relationships of activities provide a basis for organizing a business into units. The critical activities should be made the main building blocks of the business structure in order to institutionalize the role and power of the block and for the block to receive its fair share of resources. The degree of authority and independence for the blocks and their co-ordination have also to be decided.

According to Drucker, the simplest organization structure that will do the job is the best one.[6] This is confirmed by Peters and Waterman, when they use the expression: 'simple form, lean staff'.[7]

Key competencies

Once the critical activities have been identified, the staff necessary for performing the activities must be considered. This involves management, special skills and technical experts.

When businesses are following similar strategies the only way to compete is by superior implementation. You must build core competencies that rivals cannot match. In what ways can you gain a competitive edge over your rivals?

The key competencies are related to the key activities, e.g. better customer service, distribution channels, quality, innovation, merchandising skills and employee relations are obvious core competencies in any business.

It is important to build a critical mass of competencies in the activities that matter by providing administrative support, generous budgets, staffing policy, high standards and rewards and incentives.

Superior competencies are not easily duplicated by rivals so the advantage gained is likely to be sustainable over a long period of time.

This section has examined the capability of an organization but whatever change is proposed we also need some context for the change process.

The Change Process

Social aspects

The problems of implementing change normally centre around the technical and financial aspects of change in the early stages. The organization and social aspects are left till later. However, a manager should begin to think about implementation at the very outset of considering change because the organization and social aspects are also critical.

Where decisions about change have had to be made in the book so far, there has been no mention of implementation. Nevertheless, it is always important for such decisions to be made in the full knowledge of the problems of implementation. It is no good planning a change in an organization that has no chance of successful implementation. This point focuses on the importance of the Seven Ss and their linkages. Too often managers propose changes which have no chance of success because of the lack of fit between the Seven Ss.

The introduction of change involves people and the social system. Unless managers can introduce change in such a way that people will accept and support that change then the change will not be successful. Social change is a major part of the change process in any business and needs just as much effort as the changes in finance, organization or technology which managers are used to coping with.

The social change model

Rowe et al. have developed a social change model to help managers understand the ways change will be perceived by the major stakeholders in a business and the ways management can cope with resistance.[8] The procedure is as follows.

1 Identify the stakeholders and their motivating interests, their attitudes and their likely reactions to change.

2 In order to assess support for a particular change, identify the stakeholders and assign a weight from 1–10 to indicate the importance of the stakeholder to implementing the change. If the change can be made without the involvement of the stakeholder, the weight is 1. If the change cannot be carried out without the involvement of the stakeholder, the weight is 10.

3 Now score the attitude of each stakeholder towards the expected results of change, from active resistance (1) to enthusiastic support (10).

4 Multiply the importance weights by the attitude weights in order to determine the importance of the stakeholder to the change process. Important stakeholders who are resistant need special attention. Therefore, an analysis of the causes of the resistance may be required in order to deal with them.

5 Identify the social resources you have available for implementing the change. Social resources are characteristic of each stakeholder and include friendships, loyalties, habits, perceptions, psychological style, anxieties, prejudices, shared beliefs, identification with purpose, will power and dedication.

6 Finally, write a short report on the social change problem. What are the social barriers to change and in what ways can they be overcome?

A chart to help managers cope with resistance to change is given in figure 6.1.

List of stakeholders and their social resources	Importance of stakeholder to change 1–10 I	Attitude of stakeholder to change 1–10 A	Multiply I x A

Figure 6.1 A chart to help managers cope with resistance to change.

Source: Adapted from Rowe et al., 1989.

Principles of non-economic decision making

Diesing suggested three principles for making use of
above.[9] The three principles should be used to select a
series of options and the process repeated if necessary to
for social change.

(1) **Principle of Changeability**. Select the easiest possible relevant
changes within the business. Easy changes will generate less conflict and
resistance and are likely to be successful. The ease of change is based on
the concepts of introducibility and acceptability. Introducibility depends
on roles being in place in the social system that will allow the changes to
occur. Also, managers or employees must have sufficient skill to perform
those roles effectively. If roles have to be changed in order to make
progress then the people who have to change must be won over.
Acceptability involves more than gaining the approval of stakeholders. The
change must be made with the minimum of disruption, incompatibility
and conflict. Thus, change is more likely to be accepted if it is similar to
the situation it replaces and small changes are more likely to be acceptable
than large changes.

(2) **Principle of Separability**. Select a change that is sufficiently isolated
from its context for it to be implemented while protected from outside
pressures. Identifying an independent change in the business may involve
observing social relationships within a group or class of stakeholders, such
as a work group, an age group, a particular part of the organization, a
geographical region or occupational class. Alternatively, it may involve
changing a set of roles, beliefs, drives, values, rituals or symbols.

(3) **Principle of Growth**. Begin a change in such a way that extension of
change is possible. Where should the seed operation be started? What
social relationships can be changed so that a chain reaction is triggered in
the right direction? Often changes in a few activities and interactions lead
to changes in sentiments and norms. This reinforces the changes and
permits new activities to be started and the process repeated. During each
iteration the target area is increased in size and complexity.

It may well be that targets for change may not satisfy all three principles. In
that case the options should be re-examined until one is found that
introduces change easily, is easy to separate and will trigger a chain
reaction. For example:

1 Identify several changes you need to introduce. Summarize each change as an
   action to be taken in a target area, for example a new model involving improved
   technology and producing savings of 3 per cent in direct costs. A minimum
   investment of £250,000 is required for new equipment and engineering design.

2 Each change is evaluated in terms of its changeability (C), separability (S) and growth (G) using the scale from 1–10.

3 Multiply the scores to obtain a total score (C × S × G = total). The change with the highest total score is the most effective change.

The final choice must balance the social change evaluation determined above with the economic and other evaluations. The chart in figure 6.2 may be useful for organizing your thoughts.

Options for change	Comments	Rating 1–10	Scores C × S × G
A	Changeability (C) e.g. easy to change	8	
	Separability (S) e.g. reasonably separable	5	
	Growth (G) e.g. minimum growth	2	80
B	Changeability (C)		
	Separability (S)		
	Growth (G)		
C etc.			

Figure 6.2 A chart for the evaluation of social change.

Source: Adapted from Rowe et al., 1989.

In this section we have been trying to answer the following questions: What change is possible? Can it be introduced? Is it acceptable? Which is the easiest change to introduce with the social resources available?

Constraints on implementing change

Lorange identified five major trends in the environment which must be addressed during the implementation of change.[10]

1 **Attitudes**. Social attitudes change over time. Currently, attitudes towards ecology, growth, commitment and risk are in question.

2 **Politics**. Political stability, legal and fiscal systems, government attitudes to business, unions and the external stakeholders in general are important for the future of the business.

3 **Power shifts**. Where are the sources of power externally? Special interest groups and other outside pressures should be identified.

4 **Scarcity**. Shortages of natural resources – energy, water, food and raw materials – cause costs to rise. Therefore, efficiency in the use of raw materials, forecasting shortages, substitutes and alternative sources of supply must be explored.

5 **Technology**. Technological expertise is rapidly becoming the most important resource for a business and is a source of competitive advantage.

Now read Box BP6.3, which illustrates the difficulties in change policies.

BOX BP6.3

Lorange and constraints

Lorange also identified five constraints within organizations which have to be addressed:

1 **Executive obsolescence**. Environmental changes quickly make members of businesses obsolete. Ways of adapting to change must be explored to avoid the waste of human resources.

2 **Inflexibility**. Lack of communication and goal congruence between different parts of the business can cause problems.

3 **Parochialism**. The loyalty of managers to their own business rather than to the group as a whole.

4 **Power**. Where is the power? Can the CEO alter the direction of the business and reallocate strategic resources?

5 **Values, styles, traditions**. Is the culture responsive to goal modification, new business developments and environmental problems and opportunities?

Source: Adapted from Lorange, *Implementation of Strategic Planning*

The management of change

The challenge for any organization today is to manage change effectively, since failure to change successfully will rapidly threaten its ability to survive. This applies to both profit and not-for-profit organizations.

There is a difference, of course, between change which is planned and change which is unplanned. In this book we are largely concerned with planned change. Planned change is that set of activities which changes people, groups and the organization's processes and structure. This kind of change requires specific objectives which improve the organization's ability to adapt to change and also change employee behaviour. All parts of the organization are involved in becoming more adaptive and therefore organization culture has an important influence on organization adaptability.

Managers deal with change in different ways. For instance, they react to indications that change is needed and deal with problems as they arise. They may also develop a programme of planned change. However, managers today should not only plan for change but accept that change is necessary for the organization to learn, survive and be successful.

In any change situation, a person or group should be the catalyst for change or the **change agent** – the leader responsible for managing the change. Change agents may be internal or external. External change agents, such as consultants, bring in extra expertise, may be confided in, listened to and more able to make objective decisions than internal change agents. If resistance to change is expected to be high, the prestige of the external change agent may be necessary for obtaining agreement and commitment to the changes proposed.

Organization change involves changing the behaviour of people and this focuses on participation and teamwork.

Pressure for change

Hellriegal et al. believe that pressures for change in organizations come from the following factors.[11]

- **Changing technology** influences the role of management as machines take over routine, physically demanding or complex tasks. It also includes the technical knowledge managers require to integrate the functional areas. Managers also need interpersonal, communication, information processing and decision-making skills together with a positive attitude to change. The complexity of the process will require managers to be more highly trained.

- **The knowledge explosion** requires managers to find and disseminate knowledge in organizations and also obtain and create new knowledge. They will need to produce new products and services and manage people in innovative ways.

- **Rapid product obsolescence** is due to fast-changing consumer preferences and technological changes and innovations. The life cycles of goods and services are reducing dramatically and forcing organizations to shorten production lead times.

- **The nature of the workforce is changing** in the West as it grows older and more diverse in terms of gender and race. Changing values and aspirations are also affecting the rewards people seek from work and the balance they need between work and play. The mobility of the workforce and the development of human resources will become increasingly important.

- **The quality of working life** is linked to behaviour both on and off the job and influences self-esteem, job satisfaction and involvement and commitment to the organization and its goals. Improvement in performance together with better physical health and decreased absenteeism, labour turnover and accidents result from the improvement in the quality of working life.

We believe that the aspirations of an educated labour force will demand a higher quality of working life and a part in decision making. However, managerially imposed changes based on product change and technology are clearly becoming more important as environmental turbulence increases. It is important that managers take these factors into account before taking action since change may well be resisted.

Resistance to change

In spite of the pressures on organizations to change it is inevitable that change will be resisted both by people and by organizations. Resistance to change takes many forms and may vary from strikes to subtle reactions that management may never become aware of.

Hellriegal et al. believe that individual resistance to change comes from the following:[12]

- **Selective attention and retention**. People tend to select those things that fit most comfortably into their current understanding of the world they live in. In general, people only listen to or read that with which they agree, forget anything that may lead to other viewpoints and misunderstand anything that is not congruent with their current attitudes and values.

- **Habit**. People will continue as before unless a situation changes dramatically. Habits are a source of satisfaction and allow people to adjust to and cope with their world. They provide a sense of comfort and security which is difficult to overcome.

- **Dependence**. People who are highly dependent on others lack self-esteem and resist change until those on whom they depend change.

- **Fear of the unknown**. Change and its consequences mean uncertainty and some people will avoid change because of this.

- **Economic reasons**. Changes that threaten economic security. Changes in jobs may also cause a fear of not being able to perform well after the change.

- **Security and regression**. When times become difficult, insecure people regress by seeking security in their past which they believe was better.

Hellriegal et al. believe that organization resistance to change comes from the following:

- **Threats to power and influence**. Once a power base has been established, both groups and individuals will resist any changes which will affect their power and influence.

- **Organization structure**. The more mechanistic an organization, the more chance there is of filtering out new ideas which may affect the status quo.

- **Resource limitations**. Since change requires resources in terms of capital, time and people, change may be avoided because of limitations in resources.

- **Fixed investments**. Previous investment in buildings, equipment, land and people may limit the ability of an organization to change.

- **Inter-organization agreements**. These often impose obligations that limit the response of organizations to change. Typical examples are labour agreements, contracts with suppliers, licences and agreements with competitors.

From an employees' perspective, change can seem, and often is, threatening. The whole basis of working methods, customs, practices and agreements that have existed for years can be disrupted. Lay-offs and redundancies also have negative effects. The organization needs to counter its own limitations to change which range from political games to resource limitations. The force field analysis which follows takes some account of these factors but consensus is still necessary for implementation.

Overcoming resistance to change

Lewin developed a way of looking at change called force field analysis which envisages change as a dynamic balance of forces working in opposite directions at any particular point in time.[13] This means that any situation is in a state of equilibrium as a result of forces pushing against one another. The forces pushing for change are balanced by forces resisting change (see figure 6.3). Thus, in order to make a change, a manager has to modify the current balance of forces by:

- increasing the pressure for change;
- reducing or removing the resisting forces;
- changing the direction of the force.

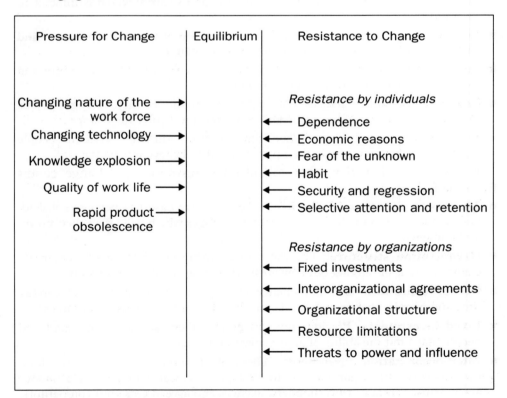

Figure 6.3 The pressures for and resistance to change in a force field diagram.

Source: Adapted from Lewin, 1951.

This model enables managers to understand the current situation and work out the factors that can or cannot be changed. For instance, any management problem can be analysed into pressure for or against the problem. The pressures for or against change may not be the same as those indicated in figure 6.3, but you should be able to insert your own forces on such a force field diagram. The diagram can be improved by indicating the strength of each factor involved, perhaps by the length of a line.

The major difficulty with this concept is the fact that it identifies the situation at a particular point in time. At other times the balance may be different. Also, each person who constructs such a figure may interpret the situation differently. However, provided managers are aware of these difficulties, force field analysis can be a useful management tool.

The approach emphasizes that we should look for multiple causes of behaviour and the forces can be of many types. The behaviour of people, groups or organizations can be assessed.

Programmes for planned change can be directed towards removing or weakening the resisting forces and creating or strengthening the driving forces in organizations.

In the long run, the choice for management is obvious: learn and innovate or stagnate and die. However, disagreement occurs about the best way to implement change, since a successful approach in one organization may not work in another. Therefore, a contingency approach should be used. To this end, the Seven Ss outlined earlier should be considered. A change in any one of these variables will affect one or more of the others. For example, a change in the organization's goals may involve a change in technology, training of employees, new administrative procedures etc. Or in certain situations the staff–style interface may be the key Ss. Therefore it is important for managers to think through the implications of the Seven Ss.

Expectations regarding change must be realistic, therefore we believe successful implementation depends on many factors:

- Clear responsibility for the change process.

- Keeping it simple by limiting your objectives to what can be successfully accomplished, given the situation and the resources available.

- Identifying and planning the necessary actions to implement change and allocate responsibility.

- Establishing 'milestones' or targets along the way by breaking change into chunks that can be easily implemented so that people are achieving success during the change process.

- Installing monitoring and control mechanisms.

- The timing of change. Can you/do you have to delay change or is it better to be decisive and then learn and adapt rather than be right? Are there special factors to take into account in your situation?

- Managing by agreement and consent.

You should now complete Activity BP6.1.

ACTIVITY BP6.1

DILUTING CULTURE?

Activity code
- ✓ Self-development
- ✓ Teamwork
- ✓ Communications
- ☐ Numeracy/IT
- ✓ Decisions

John Smythe-Jones, specialists in water treatment, effluent and drainage, was led by its founder, Smythe-Jones. With a turnover of £8,000,000 and a paper profit of £500,000, this small, tightly disciplined team of 40 people, including part-timers and associates, was very successful. Ten years before, few had heard of the firm, but now it was on the verge of a merger with a local government waterworks. It was a proposed joint venture but, if successful, it would be a *de facto* acquisition by Smythe-Jones.

The proposed merger troubled the chief executive (owner), as the cultures could clash. Further murmurings of discontent were reaching his desk from his own staff, and he had lost some very good engineers to other firms of late.

Maureen Anderson of AApma had been asked into the firm to discuss cultural change.

The firm of John Smythe-Jones was successful by any standards. Its paper profit disguised its reinvestment programme and its no-nonsense task-oriented approach.

Anderson soon realized that the Smythe-Jones reputation was well founded. It came over as a lean if not mean machine; the ethos of hard work with little time for play dominated the business; it was market-led with its service geared to the client; its core value system was known by many analysts and press commentators; and its ruthless expansionist policies meant a growth rate of some 20–5 per cent per annum for the past five years.

Smythe-Jones opened the session by noting that he was conscious that the firm was very demanding.

Smythe-Jones: 'Nonconformists are not accepted and they are counselled out if they manage to escape the selection hurdles – and that applies to the associates and part-timers as well. We believe in value consensus. We must all share and project our standard vision to our customers. Hard work is expected around here and we need to perform. The competitive environment is tough and it's dog-eat-dog. The rewards are allocated to my people accordingly. We demand loyalty and commitment from the staff.

'We're good but the casualty rate is climbing and if we merge with this other outfit I'll need even more of my people in key positions. The trouble is that some just can't keep up the pace. It is a young person's game – the stress, the changing projects, the time deadlines, the constant selling, the travel, the long hours and the disruption to leisure and family life must take their toll. It is tough, and so are we. Yet we could, and must, do better. The board believes that a change in culture can promote our business policy even more – can you change our culture?'

Anderson: 'The change really needs to come from within. Certainly I can facilitate differences in how things are done about here but this cultural thing may not be a determinant of business policy.'

Smythe-Jones: 'The values of the staff are the key success factors of this operation. The staff share our code of conduct, principles and practices. All I am asking is can we change these values so that we are even more successful? And how do we do it?'

Anderson: 'Yes, values can be modified – at least in the short term. Various methods are open to us. First of all we could examine the formal mission and stated values, then we get underneath that by looking at real behaviour rather than professed values. The value system(s) can be related back to your policy direction. The value system could include things like "innovation" and "problem solving" etc.

'We could look to your "criteria" on values and rank the professed and actual values against these criteria. Levels of risk on changes to the value systems and compatibility can be extrapolated. Experience shows that you may not like what you find when you start turning over these stones.

'Another variation is to adopt a brain-storming type of approach with the key decision makers. We can write up case histories of the organization, its context, its personality, its style, its opportunities and constraints and the position it finds itself *vis-à-vis* the product mix, for example. Again, differing perceptions can be highlighted and common denominators noted.

'The behaviour modelling approach is another variation. We can determine the ideal model that we aspire to, use key managers and senior people as the "model" and attempt to rewind "positive behaviour". To a great extent you are doing that at the moment.

'If we go for "climate" rather than "culture", it will not be so all-embracing. However, we can get a "photograph" of behaviour, reward systems, leadership style etc. on a lesser scale than the macro cultural approach. This is more piecemeal, of course, and it may suffer from attacking one or two variables when the issue is multi-faceted.

'The norms of the organization and the values of people can also be gauged from surveys and feedback sessions. These tend to be the main non-structural interventions, although a plethora of techniques exists from "leadership" to "motivating change" and "teamwork" etc. It depends a great deal on the consultant and the client – of course.

'My concern here is that your "culture", for the want of a better word, is hard-nosed and task-oriented. It is business-led – very much so, in fact. If we start to tamper with it we could be opening up Pandora's Box. We also need to be clear about the policy/culture interface.'

Smythe-Jones: 'It's not so simple.'

1 Give your views (with a rationale) on the culture/policy interface and relationship.
2 In the context of this scenario, critically appraise the options and methods outlined by Maureen Anderson.
3 Which, if any, would you recommend here, and why?

Control and Evaluation

Control is a major management function, alongside planning, organizing and leading. Planning sets direction and allocates resources. Organizing brings human and physical resources together. Leading inspires people to use the resources to the best advantage while controlling makes the right things happen in the right way, at the right time. Sound planning makes control easier.

When we examine the business environment of an organization (see Unit Four), we find that it generates a lot of information about the business. Data which cover the financial, human resources, production, operations and marketing aspects of the business will be available. These are historical data which the manager uses to measure how well the business has performed relative to past performance and on which forecasts for the future are often based.

Alongside these data, some businesses also have budgets which can be yearly to five-yearly in some cases. The examination of the variance of the current performance from the budgets is a form of control.

So control and evaluation not only occur at the end of implementation of a decision but are a process or form of monitoring which is going on all the time in any business. During the designing of plans, assigning resources and tasks, developing and communicating policies, and

---

BOX BP6.4

Objectives and milestones

The control and monitoring of the long-range business plans are key areas in the implementation phase. Goold and Quinn examine this perspective through the use and application of milestones.

This monitoring-cum-control process is seen as strategic control as opposed to the shorter time frame of budgetary control. Further, these milestones, derived from the overall plan of campaign, can be seen as a parallel process to the budgetary control mechanisms – although they have a wider strategic overview.

The setting of milestones is seen as the strategic way forward as these goals or milestones can operationalize the overall plan.

According to these writers, the milestones give the user the following advantages:

- a framework for action is rendered;
- short-term decisions do not have to be short term*ism* as the framework gives a broader context to the immediate decision;
- the milestones can also operate as some structural control mechanism over the different parts of a business empire.

Altogether, it looks a refreshing perspective on a too-narrow budget mentality and, of course, it helps to operationalize the overall policy (or policies) without losing sight of the master plan.

Source: Adapted from Goold and Quinn, *Strategic Control: strategic milestones for long-term performance*

---

developing leadership and a culture, the processes of evaluation and control must also be occurring and developing. The control and evaluation processes help managers to monitor the progress of plans. They need to know whether the gaps between the actual and the desired results are being or will be closed; also, whether changes in the environments of the business will have any effect on the objectives, so that corrective action may be taken if necessary. Unless control and evaluation are integrated in any plan it is unlikely to be successful.

Now study Box BP6.4 for a potential success story.

There is a need for control because of the changing environment, the complexity of organizations, the possibility of mistakes and the need for managers to delegate their responsibilities. Therefore, control is the process managers use to make sure that actual activities conform to planned activities. The control process is designed to measure progress towards objectives and detect deviations from the plans in time to take corrective action. Control has many faces, as is shown by the different types of control:

- **Management control** – based on past performance.
- **Real-time control** – provides current information.
- **Management by objectives** – setting objectives with frequent evaluation.
- **Performance management** – goal congruence and organization effectiveness.
- **Adaptive control** – the quickest and most effective way to respond to change.
- **Strategic control** – anticipating and developing ways to reduce potential deviations from desired objectives.

In order to operate these controls effectively, the environment must be monitored to confirm that the assumptions on which the plans were based are still valid.

An effective control system requires the identification of key success factors or parts of a business which must function effectively for the organization to succeed (see Unit Four). Hofer and Schendel have developed a useful functional area profile (see figure 6.4) which identifies key budget figures, physical and human resources, operational systems and technological capabilities.[14]

In general, managers should build the future of their business around what it does best. Success involves the integration of people, technology, production and marketing know-how into competencies in order to increase competitiveness. A core competence is something that an organization does extremely well compared to competitors.

There are many types of core competencies: manufacturing, quality control, better service, low cost, know-how, design, good locations, innovation, merchandising skills, technology, sales force, distribution channels and so on.

As we have seen, Porter's value chain concept provides a basis for comparing a business with its rivals.[15] The historical cost-accounting data need to be broken down into cost categories associated with the value chain and the products or services provided (see figures 4.1 to 4.4).

Criteria for evaluation

Before we employ these criteria, we need to be aware of what we intend to measure. Box BP6.5 indicates the type of measurement required.

Evaluation can be based on both subjective (qualitative) and objective (quantitative) criteria, depending on the purpose of the evaluation. We can adopt a qualitative or a quantitative approach, or some combination of both.

	R&D Conceive, design, develop	MANUFACTURING Operations	MARKETING Distribute/ sell/service	FINANCE Requirements	MANAGEMENT Planning/ organizing/ leading/ controlling
Key expenditures					
Physical resources					
Human resources					
Organizational systems					
Technological capabilities					

Figure 6.4 A typical functional area profile chart ready for completion.

BOX BP6.5

Long-term profitability – policy options

Schuchman examines a range of options available for management to sustain long-term profitability of the business.

The options are divided into two – increasing volume or improving productivity.

The volume subdivides into a greater expansion of the market or deeper penetration. Market expansion comes via converting new customers or by entering new areas or segments. Penetration is demonstrated by increasing the rate of usage or by taking customers from the opposition.

Improvements in productivity, according to Schuchman, seem to involve reducing costs (fixed or variable), increasing prices or improving the sales mix.

It would seem that profit maximization and cost minimization are the basic policies for achieving long-term health.

Source: Schuchman, 'Industrial marketing planning'

Qualitative criteria

Qualitative criteria are often best used in the planning stage. The questions to be answered are based on consistency, appropriateness and workability.

- Are the plans consistent with the objectives, environmental assumptions and internal conditions?
- Are the plans appropriate considering the resources, risks and time-scale?
- Are the plans feasible and stimulating?

Imagine you are the sales director for a pottery manufacturer and you have responsibility for the total sales of the firm. At a quarterly sales meeting the sales manager for the North of England stated that he had missed his sales target in the last quarter by 10 per cent, but expected to hit the target during the next quarter, whereas the sales manager for the South of England reported that he had beaten his target by 10 per cent. What should you do?

The North of England sales manager has been with the firm for a long while with a good record for reliability and accuracy. The South of England sales manager is new to the job but easily met his target sales. It seems reasonable to expect that this success can be repeated. Therefore, you decide to take no action.

Later in the week you receive the profit and loss figures for the two sales areas. You are surprised to find that the North of England area shows a higher contribution to profits than the South of England in spite of missing its targets.

On investigation you find that the South of England sales manager, in order to make a good impression, had concentrated on large existing accounts. He had persuaded them to place large orders but at a discount. The result was high sales but low profits.

Unfortunately, this move has a bad effect on the next quarter's results. The South of England falls below target by 10 per cent because its large accounts are still over-stocked. However, the North of England has made an effort to open new accounts during the previous quarter and so beat its target by 5 per cent, as predicted by the sales manager.

- This example demonstrates the link between planning and controlling.
- The standards are the sales targets agreed by the director and the two sales managers.
- The control is the quarterly sales meeting at which the sales managers report their results.
- In this example the short-term objectives of the South of England sales manager were met at the expense of the long-term goals of the firm. However, the quarterly control did not detect the trade-off till later.

Now complete Activity BP6.2 which also provides a qualitative perspective. Thereafter, the main text continues from a quantified viewpoint.

ACTIVITY BP6.2

KD DESIGNS

Activity code
- ✓ Self-development
- ✓ Teamwork
- ☐ Communications
- ☐ Numeracy/IT
- ✓ Decisions

KD stands for Kerry Designs. The firm started in Malaysia in 1985. It is a fashion company dealing mainly in smartly designed casual wear, T-shirts and jumpers, with some fashion accessories such as scarves and jewellery. The clothes were designed and sold by Kerry and manufactured to her specifications by a local textile company, ABC textiles. The designs created the uniqueness while the cotton fabric T-shirts and the heavier sweaters were manufactured to a high standard. The only outlet was a market, although it was a 'classy' market on a par with London's Covent Garden.

Kerry, an ex-art school student and a designer, at first had difficulty making a living and paying off her initial bankloan of £3,500. Thankfully, ABC textiles were not too pushy and a regular spot on the market was paying dividends. The designs were catching on and rich Western tourists soon began to invade her pitch. The T-shirts had an apparent uniqueness which flattered the wealthy Westerners. The T-shirts were not really unique, but careful merchandising helped to create a feeling of uniqueness, with no two T-shirts of the same type on display at any one time. Spares were kept in the van and could be used to replenish the stock on a half-daily basis. Soon the loan was paid off. Kerry, a tidy-minded artist, was very shrewd and lived quite frugally, preferring to reinvest the profits on building up more varied lines and new products such as belts, jewellery, bangles and earrings – all with her unique artistic eye. Her reputation was going before her.

A mutual friend introduced her to Jo Meade, an experienced marketeer and former financial manager with a multinational firm. The relationship blossomed, and soon they became the best of friends. A partnership was formed and the firm changed its name to KMD. If Kerry had the artistic prowess, Jo complemented her skills with his business acumen and his commitment to the main chance. The firm looked destined for success: the market was there, the skills were there, and both could tap the growing market for smart casualwear. The issues were really: where next, and at what pace should they develop?

The KD partnership pursued the following policies.

The first move was to go for an up-market resort in Switzerland. The company made a comprehensive agreement with the Switzotel group for designer ski suits and holiday wear. These clothes were marketed via the boutiques located in the foyers of the hotels in the group.

An exhibition at The National Art Gallery in New York the following year proved to be an enormous success and silk scarves and ties were devoured by a fashion-conscious public to the tune of £100,000.

Tangs in Singapore and Hutchins in Hong Kong followed and these prestigious outlets were selling both clothes and accessories from KD Designs by the end of that year.

Another display format has been used in linking the designer goods to painting exhibitions and to art displays of established artists.

The overall objective of the partnership is to expand and to be able to compete on similar terms with the major fashion houses. This firm targets a young to youngish-middle-aged group. It does some work for the more conservative older group but is still hitting the younger segments.

Most of the other houses in this sector have tended to flood the market with a huge presence in the High Street. The elitist image of the firm and its panderings to individuality would make such a policy unsustainable.

The geographical spread to date has been half planned and half chance. Contacts and opportunities produced the hotel contract and the American exposure. The Malaysian base is still the core base although Paris, New York and London have all opened on a small scale. A stronger presence in the European mainland is the next step.

The supplier company ABC Textiles was taken over two years ago to ensure quality standards. The production costs of KD Designs have reduced accordingly and the customer base of ABC Textiles has been added to KD. The quantity and quality issues now reinforce the core products. There are no further plans for integration.

The diversification into holiday wear still remains an adjunct to the main business rather than a pure diversification *per se*.

A strict policy of reinvestment is ongoing with between 50 and 75 per cent of net profit being ploughed back into the partnership. New materials, new equipment and new people have all emanated from this cash surplus and no cash or credit crisis with this organization is envisaged as reserves are very high.

Comment critically on the policies to date.

Quantitative criteria

In order to evaluate the effectiveness of management you can use financial data to analyse a firm's past performance and assess its current financial position. Ways of using these data for competing more effectively will be outlined.

In order to evaluate a firm's performance, we must know its objectives and be able to measure the extent to which the objectives have been achieved. For example, from a financial viewpoint, profit is an important objective of a business. However, profit is not synonymous with cash and a business must ensure it has sufficient cash to meet its obligations as they fall due. Therefore, an objective of a business might be to optimize profits while maintaining a satisfactory cash flow. There is no point in measuring profit unless it means something. This implies knowing whether the profit is good, bad or indifferent.

Profit is one of the figures quoted on the financial statements, which set out to answer the following questions.

■ What profit has the business made?

■ How much does the business owe?

■ How much is owed to it?

■ What is the cash position?

This information can be found in the four major statements:

1 Trading account

2 Profit and loss account

3 Balance sheet

4 Source and application of funds statement

These statements are normally prepared by accountants or, very often, on demand using computer packages.

In general, the procedures used for the analysis of accounts will depend on the purpose of the investigation. However, the main job is to find out as much as you can about the business and compare it with other businesses in the same industry.

The next job is to examine the accounts for the business over a number of years, usually three to five years. Once you have the accounts you need to calculate a set of ratios and trends. The actual ratios to use will depend on the business involved and the common ones will be outlined later. Use your imagination to identify figures and ratios which will be useful in your business.

To make the data meaningful we must erect criteria by which we can judge whether the figures on the statements and the ratios calculated are good, bad or indifferent. Three types of criteria are useful: budgets, past performance and comparisons with other businesses.

Budgets have two main objectives: planning and control. Therefore, target figures for the statements are useful. These could be based on the averages for the industry or the industry leaders. Comparisons of the business figures and the ratios enable the manager to plan and control the business.

A comparison with past performance indicates whether a business is doing better or worse. However, this does not indicate whether the performance is acceptable. Even if a business increases its return on capital employed from 5–8 per cent over a two-year period it still may not be doing very well.

This leads us to make a comparison with other businesses and the industry averages and leaders. However, comparisons between businesses may be fraught with errors since the environments and accounting practices may be different.

In comparing ratios remember that high ratios are not necessarily better than low ones. There may be a quality range within which performance is satisfactory but outside which either low or high performance is questionable.

Also, accounting procedures assume money values are stable. For example, assets are often valued at historical cost. This often inflates the profits of a business if fixed assets have been depreciated away, a situation often shown by businesses making profits with obsolete equipment. In such cases you should ask yourself, 'What can I expect in the future: profits, survival or liquidation?' Remember that depreciation in itself does not provide funds for the replacement of assets. If the business wishes to provide funds for the replacement of assets it must set aside each year a part of its profits that is at least equal to the depreciation. You must also take account of inflation and the advances in technology. Thus if a business is not making enough profits to do this over the long term it will not survive.

Another factor causing confusion can be differences in accounting practices, either year-on-year in a particular business or between businesses. Such differences are often difficult to identify without the help of an accountant.

The statements and the ratios you calculate from them only reflect the financial state of the business at a particular point in time. This may not represent the average position of the business. For example, if the business has a strong seasonal sales pattern, the cash debtors and stock will fluctuate in sympathy. Therefore, much will depend on the type of business and the time of year when the accounts are drawn up. If you know your business and industry you should have no trouble sorting the sheep from the goats. Nevertheless, changes from one year to the next are useful indicators of performance.

Before working out any ratios, an examination of the three major accounts should be made. First of all, go through the figures item by item. Make a column to the right of the latest entry to show the change on the previous year. Ask yourself:

- Is there any change and why?
- What is the general trend?
- Is it critical?

It is also useful to work out a few percentages such as:

$$\frac{\text{cost of sales}}{\text{turnover}} \times 100$$

$$\frac{\text{operating expenses}}{\text{turnover}} \times 100$$

$$\frac{\text{retained profits}}{\text{net profit}} \times 100$$

$$\frac{\text{dividends}}{\text{net profit}} \times 100$$

and ask yourself:

- Have these changed since last year?
- What is the trend over the past few years?

Ratio analysis

The traditional accounting statements can provide information which is useful for comparing a business's results with previous periods or with similar businesses in the same industry, the industry average or the industry leaders. Such comparisons are best done using ratios. These are useful for the interpretation of a set of accounts. However, simply calculating the ratios does not interpret the accounts but is the start of the interpretation process. The use of ratios puts the accounts into context and allows the manager to convert basic accounting data into a form that can be useful. Ratios are a way to summarize large amounts of financial data and analyse a firm's performance. Ratios enable managers to ask the right questions.

There are five broad categories of ratios:

1 **Profitability ratios** measure management's overall performance.
2 **Liquidity ratios** measure a firm's ability to meet its short-term obligations.
3 **Gearing ratios** measure the extent to which the firm is financed by debt and/or shareholders' funds.
4 **Efficiency ratios** measure how well a firm is using its resources.
5 **Investment ratios** measure how well a business is doing in the market-place.

These ratios can be used in three ways:

1 Comparison with other businesses in the same industry which are of a similar nature.
2 Comparison with the results for several years in the past to detect trends and changes.
3 Comparison against ratios set as absolute standards. For example:

profitability – gross profit margin no less than 30 per cent

liquidity – current ratio greater than 1

gearing – debt to assets ratio less than 1

efficiency – stock turnover five times per year

Normally, managers perform all three sets of calculations in order to get a feel for the financial health of the business.

Profitability ratios The statements of accounts show how much profit a business has made and managers like to be able to compare their profits with previous periods and with other businesses. However, it is difficult to compare profit figures unless they are related to the size of the business and the amount of capital invested. In order to overcome this problem we compare the profit with the capital invested or the total sales.

There are no agreed definitions for profit or capital. Therefore, you must state the definitions you use and use the same definitions all the time in order to avoid confusion.

The concept of profit most useful for our purpose is probably the net profit before tax and dividends. This profit can then be related to the amount of capital needed to finance it (total assets) or the sales producing it. Key ratios are shown in Box BP6.6.

The **gross profit margin** enables the trading profitability of the business to be determined:

$$\text{gross profit margin} = \frac{\text{sales} - \text{cost of sales}}{\text{sales}} \times 100$$

BOX BP6.6

Key profitability ratios

$$\text{gross profit margin} = \frac{\text{sales} - \text{cost of sales}}{\text{sales}} \times 100$$

This is the total margin available to cover operating expenses and still yield a profit.

$$\text{net profit margin} = \frac{\text{profit before interest and tax (PBIT)}}{\text{sales}} \times 100$$

This gives the return on sales.

$$\text{return on capital employed (ROCE)} = \frac{\text{PBIT}}{\text{total assets}} \times 100$$

This gives the return on total assets employed as a percentage.

$$\text{residual income} = \text{PBIT} - (\text{total assets} \times \text{WACC})$$

This gives the residual income as a money value.

$$\text{return on equity} = \frac{\text{PBIT}}{\text{equity}} \times 100$$

This gives the return on the shareholders' investment.

Thus it is measuring how much profit the business is earning in relation to the sales it makes. There are usually no problems comparing the gross profit margins of different businesses.

The **net profit ratio** gives the return or profit on sales and is useful for making comparisons between different periods for the same business. For our purpose, net profit or earnings will be before any interest on loan capital and before tax (PBIT). This is because we often need to compare the trading figures between businesses. The effect of tax and interest payments will be related to the individual firm rather than the industry and market.

$$\text{net profit ratio} = \frac{\text{PBIT}}{\text{sales}} \times 100$$

Nevertheless, it is difficult to compare the net profit ratios for different firms since individual circumstances vary so much. For example, each business will have different amounts of expenditure no matter how efficient the businesses are.

The **return on capital employed** (ROCE) is a very useful ratio which can be calculated in different ways. In this case, capital will include all borrowed money and on a balance sheet will be equivalent to total assets.

capital employed = total assets

= fixed assets + (current assets − current liabilities)

$$\text{return on capital employed (ROCE)} = \frac{\text{PBIT}}{\text{total assets}} \times 100$$

This can change from one year to the next, because of changes in either profit or assets or both.

A firm's performance depends on its sales, since sales generate profit. At the same time capital is employed to generate sales. Therefore, sales provide a link between profit and the capital employed.

For example, a firm with a capital of £100,000 makes a profit of £10,000 on sales of £80,000. The ROCE is therefore:

$$\frac{£10,000}{£100,000} \times 100 = 10\%$$

The net profit to sales ratio is

$$\frac{£10,000}{£80,000} \times 100 = 12.5\%$$

Since the capital employed is equivalent to total assets, we can say that the total assets have generated £80,000 sales in one year. This means the sales have 'turned over' the assets as follows:

$$\frac{\text{sales}}{\text{total assets}} = \frac{£80,000}{£100,000} = 0.8 \text{ times per year}$$

(since 12.5% × 0.8 = 10%). Therefore we can say:

net profit ratio × asset turnover = ROCE

$$\frac{\text{PBIT}}{\text{sales}} \times \frac{\text{sales}}{\text{total assets}} = \text{ROCE}$$

The return on capital employed (ROCE) is a very good measure of performance but its diagnostic ability is somewhat limited because it includes several diverse factors. McNamee believes this effect can be avoided by breaking down this ratio into two other key ratios as demonstrated above and below:[16]

$$\text{ROCE} = \frac{\text{PBIT}}{\text{total assets}} = \text{net profit ratio} \times \text{asset turnover}$$

$$\text{ROCE} = \frac{\text{PBIT}}{\text{total assets}} = \frac{\text{PBIT}}{\text{sales}} \times \frac{\text{sales}}{\text{total assets}}$$

This means that

ROCE = marketing effectiveness × production effectiveness

When the return on capital employed (ROCE) is separated into its component parts in this way, the new ratios show that any changes in ROCE can be traced to marketing or production. Thus efforts either to increase profits or to decrease shareholders' funds will increase the ROCE automatically.

This concept can be extended further by plotting the ROCE on a graph. This can be done by simplifying the equations above:

$$\text{ROCE} = \frac{\text{PBIT}}{\text{sales}} \times \frac{\text{sales}}{\text{total assets}}$$

We can now plot PBIT/sales against sales/total assets on a graph so that if we want ROCE to be 5 per cent we set up the following equations:

$$\text{ROCE} = \frac{\text{PBIT}}{\text{sales}} \times \frac{\text{sales}}{\text{total assets}}$$

5%	=	5%	×	1%
5%	=	2.5%	×	2%
5%	=	2%	×	2.5%
5%	=	1%	×	5% and so on.

The line on the graph in figure 6.5 joins all the points which represent an ROCE of 5 per cent. This line shows that it is possible to achieve an ROCE of 5 per cent by altering either the PBIT/sales or the sales/total assets or both. Lines can be drawn for any value of ROCE as shown in the graph in figure 6.6.

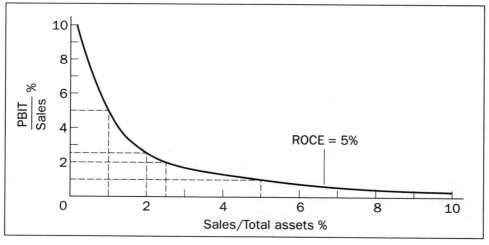

Figure 6.5 The construction of the ROCE line on a graph.

Source: Adapted from McNamee, 1985.

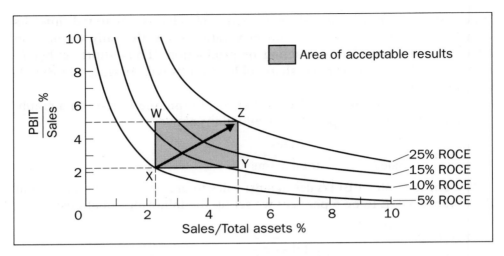

Figure 6.6 The lines for different values of ROCE and the area of acceptable results.

Source: Adapted from McNamee, 1985.

How can this concept be used to help managers plan for the future? Find out what is the best PBIT/sales ratio for your industry (say 5%), and the best sales/total assets ratio (say 5%); see the graph in figure 6.6.

If we assume the best PBIT/sales ratio and the best sales/total assets ratio in the industry are produced by different firms, then the theoretical maximum ROCE for any business in this industry is 25 per cent. Therefore, a firm with an ROCE of 5 per cent at present should move from point X to point Z. The rectangle WXYZ encloses the area containing all the possible options. Any moves that take the firm outside the rectangle will worsen the ROCE.

The firm can improve its ROCE ratio by:

- improving its PBIT/sales ratio (marketing effectiveness);
- improving its sales/total assets ratio (production effectiveness).

The theoretical maximum limit to its ROCE is 25 per cent.

This graphic approach is very useful when single ratios can be broken down into their component ratios.

Ansoff demonstrates how it is possible to optimize the return on capital employed by matching the turbulence of the environment with the aggressiveness and responsiveness of the business.[17]

Although the ROCE is in more general use for evaluating businesses and managers, the **residual income** (RI), according to Brealey and Myers, is conceptually superior to the ROCE and is a money figure rather than a ratio.[18] The residual income is found from the profit before interest and taxes (PBIT) less the capital charge. The capital charge is the total assets (from the balance sheet) times a percentage rate.

$$\begin{aligned} \text{residual income} \quad &= \text{PBIT} - \text{capital charge} \\ &= \text{PBIT} - (\text{total assets} \times \text{rate} \%) \end{aligned}$$

The rate set can be obtained from the weighted average cost of capital (Rw) where:

$$Rw = Rd(1 - Tc)D/V + ReE/V$$

Rw denotes weighted average cost of capital; Rd, current borrowing rate of the business; Tc, marginal corporate tax rate; Re, expected rate of return on the shares of the business; D, E, market values of current debt and equity; equity = number of shares $\times$ market value; and V = D + E = total market value of the business.

This rate can also be used as a discount rate for the business but remember that:

- the variables apply to the whole business;
- the weighted average cost of capital rate is correct only for projects which are just like the business;
- the rate is correct for the average project.

When this rate is used as a business benchmark it can be adjusted upwards for riskier projects and downwards for safer projects.

The advantage of the residual income (RI) over the return on capital employed (ROCE) is that:

- all investment centres will have the same profit objectives for comparable investments;
- different investment rates can be used for different types of assets.

Nevertheless, the return on capital employed is useful as a measure of past economic performance.

The rate of return on the owner's investment (equity) or **return on equity** is calculated by

$$\text{Return on equity (ROE)} = \frac{\text{PBIT}}{\text{equity}} \tag{1}$$

$$\text{ROE} = \frac{\text{PBIT}}{\text{total assets}} \times \frac{\text{total assets}}{\text{equity}} \tag{2}$$

If we plot a graph of ROCE = PBIT/total assets against total assets/equity we have a parabola of ROE similar to the ROCE in figures 6.5 and 6.6; see figure 6.7.

Considering figure 6.7, if we assume two firms with the same ROCE, one firm (Y) is earning a much higher return on equity (10 per cent) than the other firm X (5 per cent). This is because of its high total assets/equity ratio, that is, its higher proportion of debt. This means that the capital structure of X creates a disadvantage compared to Y. Therefore, in order to compete effectively it must increase its proportion of debt.

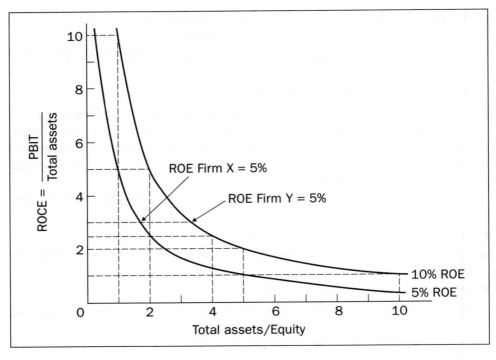

Figure 6.7 The construction of ROE lines on a graph.

Source: Adapted from McNamee, 1985.

Since

$$ROCE = \frac{PBIT}{total\ assets} = \frac{PBIT}{sales} \times \frac{sales}{total\ assets} \qquad (3)$$

we can substitute for PBIT/total assets in equation 2:

$$ROE = \frac{PBIT}{sales} \times \frac{sales}{total\ assets} \times \frac{total\ assets}{equity} \qquad (4)$$

Therefore:

ROE = marketing effectiveness × production effectiveness
× financial effectiveness

Thus, when return on equity is broken down we should be able to determine what proportion of the firm's performance is due to marketing, production or financial effects.

For example, using equation 4 we could get the following results for our firm over the past three years:

1990	*1991*	*1992*
5% × 1.5 × 2.0	6% × 1.5 × 1.8	7% × 1.5 × 2.0
ROE = 15%	ROE = 16%	ROE = 21%

The improvement in ROE is due to the marketing effectiveness or net profit/sales ratio.

If we assume that no dividends are paid then the rate of growth is equal to the return on equity.

rate of growth = return on equity (5)

Now let us go back to the concept of profit. If

total assets (TA) = debt (D) + equity (E)

and profit or return is the rate of return (R) on the total assets (TA) less the interest paid (I) on the debt (D), then:

$$\begin{aligned} \text{profit or return} &= R(TA) - ID \\ &= R(D + E) - ID \\ &= RD + RE - ID \\ &= RD - ID + RE \\ &= D(R - I) + RE \end{aligned}$$

Divide by the equity (E):

$$\frac{\text{profit}}{\text{equity}} = \frac{D}{E}(R - I) + \frac{RE}{E}$$

Therefore, using equation 5:

$$\text{return on equity (ROE)} = \frac{\text{profit}}{\text{equity}} = \frac{D}{E}(R - I) + R$$

Therefore:

$$\text{growth rate (G)} = \text{ROE} = \frac{D}{E}(R - I) + R \tag{6}$$

This is the maximum sustainable rate of growth assuming no dividends are paid.

If dividends are paid we must multiply by P (the percentage of earnings returned). Thus equation 6 becomes:

$$G = \frac{D}{E}(R - I) P + RP$$

R is related to the production policy; D/E is related to financial policy; I is related to financial policy; P is related to the dividend policy.

Therefore a manager has several possibilities available in order to increase growth:

- Increase R, the return on assets – sell more at the current price and/or increase the price.
- Increase the debt/equity ratio – borrow money.

- Reduce I, the interest paid on debt – find a cheaper source of funds.
- Increase R, the return on assets – reduce unit costs and/or produce the same quantity using less assets.
- Reduce P, the proportion of profits paid as dividends – this implies retaining a greater proportion of the profits.

Thus, the return on equity is probably the most important ratio because of its links with the capital structure, return on assets, and dividend payments. Therefore it is essential for a manager to understand these linkages in a business.

Liquidity ratios The total amounts of debtors and creditors can be found from the balance sheet but whether they are high or low, good or bad is best determined using liquidity ratios. Liquidity is a measure of the ability of the business to meet its current liabilities when they are due. The term 'current' means payable or receivable in the next twelve months. Some businesses trade in cash and may have a current assets ratio of less than 1. In this case, the cash flow is very important for meeting immediate liabilities.

During times of high inflation or when starting a business, adequate liquidity is particularly important. The liquidity of a business is related to its cash flow which should also be determined; this is discussed in a later section.

The current liabilities must be paid out of the current assets. If these are not sufficient the fixed assets will become eroded as they are liquidated to meet the liabilities, unless a loan is negotiated, of course.

The **current ratio** is

$$\frac{\text{current assets}}{\text{current liabilities}}$$

Usually one expects this ratio to be greater than 1:1 in the long run since current assets should be greater than current liabilities. A current ratio of 2 or 3 is usually aimed for. However, the proportion of the various types of current assets is also important. For example, consider a business with the following current ratio:

$$= \frac{\text{current assets}}{\text{current liabilities}} = \frac{£20,000}{£10,000} = 2:1$$

This is within the usual requirement of 2 to 3 so it appears to be satisfactory. However, if we now look at the current assets:

Stock	£17,000
Debtors	£2,500
Cash	£500
Total current assets	£20,000

we can see that, if the stock will take a long time to turn into cash because, for example, much of it is obsolete and so difficult to sell, there may be a problem. Consequently, the **acid test ratio** is often used:

$$\text{acid test ratio} = \frac{\text{current assets} - \text{stock}}{\text{current liabilities}}$$

$$= \frac{£20,000 - £17,000}{£10,000}$$

$$= \frac{£3,000}{£10,000}$$

$$= 0.3:1$$

In this case an acid test ratio of less than 1:1 requires an immediate investigation of both the current assets (less stock) and the current liabilities.

Liquidity ratios less than 1:1 do not always mean the position is critical but they do require investigation and remedying if necessary. It is often useful to compare these ratios with the industry average or with the industry leaders. Ratios less than 1 can often be found in stable industries, but if your industry is not stable, be careful.

A high liquidity ratio is not necessarily good or bad since a high ratio may mean a business is not using its current assets efficiently. On the other hand, the business may be using a high ratio as a shield against future uncertainty.

From an analytical viewpoint many managers start with the liquidity ratios since these indicate how pressing the commitments are and the time available for taking action.

Gearing or leverage ratios These ratios emphasize who provides the capital for the business, the owners or outside creditors such as the banks or both. Those businesses with a high proportion of debt in their capital structure are called highly geared or levered.

The most commonly used ratio is the **total debt/total assets ratio** taken from the balance sheet. This is a measure of the total funds provided by debt. A ratio greater than 0.5 is usually considered safe for firms in stable industries.

$$\text{The \textbf{debt/equity ratio}} = \frac{\text{total long-term debt}}{\text{total equity}}$$

This ratio uses accounting or book values rather than market values. The market values can be used to determine whether a business will get its money back. Market values include intangible assets generated by advertising, research and development and training. Such assets are not easily sold and may disappear if the business gets into difficulties. Therefore, it is probably best for our purposes to ignore the market and follow the accountant in this case.

Take care in comparing the capital structure of businesses since the decision whether or not to incur long-term debt must take into account four factors: taxes, risk, asset type and financial slack. These, of course, vary for each business. The aim should be to choose the capital structure that maximizes the value of the business. Businesses with safe, tangible assets and a large taxable income to shield can be expected to have a larger debt than an unprofitable risky business with intangible assets.

There is also a 'pecking order theory' which indicates that businesses use internal finance if possible but choose debt over equity finance when external funds are needed. Thus, without the financial slack mentioned earlier, a business may be forced to issue undervalued shares or miss an investment opportunity.

The other measure of capital structure is the **debt coverage ratio** which shows the business's ability to cover the fixed charges.

$$\text{debt coverage} = \frac{\text{PBIT}}{\text{interest paid}}$$

These ratios can also be compared to the industry averages or leaders in the industry.

Efficiency ratios The normal accounting statements do not measure the efficiency of a business. Therefore we must calculate a few ratios which will tell us how successful the management have been in using the resources of the business.

The **sales/stock ratio** is often used to indicate average stock levels but is this true given that we are comparing sales at output prices with stock at input prices? Perhaps it would be more sensible to relate stock to cost of sales. However, provided you keep the profit margins constant the stock/sales ratio can be useful over several years.

The **stock turnover ratio** shows the rate at which a business turns over its stock. The number of times stock is turned over depends on the industry but a figure between 5 and 10 seems a good target.

$$\text{stock turnover} = \frac{\text{cost of sales}}{\text{average stock}}$$

The sales revenue may be used instead of cost of sales if the accounts do not provide the figures. The stock in the balance sheet may also have to be used instead of the average stock if the opening and closing figures cannot be found.

The greater the turnover, the more efficient the business is and the stock turnover ratio can often be compared to competitors or the industry figures.

The **sales to total assets ratio** indicates the extent to which assets are working.

$$\text{sales/assets} = \frac{\text{sales}}{\text{average total assets}}$$

A comparison with the industry average or leaders is useful.

The **sales to working capital ratio** can be measured more accurately than the sales to total assets ratio and therefore may be more significant. If

$$\text{working capital} = \text{current assets} - \text{current liabilities}$$

and

$$\text{average working capital} = \frac{(\text{starting} + \text{ending})}{2}$$

then

$$\text{sales to average working capital} = \frac{\text{sales}}{\text{average working capital}}$$

The **average collection period** measures the speed customers pay their bills.

$$\text{average collection period} = \frac{\text{average debtors}}{\text{average daily sales}}$$

Instead of 365 days you can use 12 months or 52 weeks. Average figures are obtained by adding start and end of year figures and dividing by two.

Investment ratios Sometimes it is useful for a manager to combine accounting figures with market-based ratios.

The **payout ratio** measures the proportion of profits (earnings) which are paid out in dividends.

$$\text{payout ratio} = \frac{\text{dividend}}{\text{earnings per share}}$$

In general, managers do not like to cut dividends if there is a fall in profits. Therefore, if profits vary year on year managers tend to set a low payout ratio. However, if profits fall unexpectedly, the payout ratio will tend to rise temporarily. On the other hand, if profits are expected to rise in the future, managers may feel safe in paying higher dividends than usual.

Profits which are not paid out as dividends are ploughed back into the business. Therefore:

$$\text{proportion of profits ploughed back} = 1 - \text{payout ratio}$$

$$= 1 - \frac{\text{dividend}}{\text{earnings per share}}$$

The profits ploughed back into the business have to be large enough to fund future development and the replacement of wasting assets.

The **price/earnings ratio** is a useful measure of the esteem in which the business is held by investors.

$$\text{price/earnings ratio} = \frac{\text{share price}}{\text{earnings per share}} \tag{1}$$

It is generally accepted that

$$\text{share price (P)} = \frac{\text{expected dividend}}{R - G} \tag{2}$$

where R is the return expected by investors from similar investments, and G the expected rate of dividend growth.

Substituting for share price in equation 1:

$$\frac{\text{price}}{\text{EPS}} = \frac{\text{dividend}}{\text{EPS}} \times \frac{1}{R - G} \tag{3}$$

Therefore, a high price/earnings ratio can indicate:

■ that investors expect dividends to grow (G);
■ that investors are content with a low return (R);
■ that the business will achieve average growth while paying out a high proportion of earnings (dividend/EPS).

The **dividend yield** measures the rate of return an investor gets when shares are purchased at the current market price at the declared dividend rate.

$$\text{dividend yield} = \frac{\text{dividend per share}}{\text{share price}} \tag{4}$$

If the business expects a steady rate of growth in dividends we can use equation 2:

$$\text{share price} = \frac{\text{dividend per share}}{R - G}$$

Then

$$\text{share price} \times (R - G) = \text{dividend per share}$$

Substituting for the dividend per share in equation 4:

$$\text{dividend yield} = \frac{\text{share price} \times (R - G)}{\text{share price}} = R - G$$

Therefore, a high yield indicates that either investors expect low dividend growth or they require a high return.

Cash flow

Of course, profit is not synonymous with cash. A business may be showing a profit but be short of cash and running an overdraft. The reason for this

'X' Limited		
Source of funds:	£	£
Profit before tax		80
Adjustment for items not involving the movement of funds:		
Depreciation		10
Total generated from operations:		90
Funds from other sources:		
Issue of shares for cash	70	
Issue of debentures for cash	30	
		100
Total funds		190
Application of funds:		
Dividends paid	(25)	
Tax paid	(35)	
Purchase of fixed assets	(30)	(90)
Net increase in funds:		100
Increase/decrease in working capital:		
Increase in stocks	25	
Increase in debtors	85	
(Increase) in creditors	(8)	
Movement in net liquid funds:		
(Decrease) in cash balances	(2)	100

Figure 6.8 A typical source and application of funds statement.

is that accounting procedures measure income according to the accrual concept – the matching of revenues and expenses (exchange values), not receipts and expenditures (cash exchange). The source and application of funds statement endeavours to redress the balance and highlights the reasons for changes in the liquidity of a business.

The funds statement (see figure 6.8) shows where the funds have come from and where they have gone to. Funds may be generated by the business or come from outside it. Funds may be disposed of by investing them in the working capital or spending them outside the business.

In figure 6.8 it is obvious where the funds have come from, how they have been used and the changes in working capital during the year.

The source and application of funds statement can be used to control the business. However, simply increasing stocks to increase working capital, for instance, is not sensible since cash is tied up and possibly

Ratios	1991	1992	1993	1994	Trend	Standard	Comment
Profitability: Gross profit margin Net profit margin ROCE RI Return on equity							
Liquidity: Current ratio Quick ratio							
Leverage: Total debt/Total assets Debt/Equity PBIT/Interest							
Efficiency: Cost of sales/Stock Sales/Total assets Sales/Working capital Debts/Daily sales							
Investment: Dividend/EPS P/E ratio EPS Dividend yield							

The Trend column is completed using arrows ↑ up, → neutral, ↓ down.
The Standard column should indicate the target ratio or industry average.
The Comment column can be used as necessary.

Figure 6.9 Summary of the financial position of the business.

wasting away when used in this way. Therefore, you need to think carefully about the significance of each of these figures.

You are recommended to produce a chart such as the one in figure 6.9 to summarize the financial position of the business. The list can be extended as necessary but choosing standards and tolerance limits is not easy. You can also compare the results with competitors or industry norms. It is best to identify critical success factors (see Unit Four) and the measures needed to judge whether the success factors are being achieved.

In order to practise the use of ratios and the analysis of financial statements you should now work through Activity BP6.3.

ACTIVITY BP6.3

CASH COMPANY PLC

Activity code
✓ Self-development
✓ Teamwork
✓ Communications
☐ Numeracy/IT
✓ Decisions

Trading, profit and loss account for the year to 31 March 1992:

	1991 £'000	1992 £'000
Turnover	2015	2524
Cost of sales	782	1080
Gross profit	1233	1444
Operating expenses	995	1208
Operating profit	238	236
Royalties	17	16
PBIT	255	252
Interest	(24)	(50)
Tax	(85)	(71)
Profit for year	146	131
Dividends	47	47
Retained profit	99	84

Balance sheet at 31 March 1992:

	1991 £'000	1992 £'000
Fixed assets	702	797
Current assets:		
Stock	668	758
Debtors	153	209
Cash	44	43
	865	1010

	1991 £'000	1992 £'000
Current liabilities:		
Short-term borrowing	342	81
Bills of exchange	11	23
Taxation	121	50
Dividend proposed	30	30
Creditors	250	361
	754	545
Net current assets	111	465
Total assets less current liabilities	813	1262
Amounts due after 1 year:		
Loans	65	421
Tax	5	10
Creditors	21	15
	91	446
Provisions	(11)	21
Net assets	733	795
Capital and reserves:		
Called-up share capital	99	99
Share premium account	214	214
Profit and loss account	420	482
Shareholders' funds	733	795

Source and application of funds for the year to 31 March 1992:

	1991 £'000	1992 £'000
Sources of funds:		
PBIT	231	203
Adjustments:		
Non-cash items	104	125
Funds generated from operations	335	328
Funds from other sources:		
Sale of fixed assets	20	14
Loans	16	391
	371	733
Applications of funds:		
Increase in fixed assets	288	253
Dividends paid	47	47
Goodwill from acquisitions	15	5
Repayment of loans	23	107
Tax	96	107
	469	442

	1991 £'000	**1992** £'000
Increase/(decrease) in working capital:		
Stocks	213	90
Debtors	32	56
Creditors	(66)	(114)
	179	32
Total application of funds	648	474
Net movement of funds	(277)	259

1 Study the above statements of accounts, make the necessary calculations and complete a chart like the one in figure 6.9 for the years 1991–2.

2 Comment on the results for the year to 31 March 1992.

Assume the following:

■ 1,980,000 authorized, issued and fully paid-up shares at 5p each

■ Share price at 31 March 1991 = £1.30

■ Share price at 31 March 1992 = £1.25

Other measures of performance

Rowe et al. suggest another approach to measuring performance which involves the identification of four indicators: efficiency, effectiveness, equity and responsiveness.[19]

Efficiency – doing things right – is the ratio of output produced to input consumed. For example one could use:

$$\text{return on investment} = \frac{\text{profits}}{\text{investment}}$$

Effectiveness – doing the right things – is the degree to which a target has been achieved, such as market share.

Equity is the fairness, impartiality or equity with which an organization's stakeholders are treated. It is directly related to social responsibility because of the concern for stakeholders such as shareholders, customers, employees and the community. Equity is becoming an increasingly important measure of performance as the twentieth century draws to a close. Major stakeholders should be identified and measures decided upon.

Responsiveness is the extent to which the organization satisfies the demands placed on it, such as average service time per customer.

Drucker suggested eight key areas in which objectives should be set and measures of performance reported: marketing, innovation, human organization, financial resources, physical resources, productivity, social responsibilities and profit.[20] A chart can easily be constructed and filled in.

You should now complete the final two Activities, BP6.4, which is concerned with the success or otherwise of some company policies, and BP6.5, which involves a review of the concept of policy. To finish off, study Box BP6.7 on page 283.

ACTIVITY BP6.4

THE BEST-LAID PLANS OF MICE AND MEN

Activity code
☑ Self-development
☑ Teamwork
☑ Communications
☑ Numeracy/IT
☑ Decisions

The following examples of both unsuccessful and successful policies have been adapted from *Business Week*.

Your task is to comment on the causes of relative failure (1–5) and success (6–10) and to extrapolate any themes.

Plan	Outcome	Comment/themes
COMPANY 1 To diversify coal, gas, oil and exploration and tracking.	Gas shortages did not occur and higher prices which were expected did not materialize.	
COMPANY 2 To create fast food outlets at the bottom end of the market.	Up-market restaurants snapped up any available growth including this target segment.	
COMPANY 3 To focus on cement and related sectors while selling off other areas.	Cement shortages occurred and higher prices did not materialize.	

Plan	Outcome	Comment/themes
COMPANY 4 To build on reputation for mowers and snow-blowers by expanding into other home-care products.	Snowless winters. Distribution difficulties.	
COMPANY 5 To make alliances with independent carriers and to persuade regulators to hold Greyhound to 67 per cent of inter-city traffic.	Deregulation and opposition of competition put on war footing.	
COMPANY 6 To offset the cycle of its manufacturing business.	Expanded into financial and protective services (one-third of its earnings at that time).	
COMPANY 7 To move towards an electronics company away from industrial and electrical manufacturing.	Bought nine high-tech firms and disposed of old lines.	
COMPANY 8 To refocus on core business (grocery and food).	New product development and better marketing and disposing of non-core areas, e.g. petfood.	
COMPANY 9 To become less vulnerable to savings and movements in housing.	Moved into kitchen cabinet fabrications.	
COMPANY 10 To diversify into non-sweets/chocolate services.	New products (sweets) snacks, pasta and restaurant divisions.	

Source: The cases have been adapted from *Business Week*, 'The new breed of strategic planner – number crunching professionals are giving way to line managers'

ACTIVITY BP6.5

FACTORS ON EVALUATION

Activity code
- ✓ Self-development
- ✓ Teamwork
- ✓ Communications
- ☐ Numeracy/IT
- ✓ Decisions

Effective business policy is a process involving two related stages. The first involves deciding what to do and the second involves doing it. The formulation phase links environmental opportunity to internal capacity while results can be achieved through systems, organizations, targets, leadership and so on.

Your role is to reflect upon the main phases of policy formulation and subsequent goal achievement which we have tried to cover in this volume and to list these factors with a view to being able to audit, if not evaluate, a given policy in practice. One or two examples are given.

Formulation

Phase/stage	**Comment**
e.g. identifying an opportunity	Conducting an environmental scan of the wider environment and possibly the competitive environment for a potential opportunity.

Implementation

Type/factors involved	**Comment**
e.g. organization/structure	The nature or type of the skeleton of the organization may reflect the policy. Some argue that the structure is the means to meeting policy objectives.

BOX BP6.7

Policy – success and failure

According to Alexander's research of 93 companies and 127 American government agencies, some similar difficulties existed in policy in two out of three organizations in the sample. The problems included:

- the implementation phase took longer than first expected;
- (major) unforeseen problems occurred;
- unpredictable events (external) often occurred;
- short-term crises and competing activities deflected effort within the organization;
- co-ordination was poor.

Better planning with targets and forecasts could help, as well as better managerial control and focus. Above all, though, the policy needs to have tolerance levels inbuilt as rigidity in the face of unpredictable events means that the organization is at the mercy of external forces. Focus is necessary but so is a degree of flexibility, with contingency plans for potential scenarios.

Source: Alexander's research at Virginia Tech is adapted from *The Economist*, 'Putting planners on the shop floor'

Notes

1 Charlesworth, *Revolution in Perspective*.
2 Ansoff and McDonnell, *Implanting Strategic Management*.
3 Ibid.
4 Ibid.
5 Drucker, *Management: tasks, responsibilities, practices*.
6 Ibid.
7 Peters and Waterman, *In Search of Excellence*.
8 Rowe et al., *Strategic Management: a methodological approach*.
9 Diesing, *Reason in Society*.
10 Lorange, *Implementation of Strategic Planning*.
11 Hellriegal et al., *Organisational Behaviour*.
12 Ibid.
13 Lewin, *Field Theory in Social Science*.
14 Hofer and Schendel, *Strategy Formulation: analytical concepts*.
15 Porter, 'From competitive advantage to corporate strategy'.
16 McNamee, *Tools and Techniques for Strategic Management*.
17 Ansoff and McDonnell, *Implanting Strategic Management*.
18 Brealey and Myers, *Principles of Corporate Finance*.
19 Rowe et al., *Strategic Management: a methodological approach*.
20 Drucker, *Management: tasks, responsibilities, practices*.

Conclusions

In this book we have tried to draw your attention to, and develop your skills in, some of the key business policies which will enable you to make a success of your business. For instance, to be successful, managers must:

- have a vision of the future which can be easily transmitted to other members of the organization who can also identify with it;
- develop peripheral vision;
- continually look for a sustainable competitive advantage;
- control costs and cash flow and invest in the future;
- search for and satisfy customer needs;
- demand quality, service and integrity;
- observe the environment external to their organization in order to respond to and anticipate change: to identify the opportunities and threats and plan for them, perhaps changing threats into advantages;
- observe the competitive environment in which their organization operates so that they can develop a sustainable competitive advantage;
- analyse their organization so that they understand its strengths and weaknesses and can capitalize on them and again develop a sustainable competitive advantage;
- make the correct decisions; management is also about decision making and this book set out to identify the key decisions managers must make for an organization to be successful. Correct decisions depend on information and this book has focused your attention on the information important for policy decision making;
- manage their organization effectively. Management is about planning, organizing, leading and controlling in order to achieve objectives through people and needs many skills and knowledge inputs.

This book has focused on some of these key policy attributes. The whole *Effective Management* series covers the breadth and depth of management and supplements this book to develop the complete effective manager.

On looking back over the past two decades, there has been a growing emphasis on the environment and an appreciation of the many ways we interact with it. This pressure to understand and manage our environment is now beginning to be appreciated by the business world. It is only by appreciating our environment in all its guises – natural, external, competitive and business – that managers will be successful in the future. Thus we have tried to provide a coherent view of the managerial tools which can be used to take advantage of and shape the business environment for a new and successful future.

Bibliography

Abell, D. F. and Hammond, J. S., *Strategic Market Planning: problems and analytical approaches* (Prentice Hall, Englewood Cliffs, NJ, 1979).

Allen, M. G., 'Diagramming GE's Planning for What's WATT', in *Corporate Planning: techniques and applications*, eds R. J. Allio and M. W. Pennington (AMACON, New York, 1979).

Altman, E. I., 'Financial ratios, discriminant analysis and the prediction of corporate bankruptcy', *Journal of Finance*, 23, 4 (1968).

Anderson, A. H., *Successful Training Practice* (Blackwell, Oxford, 1994). The rest of the *Effective Management* series co-ordinates our work.

Ansoff, I. H. and McDonnell, E. J., *Implanting Strategic Management* (Prentice Hall, Englewood Cliffs, NJ, 1990).

Argenti, J., *Corporate Collapse* (McGraw Hill, New York, 1976).

Argyris, C. and Schon, A., *Organisational Learning: a theory of action perspective* (Addison-Wesley, Reading, MA, 1978).

Armstrong, J. S., 'The value of formal planning for strategic decisions: review of empirical research', *Strategic Management Journal*, 3 (1982), pp. 197–211.

Backman, J. and Czepoel, J. (eds), *Changing Market Strategies in a New Economy* (Bobbs-Merrill Educational Publishing, Indianapolis, 1977).

Bates, D. L. and Eldredge, D. L., *Strategy and Policy, Analysis, Formulation and Implementation* (W. C. Brown, Dubuque, Iowa, 1980).

Beer, M., Spector, B. A., Lawrence, P. R., Mills, D. Q. and Walton, R. E., *Human Resource Management* (Free Press, New York, 1985).

Biggadike, E. R., *Corporate Diversification: entry, strategy, and performance* (Harvard University Press, Cambridge, MA, 1979).

Brealey, R. A. and Myers, S. C., *Principles of Corporate Finance* (McGraw Hill, Singapore, 1988).

Burns, T. and Stalker, G. M., *The Management of Innovation* (Tavistock Publications, London, 1961).

Business Technician and Education Council (BTEC), 'Common skills and experience of BTEC programmes' (BTEC, London, n.d.).

Business Week, 'The new breed of strategic planner – number crunching professionals are giving way to line managers', 17 September 1984.

Business Week, 'Who's excellent now?', 5 November 1984.

Chandler, A. D., *Strategy and Structure: chapters in the history of American industrial enterprise* (MIT Press, Cambridge, MA, 1962).

Charlesworth, M., *Revolution in Perspective* (Eurobooks, History Book Club, London, 1972).

Christensen, C. R., Andrews, A., Bower, J. L., Hamermesh, R. G. and Porter, M. E., *Business Policy – Text and Cases* (Irwin, Holmewood, Ill., 1982).

Cowe, R., 'As Clark loses its footing, the family falls out over chairman', *Guardian*, 8 October 1992.

Cravens, D. M., *Strategic Marketing* (Irwin, Holmewood, Ill., 1982).

Cravens, D. M., Hills, G. E. and Woodruff, R. B., *Marketing Decision Making: concepts and strategy* (Irwin, Holmewood, Ill., 1980).

DeLozier, M. W. and Woodside, A., *Marketing Management: strategies and cases* (Charles E. Merrill, Columbus, 1978).

Diesing, P., *Reason in Society* (Greenwood Press, Westport, Conn., 1962).

Drucker, P. F., *Management: tasks, responsibilities, practices* (Harper & Row, New York, 1974).

The Economist, 'Putting planners on the shop floor', 5 November 1983.

Eison, I. I., *Strategic Marketing in Food Service* (Lebhar-Friedman Books, New York, 1989).

Elliott, J., 'Where green signals growth', *Financial Times*, 4 May 1990.

Emerson, R. L., *Fast Food: the endless shakeout* (Lebhar-Friedman Books, New York, 1979).

England, G. W., 'Organisational goals and expected behaviour of American managers', *Academy of Management Journal*, 11 (June 1967).

England, G. W., 'Managers and their value systems', *Colombia Journal of World Business*, 13, 2 (summer 1987).

Freeman, R. E., *Strategic Management: a stakeholder approach* (Pitman, London, 1984).

Furst, S. and Sherman, M. (eds), *The Strategy of Change for Business Success* (Clarkson N. Potter, New York, 1969).

Garvin, D. A., 'Competing on the eight dimensions of quality', *Harvard Business Review* (Nov.–Dec. 1987), pp. 101–9.

Goold, M. and Quinn, J. J., *Strategic Control: strategic milestones for long-term performance* (Business Books, London).

Gorb, P., 'Design profitability and organisational outcomes', *Proceedings of the Royal College of Art 'Design Policy' Conference*, 4 (Design Council, London, 1984).

Greiner, L. E., 'Evolution and revolution as organisations grow', *Harvard Business Review* (July–Aug. 1972).

Hamel, G. and Pralahad, C. K., 'Strategic intent', *Harvard Business Review* (May–June 1989), pp. 63–76.

Hanan, M., *Life Styled Marketing: how to position products for premium products* (AMACOM, New York, 1980).

Hax, A. and Majluf, N. S., *Strategic Management: an integrative perspective* (Prentice Hall, Englewood Cliffs, NJ, 1984).

Hayes, R. H. and Wheelwright, S. C., *Restoring our Competitive Edge – Competing through Manufacturing* (Wiley, New York, 1984).

Hedley, B., 'The fundamental approach to strategy development', *Long Range Planning*, 9 (Dec. 1976).

Hedley, B., 'Strategy and the "business portfolio"', *Long Range Planning* 10 (1977).

Hellriegal, D., Slocum, J. W. and Woodman, R. W., *Organisational Behaviour* (West Publishing Co., St Paul, Minn., 1989).

Henderson, B. D., 'The experience curve', in *The Growth Share Matrix of the Product Portfolio* (The Boston Consulting Group, Boston, *Perspectives*, 135, 1973).

Hofer, C. W., *Conceptual Constructs for Formulating Corporation and Business Strategies* (InterCollegiate Case Clearing House, Boston, No. 9-378-754, 1977).

Hofer, C. W. and Schendel, D., *Strategy Formulation: analytical concepts* (West Publishing Co., St Paul, Minn., 1978).

Hurd, D. A., 'Vulnerability analysis in business planning', *SRI International Research* Report No. 593 (1977).

Jauch, L. R. and Glueck, W. F., *Business Policy and Strategic Management* (McGraw Hill, New York, 1988).

Jones, J. A. G., 'Training intervention strategies', ITS Monograph no. 2 (Industrial Training Service Ltd, London, 1983).

Kelly, E. J., *Marketing Planning and Competitive Strategy* (Prentice Hall, Englewood Cliffs, NJ, 1972).

Kiechel, W., 'Corporate strategists under fire', *Fortune*, 27 December 1982.

Kotler, P., *Marketing Management* (Prentice Hall, New York, 1980).

Laurence, B., 'Old-fashioned way ahead at John Lewis', *Guardian*, 1 February 1993.

Lawrence, P. R. and Lorsch, J. W., *Organisation and Environment* (Harvard Business School Press, Boston, 1986).

LeBell, I. and Krasner, O. J., 'Selecting environmental forecasting techniques for business planning requirements', *Academy of Management Review*, 4, 3 (1977).

Lewin, K., *Field Theory in Social Science* (Harper & Row, New York, 1951).

Levitt, T., 'Marketing myopia', *Harvard Business Review* (July–Aug. 1960).

Lorange, P., 'Where do we go from here: implementation challenges for the 1980s', in *Implementation of Strategic Planning* (Prentice Hall, Englewood Cliffs, NJ, 1982).

Luck, D. J. and Ferrell, O. C., *Marketing Strategy and Plans: systematic marketing management* (Prentice Hall, Englewood Cliffs, NJ, 1979).

Mainer, R., *The Impact of Strategic Planning on Executive Behaviour* (Boston Consulting Group, Boston, 1968).

Management Charter Initiative (MCI), *Diploma Guidelines* (MCI, London, n.d.).

Management Consultants News, *Multi Dimensional Data Sensor* (Prize Marketing Publications Ltd, 4, 3).

Martin, W. and Mason, S., *Leisure and Work: the choices for 1991 and 2001* (Leisure Consultants, Sudbury, Suffolk, 1978).

McKiernan, P., 'Strategy formulation and the growth share matrix', in P. McKiernan, *Strategies of Growth, Maturity, Recovery and Internationalization* (Routledge, London, 1992).

McNamee, P. B., *Tools and Techniques for Strategic Management* (Pergamon Press, Oxford, 1985).

Mintzberg, H., 'Five Ps for Strategy', *California Management Review*, in *The Strategy Process*, eds H. Mintzberg and J. B. Quinn (Prentice Hall, Englewood Cliffs, NJ, 1987).

National Economic Development Office and Manpower Services Commission, *Competence and Competition, Training and Education in the Federal Republic of Germany, the USA and Japan* (NEDO/MSC, London, 1984).

Newspaper Advertising Bureau, *Eat and Run: a national survey of fast food chain patronage* (Newspaper Advertising Bureau, New York, 1978).

Olins, W., *The Corporate Personality* (Design Council, London, 1978).

Olins, W., *The Wolff Olins Guide to Corporate Identity* (Wolff Olins, London, 1983).

Particelli, M. C., 'The Japanese are coming: global strategic planning in action', *Outlook*, 4 (Booz, Allen and Hamilton, New York, 1981), pp. 36–44.

Pascale, R. T., 'Perspectives on strategy: the real story behind Honda's success', *California Management Review*, XXVI (1984), pp. 47–72.

Pascarella, P., 'Strategy comes down to earth', *Industry Week*, 9 January 1984.

Peters, T. J. and Austin, N., *A Passion for Excellence* (Random House, New York, 1985).

Peters, T. J. and Waterman, R. H., *In Search of Excellence* (Harper & Row, New York, 1982).

Pilditch, J., *Talk about Design* (Barrie and Jenkins, London, 1976).

Porter, M. E., *Competitive Strategy: techniques for analyzing industries and competitors* (Free Press, New York, 1980).

Porter, M. E., 'From competitive advantage to corporate strategy', *Harvard Business Review*, 45 (May–June 1987), pp. 46–9.

Prahalad, C. K. and Hamel. G., 'The core competence of the corporation', *Harvard Business Review*, 68 (1990), pp. 79–93.

Prescott, J., 'Airline affair more than a commercial dispute', *Guardian*, 20 March 1993.

Quinn, J. B., *Strategies for Change: logical incrementalism* (Irwin, Holmewood, Ill., 1980).

Quinn, J. B., 'Honda Motor Company, Case 1–10', in *The Strategy Process: concepts and cases*, eds H. Mintzberg and J. B. Quinn (Prentice Hall, Englewood Cliffs, NJ, 1990).

Rathmell, J. M., *Marketing in the Service Sector* (Winthrop Publishers, Cambridge, MA, 1974).

Rodger, I., 'Clocking on to diversity', *Financial Times*, 18 July 1990.

Rowe, A. J., Mason, R. O., Dickel, K. E. and Snyder, N. H., *Strategic Management: a methodological approach* (Addison-Wesley, Reading, MA, 1990).

Sasser, E. W., Olsen, P. R. and Wyckoff, D. D., *Management of Service Operations* (Allyn and Bacon, Boston, 1978).

Sathe, V., 'Implications of corporate culture: a manager's guide to action', *Organisational dynamics*, 12 (1983), pp. 5–23.

Schein, E. H., *Organisation, Culture and Leadership* (Jossey-Bass, San Francisco, 1985).

Schoeffler, S., 'Nine basic findings on business strategy', *PIMS Letter*, No. 1 (1984).

Schoeffler, S., Buzzell, R. D. and Heany, D. F., 'Impact of strategic planning on profit performance', *Harvard Business Review* (March–April 1974).

Schuchman, A., *Industrial Marketing Planning* (Seminar, University of Bradford, July, 1975).

Shama, A., *Marketing in a Slow Growth Economy: the impact of stagnation on consumer psychology* (Preager, New York, 1980).

Shetty, Y., 'New look at corporate goals', *California Management Review*, 22 (Winter 1979).

Slatter, S., *Corporate Recovery: successful turnaround strategies and their implementation* (Penguin, London, 1984).

Slocum, J. W. and Sims, H. P., 'Typology for integrating technology organisation and job design', *Human Relations*, 33 (1980), p. 196.

Spinks, P., 'Dutch eco laws prompt Shell to clean up Rotterdam refinery', *Guardian*, 16 January 1993.

Spranger, E., *Types of Men* (Niemayer, Halle, Germany, 1928).

Steiner, P. O., *Mergers: motives, effects, policies* (University of Michigan Press, Ann Arbor, 1975).

Technomic Consultants, *Dynamics of the Chain Restaurant Market 1978, including 'Top of the Pyramid': a comprehensive study of the trends in the chain restaurant market* (Technomic Consultants, Chicago, 1978).

Thompson, A. A. and Strickland, A. J., *Strategic Management: concepts and cases* (Irwin, Holmewood, Ill., 1992).

Thornhill, J., 'Why eight is a lucky number', *Financial Times*, 13 December 1990.

Topalian, A., 'Corporate identity: beyond the visual overstatements', *International Journal of Advertising*, 3 (1984), pp. 55–62.

Topalian, A., 'Developing a corporate approach to design management', paper presented at the Olivetti Design Management Symposium, University of Munich, 28 June, 1984.

Topalian, A., *Jaguar Cars Limited: upgrading the design and service of the dealership network* (Alto Design Management, London, 1988).

Topalian, A., *Design Management at WH Smith Group PLC* (Alto Design Management, London, 1988).

Topalian, A., 'Organisational features that nurture design success in business enterprises', *Proceedings of the 2nd International Conference on Engineering Management*, Toronto (1989).

Training Commission/Council for Management Education (CMED), 'Classifying the components of management competencies' (Training Commission, London, 1988).

Uttal, B., 'The corporate culture vultures', *Fortune*, 17 October 1983.

Vaughan, C. L., *Franchising: its nature, scope, advantages and development* (Lexington Books, Lexington, 1979).

Waterman, R. H., *The Renewal Factor: how the best get and keep the competitive edge* (Bantam, New York, 1987).

Waterman, R. H., Peters, T. J. and Phillips, J. R. 'Structure is not organisation', *Business Horizons* (June 1980).

Wilson, D. C., *A Strategy of Change* (Routledge, London, 1992).

Woodward, J., *Industrial Organisation: theory and practice* (Oxford University Press, London, 1965).

Worcester, R. M., 'Research and the corporate image', Market Research Society, Annual Conference Papers (March 1970), pp. 125–38.

Wyckoff, D. D. and Sasser, E. W., *The Chain Restaurant Industry* (Lexington Books, Lexington, 1978).

Zakon, A. J., *The Beliefs Audit* (Boston Consulting Group, Boston, *Perspectives*, 282, 1985).

Index